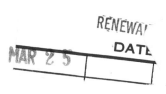

A New Deal for Workers' Education

A New Deal for Workers' Education

The Workers' Service Program
1933–1942

Joyce L. Kornbluh

University of Illinois Press
Urbana and Chicago

Publication of this work was supported in part by
a grant from the Andrew W. Mellon Foundation.

© 1987 by the Board of Trustees of the University of Illinois
Manufactured in the United States of America
C   5   4   3   2   1

This book is printed on acid-free paper.

Library of Congress Cataloging-in-Publication Data
Kornbluh, Joyce L.
  A new deal for workers' education.
  Bibliography: p.
  Includes index.
  1. Labor and laboring classes—Education—United States.
2. Adult education—United States.   3. United States—Social
conditions—1933–1945.   I. Title.
LC5051.K67   1987   374'.973   86–25048
ISBN 0-252-01395-6

In memory of George Guernsey,
Associate Director, CIO Department of Education and
Research, 1945–1955, and Assistant Director, AFL-CIO
Department of Education, 1955–1974, for his inspiration
and commitment to workers' education.

Contents

Abbreviations

ACWA	Amalgamated Clothing Workers of America
AFL	American Federation of Labor
ASW	Affiliated Schools for Workers
CIO	Congress of Industrial Organizations
CWA	Civil Works Administration
EEP	Emergency Education Program
FERA	Federal Emergency Relief Administration
FWA	Federal Works Administration
ILGWU	International Ladies Garment Workers Union
NCELE	National Committee for the Extension of Labor Education
NRA	National Recovery Administration
NYA	National Youth Administration
UAW	United Auto Workers
WPA	Works Progress Administration
WEB	Workers' Education Bureau
WTUL	Women's Trade Union League

Acknowledgments

The research for this study was started in 1968 when Eugene Power of University Microfilms, Inc. gave me a gift of Hilda W. Smith's unpublished report of her Federal Emergency Relief Administration (FERA) and Works Progress Administration (WPA) experiences, "People Come First." I am grateful to Mr. Power for starting me on a long research process that has taken me to many libraries and archives over the past nineteen years, and to interview many of the participants of the New Deal's workers' education projects.

In the course of this study, I was aided by some special grants that enabled the research: a seed money grant from the Center for Continuing Education for Women at the University of Michigan covered some expenses of the research that led to co-authoring the chapter, "Labor Education and Women Workers: An Historical Perspective," in *Labor Education for Women Workers*, edited by Barbara Mayer Wertheimer (Philadelphia: Temple University Press, 1981). A grant from the Eleanor Roosevelt Foundation covered my expenses for two weeks' research in the WPA Archives of the Franklin Delano Roosevelt Library in Hyde Park, New York. A Rackham Fellowship enabled me to take a year's leave of absence from the Labor Studies' Center at the Institute of Labor and Industrial Relations, the University of Michigan, to write this study. The Eggertsen National Award in the History of Education helped finance manuscript revisions for publication. I am grateful for that support.

I am especially appreciative of the archivists and librarians who have been helpful in this research: Debra Bernhardt and Jon Bloom at the Tamiment Collection at New York University; Eleanor Lewis at the Sophia Smith Collection at Smith College; Patricia King at the Schlesinger Library, Radcliffe College; Dione Miles at the Archives of Labor and Urban Affairs, Wayne State University; Richard Strassberg at the Archives of the New York School of Industrial and Labor Relations at Cornell University; and Lucy West at the Bryn Mawr College library. They have helped make my stay at their libraries personally and professionally rewarding.

I would also like to thank the following persons whom I interviewed for this study: Jack Barbash; Wilbur Cohen; Alice Cook; Nelson Cruickshank; Frank Fernbach; Sara Fredgant; Harry Gersh; Marguerite Gilmore; William Haber; Miles Horton; Dorothy Jorgenson; Frank Marquart; Larry Rogin; Hilda W. Smith; Caroline Ware; and B. J. Widick. The time together with these former instructors, administrators, participants, and supporters of the FERA and WPA workers' education projects enriched my perspectives.

Larry Berlin, William Cave, Daniel Fusfeld, and Robin Jacoby from the faculty of the University of Michigan were of great support in their encouragement and suggestions for this study. Judith McCulloh, executive editor at the University of Illinois Press, has been a delightful supporter during all the phases of getting this book into print. Ellen Ilfeld and Steve Babson, both accomplished writers and social critics, were invaluable for their editing help. I am grateful to Steve for sharing his knowledge and commitment to the labor movement and workers' education.

Jackie Rodgers has my sincere appreciation for her outstanding word-processing abilities and her sensitivity to deadlines. I appreciate the support of Malcolm Cohen, Director of the University of Michigan Institute of Labor and Industrial Relations. My family, who has lived with this research-in-progress for more than a decade, continues to have my love and gratitude.

A Practitioner's Preface

In April 1948, a month before I graduated from the University of Pennsylvania, I was hired by Dr. Benjamin Barkas, a professor of adult education at Temple University, to work with him and Haines Turner in a workers' education extension project. The project was run by the Philadelphia Board of Education's Adult Education Division in cooperation with Pendle Hill, a Quaker education center in the Philadelphia suburbs. Barkas and Turner, educators and visionaries—one a socialist, the other a Quaker—courageously hired a cluster of young college graduates for an internship that was to shape and inform our lives. They had the full support of Dr. Paul Sheats, the director of adult education for the Philadelphia Board of Education.

Emory Via, Jack Beidler, Nora Seligman, and I were given a range of assignments that included writing materials, organizing conferences, setting up a strike library, and helping teach workers' classes. My first task was to develop a stewards' training manual. This was quite a challenge since I had never worked in industry, processed a grievance, or spent much time on a factory floor. In field testing the manual with UAW members who were on strike against the Budd Locomotive Company in Nicetown, an industrial neighborhood in Philadelphia, I learned some of the basic lessons for workers' educators—to listen and to learn from the participants, to use their experiences as the basis of class discussions, to keep a sense of humor, and to be flexible in a wide range of situations where it is frequently the instructor who experiences the greatest learning.

It was not until I did the research for this book—a process that took me to more than a dozen libraries and archives over the past nineteen years—that I learned that the workers' education project at the Adult Education Division of the Philadelphia Board of Education was the direct outgrowth of the active labor education advisory committee that had been developed in that city in 1933–1934 as part of the New Deal's Emergency Education Program (EEP). It was of personal, as well as scholarly, interest to learn that Hilda Worthington Smith, named Specialist of Workers' Education by Harry Hopkins in September 1933, had gone to Philadelphia to pilot some of her projects soon after she was hired.

Growing up in Philadelphia during the Depression, I could not help but be affected by the WPA programs that involved members of my family. My Russian-born grandmother who told me, "I want to learn a little English before I die," took WPA Americanization classes that met in the neighborhood elementary school. My father, a social studies teacher, taught WPA civics classes to foreign-born South Philadelphians in a junior high school building. In third grade, I spent Saturdays at the New Theater, a WPA-supported theater project, where I took classes in stage craft and improvisation and acted in *The Emperor's New Clothes* and *The Revolt of the Beavers*. It was, however, a recent surprise to see my mother's name in the Temple University Urban Archives on a list of members of a citywide New Deal education and recreation advisory committee. She was a delegate to that citizens' committee from the Parent-Teacher Organization of my grade school.

Over the past thirty-nine years, I have continued the workers' education internship I started under Ben Barkas in Philadelphia in 1948, working for unions and universities in several cities around the country: developing workers' education programs, teaching credit and noncredit classes, writing books and materials, lobbying for legislation and new social policies, and taking time off periodically to research and compile some publications that might be of use in this field.

Along the way, I have continued to learn from the participants in our programs and from my colleagues and special mentors: Ben Barkas, Arthur Carstens, Kermit Eby, Miles Horton, George Guernsey, Larry Rogin, Bill and Mary Elkuss, Harvey Friedman, Jacqueline Kienzle, Marjorie Rachlin, Alice Hoffman, John Edelman, Brendan Sexton, Alice Cook, Sara Fredgant, Barbara Wertheimer, and Hy Kornbluh. There are many more. We have also learned from the many young people who have been interns in the Labor Studies Center at the University of Michigan. This book is dedicated to all of them—my old workers' education colleagues and my new ones—who share a commitment to the ability of working-class adults to continue to learn and to grow, to the need for industrial democracy and economic justice, and to the potential of education in empowering workers and building a democratic and vital labor movement. By learning more about the scope, achievements, and limitations of these New Deal workers' education and workers' service programs, I hope that we can all enhance our understanding and sophistication as labor educators plan policies and programs for the years ahead.

This study, however, must acknowledge and honor our debts to Hilda Worthington Smith (1890–1984), whom we all called Jane, who made these events happen in the 1920s and 1930s through her visions and persistence. Her work has helped us all learn, in the words from one of her poems, "what dreams may grow," and the difficulties and challenges of devising educational strategies that might lead to social change.

A New Deal for Workers' Education

1

Introduction

What do I want from workers' education? I want workers' education to teach me the truth about our economic system, our government, laws, customs, and traditions. I want workers' education to give me that which no other educational institution has given me since I first entered the public schools and which I cannot obtain anywhere else.

—Nettie Silverbrook,
January 1928[1]

Dear Sirs:

This is James Washington.

I have learned to read and write. I have learned to plant corn and grass and flowers and raise fruit and potatoes and raise cattle and how to save my soil and how to plant peas and how to save my teeth from decay. I have learned how to sleep well and how to save my wife from walking too much and how to cook corn and how to bake bread. I have learned about the Lord and to say the Lord's prayer and this is all I have to say at this time. So I will close.[2]

James Washington was one of several million adults who participated from 1933 to 1942 in the first nationwide, federally supported adult education program in the United States. Started as a relief project by the Roosevelt Administration, the New Deal's Emergency Education Program (EEP) soon established itself as one of the most innovative and controversial education efforts in the nation's history. Each year, the EEP put as many as 200,000 teachers, administrators, and clerical employees to work organizing a remarkably wide range of classes in an equally varied range of settings. Under their tutelage, unemployed workers and impoverished farmers learned vocational skills at public schools and worksites; jobless women studied parenting, homemaking, or first aid at YWCAs or hospitals; the illiterate mastered reading and writing at migrant camps; the foreign-born learned the rudiments of naturalization at Salvation Army shelters; the blind took courses in Braille and lip reading at churches and private homes; and hundreds of thousands of men and women attended classes in workers' education, safety, health, and general education in union halls and neighborhood schools.[3]

Mobilized in response to the Great Depression and mounting disillusionment with our country's economic system, these emergency efforts succeeded in raising the basic minimum level of education, especially of poor people and minority people, in a number of areas in the nation. Although New Deal efforts aimed primarily to reduce unemployment and dispense welfare funds, and did little to change the distribution of opportunity in public school systems or the way public education was financed and administered, a number of these emergency education projects influenced education programming in formal as well as informal settings following the New Deal decade.[4]

According to historian C. Hartley Grattan, the effect of this educational revival was to "introduce thousands of people to adult education for the first time, spreading the idea to groups of people and to geographic areas that hitherto had never been able to experience it and judge its utility." Even more significant, as Malcolm Knowles underscored, the New Deal adult education programs served in "broadening of the curriculum and the freeing of the adult schools' methodology from the shackles of traditional classroom procedure."[5]

From 1933 to 1936, public opinion was favorable, for the most part, to New Deal education programming as a form of temporary work relief. After 1936, however, opposition to many New Deal projects increased because of the alleged use of relief funds for political purposes. Public and political resistance to the continuation of large-scale, federal government spending further weakened the New Deal's EEP. In 1938, the *Spokane Spokesman Review* reflected widespread attitudes toward federally financed emergency programs when it noted editorially that New Deal projects included both nursery school and adult education. "Thus," the article stated, "as in Russia, the philosophies and tenets of the New Deal are taken to the people from the cradle to the grave."[6] Such allegations about the radical nature of the New Deal's educational projects, together with administrative problems within the programs and political divisions among their supporters, finally scuttled the government's educational initiatives in the late 1930s and early 1940s.

This study focuses on one component of that federal initiative, the Workers' Education Project, reorganized and renamed the Workers' Service Program in 1939, the first government sponsored, national workers' education program in this country. Rough estimates suggest that close to a million workers were reached by the EEP's workers' education activities between 1933 and 1942 when the New Deal projects were shut down. During each year in the nine-year period, from 500 to 2,000 relief instructors taught workers' classes organized in cooperation with unions, public schools, YWCAs, settlement houses, and community organizations in thirty-four states. Seventeen states were involved throughout the entire ten years of the government program. In addition, a network of residential teacher training centers was developed in the summers of 1934 and 1935, and a little known program of educational camps for jobless women, initiated by the workers' education program, lasted from 1934 to 1937.[7]

The New Deal workers' education program disseminated information about workers' rights under the Roosevelt Administration. Its written policy statements supported workers' rights to organize and bargain collectively in unions of their own choosing. Classes focused on social issues as well as on working conditions and workplace problems. In addition to courses in general adult education and social studies, union members could request classes in public speaking, parliamentary procedure, union administration, labor law, and collective bargaining. Conferences and forums on current events were scheduled in many areas of the country. Libraries were set up in union halls. State and local advisory committees were organized to link the program with the labor movement and community organizations, and to develop an infrastructure that, it was hoped, would continue the programming after the New Deal's demise.[8]

One labor educator called the New Deal workers' education program "the greatest impetus ever given to workers' education in the United States," and a 1956 report on labor education stressed the importance of the mark it had made on workers' education in this country. Several other studies of workers' education have paid tribute to its important contributions. Yet, despite these evaluations, there has been no full-length study of the history of the federal program, the context in which it developed, and the ways it shaped and reflected the contributions, contradictions and problems of the New Deal's FERA and WPA programs.[9]

I

This study takes as its point of departure Clarke A. Chambers's thesis, in *Seedtime of Reform*, that the reform impulse in the years between the end of World War I and the inauguration of Franklin Roosevelt had an impact on the New Deal years. In 1963, Chambers wrote:

> From progressivism and from the reform movements in the postwar decade [the New Deal] drew both its methods of analysis and its spiritual inspiration. . . . Out of pressing need, the New Deal evolved a program; from the past it drew its inspiration. The inventiveness of the New Deal operated more in the arena of program than abstract policy. That it was not devoid of lively and viable theories, however, is absolutely clear. It succeeded, where it did succeed, not only because it proposed real, if always partial, answers to real and present problems; it succeeded also because its idiom drew from a tradition still revered in the American heart. It owed a profound debt to those reform and welfare leaders who

had pioneered new programs and kept alive the tradition of humane liberalism in the years of normalcy.[10]

Chambers's general observations about the roots of New Deal reformism can be extended still further in the case of New Deal educational programming. Indeed, the "seedtime" of the Roosevelt Administration's EEP stretched back well beyond the 1920s to the beginnings of large-scale industrial development in this country. It was influenced by the movement of native-born workers from small-town communities to rapidly growing urban areas, and by the appearance in American cities of a "rootless," often foreign-born population.

Observers had noted the existence of a growing urban proletariat before the Civil War; the draft riots of 1863 gave some inkling of its potentially volatile nature. But the onset of the industrial depression in 1873 brought this new class to public attention with special force and suggested a new role for education to mitigate the effects of social turmoil in these pivotal years of industrial and urban growth.

As the nationwide boom in railroad construction faltered and collapsed in 1873, relief applicants besieged Boston's Overseers of the Poor as if "some great fire or more serious calamity" had struck the community. A "homeless, houseless" army of 7000 unemployed workers and drifters sought overnight shelter in Detroit's police stations in 1874–1875—a staggering increase from the 500 public lodgers listed a decade earlier in 1865–1866. Over 400,000 transients bedded down in New York City's police stations during the depression's second year, and citywide arrests for vagrancy soared to over one million in 1877.[11]

These transients emerged from the growing slum districts that evoked in their very names a sense of foreboding: Kerosene Row, Poverty Gap, Hell's Kitchen, and Bandit's Roost. In 1877, foreboding turned to panic among business and professional leaders when a wave of strikes and riots flared across the United States. Sparked by wage cuts on the nation's railroads, the conflict spread to nearby factories and slums, pitting large crowds of workers and unemployed against police, militia, and U.S. Army troops. Over 100 died in two weeks of bitter violence.

The Great Strike of July 1887, marked a watershed in American life. "The extremes of wealth and poverty are now to be seen here as abroad," the *Chicago Tribune* observed in a poststrike editorial entitled "The Dangerous Classes." "The rich growing rich and the poor poorer—a fact to tempt disorder." Significantly, some community leaders believed that augmented militias and new armories were not enough to counter this new threat to social order and that the education process must infuse new cohesion into threatened communities. One Chicago minister, quoted in the *Tribune*, argued that laboring men—"the very sight of whom are a disgust"—were still a part of the American community no matter how loathsome or violent. "In some sense," he continued, "we are responsible . . . to do all we can to raise them out of ignorance." Within one year, his middle-class compatriots had enlisted educational reformers to join temperance organizers and Christian missionaries in such an educational effort.[12]

Churchmen and missionaries were not alone in their negative assessment of the "dangerous classes" and in their positive prescription of education to spread nativist values to new ethnic and urban populations. Skilled workers were no less alarmed by the appearance of an unskilled and transient proletariat, although they blamed the sweat-shop capitalist for this destabilizing blight as often as they blamed intemperance or sin. "That man who passes yonder with heavy footstep, hair unkempt, person dirty, dinner bucket in hand, and a general air of desolation," said a Pittsburgh glass blower in 1884, "is a 12-hour-a-day wage slave." The remedy for such industrial degradation was shorter hours, union working conditions, and education. "We must get our people to read and think," declared Robert Howard, a spinners' leader in Fall River, Massachusetts, "to look for something higher and more noble in life than working along in that wretched way from day to day and from year to year."[13]

From year to year, however, the blight of "wage slavery," poverty, and unemployment grew steadily more worrisome. The urban proletariat grew larger and more alien as 15 million immigrants entered the United States between 1890 and 1914. Economic slumps in 1884, 1893, 1904, 1907, 1912, and 1921 periodically added millions of transient workers to this depressed population, while mechanization and deskilling of work steadily undermined the position of many skilled craftsmen. Even as the middle class grew and some workers prospered, America's slums harbored a growing and potentially volatile mass of downtrodden workers.[14]

Reformers portrayed this impoverished underclass in a multitude of roles—as incendiaries, parasites, strikebreakers, sinners, or victims—and frequently regarded their presence as a threat to the Republic. Liberal crusader Jacob Riis expressed this prevailing mood of anguish and anxiety in his book, *The Battle with the Slum*. "The slum," he wrote in 1902, "stands for ignorance, want, unfitness, and mob rule in the day of wrath. . . . When the slum flourishes unchallenged in the cities . . . patriotism among their people is dead."[15]

II

Restoring or inculcating patriotism (of one sort or another) and promoting citizenship activities were prime tasks of adult educators from the 1870s through the post-World War I years. The ideal bond of loyalty was construed in different ways—to God, nation, trade, employer, or class. The prevailing notion was that continuing change in an industrial society required continuing education to reorient and invigorate the dislocated worker.

Many reformers were deeply troubled about the changing relationships of people caught in transition from traditional small-town society to urban industrial areas. They sought methods to initiate or enhance participation in social institutions that rapidly were becoming centralized, bureaucratized, and alienated from the myths and visions of the face-to-face character of small-town life. Many viewed education as a moral process: enhancing the intelligence of workers so that they could help overcome the evils of their times.

Numerous approaches to these educational tasks emerged between the 1870s and the 1930s, which contributed in their own ways to the substance or context of the New Deal's EEP. First on the scene were Protestant evangelists. "Adult education" was intrinsic to their earthly mission and to the evangelical and temperance crusades that had focused on the urban poor even before the Civil War. After 1870, evangelism established an organized and sustained presence in the slums: New York's YMCA set up its Bowery Branch in 1872; John McAuley opened his Water Street Mission that same year, and the Salvation Army started its first mission in 1880.

Beyond their goal of spiritual regeneration for the masses, the missions also claimed a social dividend. "It is gratifying," one New York mission reported in 1883, "that the importance and value of this work of the Mission has commended itself more and more to businessmen. Its reformatory influence upon the lawless and dangerous classes is a matter of record." [16]

Not every slum evangelist, however, construed religion's role in such narrowly conservative terms. Beginning in the 1880s, the Social Gospel movement preached a reformist doctrine that called for regulation of large corporations, prohibitions on child labor, and progressive taxation of income and inheritances. From the 1880s through the first part of the new century, socially conscious ministers spread the message that the wealthy should behave righteously to solve social unrest. The rich and the middle classes must form an "intelligent and humane public opinion" to ameliorate industrial conflict and advance industrial peace.

Popular education had a leading role in remaking social institutions by raising individual consciousness about social and economic evils. Christian principles applied to social problem solving would help "cultivate the social temper, the habit of cooperation, the spirit of service, and the consciousness of fraternity," as Social Gospel leader Washington Gladden wrote in 1902. [17]

However much the "reformatory influence" of Protestant missions commended itself to businessmen, many corporate leaders concluded they would have to intervene directly in the education of the "dangerous classes" to insure a loyal and efficient workforce. "It is the testimony of most writers," observed

William Tolman in his 1909 study, *Social Engineering*, "that department store employees . . . are often supremely uninterested and regardless (sic) of the fact that their employer's welfare is identical with their own. Such indifference is due to the lack of comprehensive training."[18]

"Comprehensive training," as implemented by America's biggest companies after 1900, had several goals. By countering the traditional (though partially decayed) craft-control of apprenticeship, companies hoped to wean their skilled workers away from unions and wed them to the corporation. Corporate-controlled vocational education would do so by inculcating values, skills, and aspirations consistent with the companies' "scientific" redivision of labor. For the less-skilled and the foreign-born worker, English courses and Americanization classes would teach the language skills and work habits appropriate for mechanized mass production.

Discipline, consumerism, and conformity were the cultural norms stressed in these explicitly assimilationist programs. Only the biggest corporations could afford such comprehensive social engineering, and in many cases, even they preferred to socialize the costs by transferring responsibility to the public schools. Detroit, for example, provided singular examples of both strategies in the early twentieth century.

The Ford Motor Company's English School and Sociological Department, founded in 1914, and its Apprentice School, organized in 1923, exemplified company- financed and controlled education programs. Many smaller companies, however, saw no return in training workers who might subsequently leave their employ. The majority, therefore, backed publicly funded programs such as the public schools' evening English classes. In Detroit, the Americanization Committee of the Board of Commerce promoted these citizenship programs along with Cass Technical School's continuation classes for apprentices, organized by the Employers' Association of Detroit in 1913.[19]

Ideally, as articulated by Boyd Fisher, vice president of the Executives' Club of Detroit, these worker education programs would extend "factory discipline into the whole life of the workman." The employer would thus become, in Fisher's words, "a co-partner with the teacher, the minister, and the social worker in the business of reforming men."[20]

III

As a distinct branch of adult education, workers' education developed in the nineteenth century as a response by early reformers to the needs of workers to better understand the economic and social changes brought about by the Industrial Revolution. Some aspects of workers' education were rooted in British and European adult and workers' education programs, and were aided by the influx into the United States of European union activists and socialists.

During these early years, education projects were conducted by individual philanthropists, organizations aiding the assimilation of European immigrants, various branches of the Socialist movement, and reformers designing education programs specifically for women workers.

Diverse and often overlapping goals of workers' education during these formative years included raising workers' educational levels, stimulating their cultural interests, aiding their citizenship efforts, increasing their understanding of unionism, training them for union activism, helping them understand the society they wanted to change, and radicalizing the labor force. By the 1930s, the goals of workers' education remained unclear and the tensions generated by divergent philosophies and conflicting types of programs would be reflected in the experiences and crises of the New Deal's workers' education projects.[21]

By and large, these early workers' education activities in the nineteenth and early twentieth centuries took place outside the trade union movement. Organized in 1886, the American Federation of Labor (AFL) put its efforts into expanding free public school education and withheld support for workers' education for almost forty years because of its distrust of middle-class intellectuals and left-wing activists.

In goals and content, a limited number of trade union education programs reflected the diverse and fragmented nature of a hard-pressed union movement. In an era characterized between 1900 and 1930 by open–shop union busting and left-wing ferment, AFL's craft unions generally found themselves on the defensive, beset by challenges from antiunion employers as well as from more radical labor groups. Conservative trade unions responded with educational efforts that promoted a "craft culture" of sobriety, respectability, brotherhood, and hard work. Left-wing unions, particularly in the needle trades, combined their advocacy of social change and industrial unionism with an assimilationist curriculum aimed at their foreign-born constituents.

The educational efforts of both wings of the labor movement paralleled certain features of corporate and evangelical teaching. The AFL's Labor Forward campaign from 1912 through 1916 consciously adopted the methods and much of the message of the Social Gospel movement's Men and Religion campaign of 1911–1912. In these same years, the International Ladies Garment Workers' Union (ILGWU) and the Amalgamated Clothing Workers of America (ACWA) both put considerable emphasis on teaching English and citizenship skills to foreign-born workers. Yet AFL and left-wing unions also promoted ideas, including the efficacy of collective strike action and the immorality of sweat-shop entrepreneurship, that put them at odds with business leaders and conservative evangelists.[22]

During World War I, trade union membership experienced a temporary spurt as a result of a no-strike pledge made by AFL President Samuel Gompers in exchange for government and industry recognition of expanded organizing and bargaining rights for labor. This, in turn, stimulated workers' education programs in the needle trades and in some city labor councils. Both the ILGWU and the ACWA set up education departments at their national headquarters in New York City and started a United Labor Education Committee, backed largely by the needle trades. Between 1918 and 1921, a number of city labor federations also started evening classes for workers, usually taught under the auspices of colleges and universities.

By 1921, there were upward of seventy-five workers' "colleges," "temples," and study programs located in twenty-one states across the country. Their curricula reflected the varied goals of a growing workers' education movement. Many, such as the Boston Trade Union College that opened in 1919 under the sponsorship of the Boston central labor union, offered classes in effective writing and speaking, economics, literature, law, science, and recreation taught by instructors from the faculties of nearby schools. The St. Paul, Minnesota Labor College attempted "to provide trained and educated workers for labor, . . . [to create] better citizens, . . . to afford some enjoyment of life hitherto denied." The Trade Union College of Greater New York proposed to "train American workers to think fundamentally and constructively about economic questions." Several faculty members at Amherst College in Massachusetts taught off-campus classes for workers "as an expression of the belief that an opportunity for liberal education should be open to all who feel its need." [23]

To meet the need for a national center that could act as a clearinghouse for these activities, the Workers' Education Bureau (WEB) was organized at an April 1921 conference in New York City. James Maurer, a socialist and president of the Pennsylvania Federation of Labor, was elected president, and Spencer Miller, Jr., a graduate of Columbia University Teachers' College, was elected secretary, an executive office he held for the next thirty years. [24]

The purpose of the WEB was "to collect and disseminate information about the education efforts of any part of organized labor; to coordinate and assist the educational work now carried on by organized workers; and to stimulate the creation of additional [workers' education] enterprises throughout the United States." This confederation of workers' education programs, the first such national organization in the country, was given approval and some financial support by the AFL and soon counted as affiliates hundreds of AFL local unions, city and state federations, and some international unions. [25]

The WEB program focused much of its energy on developing reading materials to help union members understand economic and social problems, and to aid local unions in stabilizing their membership. Pamphlets on union administration, the function of the shop steward, and labor history were issued in a series called the Workers' Bookshelf, praised by progressive educator Harry

Overstreet as "the first serious and sustained attempt to give authentic recognition to the thinking worker." Early in 1926, Miller reported an enrollment of 40,000 students in workers' study groups or "colleges" financed by labor unions in over 300 industrial centers in thirty states.[26]

The labor movement's growing utilization of college faculty was underlined in 1921, when the University of California at Berkeley, in cooperation with the California State Federation of Labor, established the nation's first labor extension service. The following year, Syracuse University followed the California example by offering labor extension classes in economics to workers, and similar programs were started in the same time period by Harvard, the Massachusetts Institute of Technology, Tufts, Amherst, the University of Cincinnati, and the University of Oklahoma.[27]

Establishment of university and college extension programs not only gave legitimacy to the labor movement's educational aims but also ratified the cautious tenor of most workers' education. Since the content of such programs had to meet the approval of university officials as well as sponsoring AFL unions, the curricula tended to reflect a moderately liberal agenda. A mild reformism and a focus on the organizational needs of "responsible" unions were acceptable. Advocacy of more fundamental social change was not, and teaching about industrial unionism was suspect. Tension between these poles of workers' education, already evident in the 1920s, would become salient issues in the New Deal's EEP.

IV

As with most New Deal reforms, the EEP owed a great debt to the Progressive movement. Defining the parameters and origins of this diffuse reform crusade is difficult, but among its earliest manifestations in the field of education, the settlement house movement of the 1880s and 1890s set the stage for much of what followed.

In this and other reform campaigns stressing education, the prominent role played by middle- and upper-class women foreshadowed key elements of the EEP. Colleges and universities had finally opened their doors to women after the Civil War, beginning with Vassar in 1865, Wellesley and Smith in 1875, and Mount Holyoke, Bryn Mawr, and Barnard in the 1880s. Women who graduated from these elite institutions, however, found most avenues of professional advancement barred. Social work and education were among the exceptions, and the settlement house movement and such related organizations as the YWCA Industrial Department, combined these disciplines with a crusading commitment to working among the poor.

In this regard, the movement borrowed from precedents established by mission evangelists and the Social Gospel advocates. Indeed, many settlement house founders came from religious backgrounds—Jane Addams and Ellen Gates Starr, co-founders of Chicago's Hull House, were both educated in a women's seminary—but the educational programs they established were primarily secular. Enlightenment and self-improvement, not salvation, were the goals for most of the approximately 100 settlement houses established between 1886 and 1900. In addition to courses in cooking, vocational skills, English, and "Americanization," settlement houses and YWCA industrial girls' clubs also organized classes and discussion groups on current events, literature, music, and drama. Settlement house and social work leaders, such as Grace Coyle, a staff member of the YWCA Industrial Department, pioneered the use of group work methods, which became the dominant pedagogy of workers' education.[28]

Some of the movement's founders assumed that exposure to "higher" culture and middle-class norms would "elevate" the masses. Most reformers recognized the need to reconstruct political and economic life along more democratic lines, but even when they advocated specific reforms, progressives still subscribed to the liberal faith in education and moral suasion as the primary agents of social change. As progressives saw it, only an educated citizenry could shoulder the task of reforming society, and publicly supported education was, they concluded, the only adequate means of providing instruction on such a large scale.

Advocacy of night classes for adults easily merged with the social-control agenda of businessmen—an agenda shared by some progressives—and helped produce a proliferation of adult education programs after 1900. By 1910, more than 100 public schools in New York City offered night classes in language, sciences, commercial subjects, domestic arts, and vocational skills.

In New York and elsewhere, much of this curriculum promoted middle-class cultural norms and industrial discipline, but a sizeable number of progressives also believed that unions played a positive role in checking the abuses of big business. Some settlement houses invited union members to participate in their classes and discussion groups. The Women's Trade Union League (WTUL), formed in 1903 by social workers, wealthy gentlewomen, and some women workers, established a Training School for Active Workers in cooperation with Chicago's Northwestern University, and raised scholarship funds for young women to learn economics, civics, collective bargaining, office work, and union organization.[29]

This widening ferment for adult education eventually generated a distinctive methodology, brilliantly articulated in 1916 by John Dewey in *Democracy and Education*. Dewey's assertion that the *process* of a democratic education would lead to a democratic society became the maxim of adult educators in general, and workers' education leaders in particular. As they developed teaching methods that would democratize classrooms in settlement houses, night schools, union halls, and university extension programs, workers' educators settled on four major principles: (1) involving participants in developing curricula based on their own needs and interests; (2) opposing the isolation of schooling from the real world; (3) building learning experiences around real-life situations; and (4) viewing the education process as a means of social change.[30]

All of this put workers' education leaders at odds with traditional academic curricula that isolated schooling from the community. Progressive educators—influenced by William Kilpatrick's concept of the project method, first outlined in 1918, to build a curriculum around "wholehearted, purposeful activity in a social situation"—focused on developing methods that would prepare students for social living. Participants at the 1922 national conference of the Workers' Education Bureau (WEB) in New York City applauded when speaker Kilpatrick, an eminent professor at Columbia University Teachers' College, asked: "Is it not possible to apply in the teaching of adults a principle that is gaining great acceptance in the case of younger people—that learning comes best when it comes in connection with some purpose the learner feels?"[31]

Addressing himself to the problems of adult instruction during the day-long session on methods of teaching workers, Kilpatrick stressed the need for participant-oriented curricula led by instructors who raise questions, refrain from imposing convictions, recognize diversity of opinion, and avoid propaganda. "This method," he stated, "looks towards democracy. If the instructor is democratic at heart, he has by this method the chance to be democratic in fact."[32]

The leaders of the workers' education movement in the 1920s—most of them college-educated and middle-class, and many from the graduate programs at Columbia University—developed new institutional contexts and programs where they tested and refined these progressive education theories for their adult worker constituency. They articulated the aims of progressive educators by pragmatically developing classroom techniques for their worker-students: active advisory committees with members from workplace and community organizations; learning experiences through small discussion groups, panels, field trips, forums, workshops, and self-government activities; use of community resources; and a new role for the teacher as a collaborator in the learning process.[33] Many of these educators were inspired by workers' education developments in Europe, especially in Great Britain and Scandinavia, where unions, community organizations, and government supported well established programs offering a wide range of education for adult working-class students.

In developing their philosophies and programs, adult and workers' education leaders were influenced by a British publication, *The 1919 Report*, called by one educational historian "probably the most important single contribution ever made to the literature of adult education." Initiated by the British Prime Minister Lloyd George at the end of World War I, *The 1919 Report* was an analysis of adult education activities in Britain written by members of a Cabinet Reconstruction Committee that included British social philosophers R. H. Tawney and Albert Mansbridge.

In the context of a world convulsed by the aftershocks of the Russian revolution, the report stressed the importance of adult education to the functioning of a democratic society. The committee recommended that the state support and fund adult education as a permanent national program, and that universities establish extension services and departments to develop adult education programs as one of their major responsibilities.[34]

Following the traumas of World War I and the wave of strikes and urban riots that swept the United States in 1918–1919, support was intensified for programs that aimed to broaden the base of democratic participation in society and to train citizens who were literate, loyal, knowledgeable, and articulate on behalf of liberal capitalism and political democracy. In 1919, the Progressive Education Association was formed. In 1922, the National Council on Social Studies was organized to advance the use of history, economics, and social civics to help students think more constructively on domestic as well as international problems. In 1923, the University Extension Association set up a permanent committee on workers' education; in 1926, the American Association for Adult Education was founded; in 1929, the influential *Journal of Adult Education* was started.[35]

An adult education literature emerged that was to influence practitioners in both the fields of adult education and workers' education; it included: John Dewey's *Democracy and Education*; James Harvey Robinson's *The Mind in the Making* (1921) and *The Humanizing of Knowledge* (1924); Eduard Lindeman's *The Meaning of Adult Education* (1926); Horace Kallen's *Education, the Machine and the Worker* (1926); A. L. Hall-Quest's *The University Afield* (1926); J. K. Hart's *Adult Education* (1927); Dorothy Canfield Fisher's *Why Stop Learning* (1927); Frederick Keppel's *Education for Adults* (1933); and Edward Thorndike's *Adult Learning* (1929).[36]

A close relationship developed between a number of these adult education theoreticians and workers' education practitioners, especially those in the New York area. In addition to Kilpatrick, outstanding educators such as Lindeman, Robinson, Hart, Overstreet, and Charles Beard visited workers' education classes, contributed to workers' education periodicals, and corresponded with workers' education activists. Robinson edited a series of monographs for the Workers' Bookshelf, the publication program sponsored by the WEB. Lindeman served as WEB research director for a short time in the late 1920s. Lindeman, Beard, Overstreet, and Kilpatrick were frequent speakers at workers' education conferences and workshops. Dewey was active in the American Federation of Teachers, the union to which a number of the workers' education practitioners belonged.[37]

All of these theoreticians and practitioners helped prepare the ground for the New Deal's EEP. None, however, rivaled the influence of Hilda Worthington Smith, who helped found the Bryn Mawr Summer School for Women Workers in 1921, served as its director until 1933, and was head of the New Deal's workers' education projects between 1933 and 1942.

Smith was the embodiment of the liberal patrician who so often figured in the leadership of the Progressive movement. This genteel and gracious woman was born in New York City in 1888, into a wealthy and well-connected family that summered at its Hudson River estate across from the Roosevelt home at Hyde Park. She was educated at private schools and at Bryn Mawr College where she received a rigorous education, played basketball, and was elected president of the student council, a formative experience in her early years. She later recalled that she learned at Bryn Mawr how the objectives of self-governing groups could be obtained "through analysis of problems and group decisions."[38]

Smith stayed at Bryn Mawr College for a master's degree, working with community suffrage groups and with factory women at a Philadelphia settlement house as part of her volunteer field work. After taking a diploma at the New York School of Philanthropy (later named the New York School of Social Work), she returned to the town of Bryn Mawr to direct a community center that provided, as a result of her leadership, lunches for schoolchildren, a library, a gym for teenagers, clubs for adults, and night classes for town workers. In 1919, the dominant and creative Bryn Mawr College President, M. Carey Thomas, tapped Smith to serve as dean at Bryn Mawr College. In that role, she administered college programs, counseled undergraduate women, and arranged night classes for the college gardeners and service employees.[39]

In 1921, President Thomas asked Smith to head the Bryn Mawr Summer School for Women Workers, a pioneer venture in workers' education that Thomas helped start on her campus after visiting Workers' Education Association programs in England. This opportunity melded Smith's interests in social work and education, and was a turning point in her career.

With strong support from the WTUL, the YWCA Industrial Department, federal and state agencies that dealt with women workers, and the needle trades unions, Smith developed an innovative summer program that from 1921 to 1936 annually raised scholarship funds for approximately a hundred women factory workers who came together on the lush Bryn Mawr campus with about fifty staff drawn mostly from eastern colleges. During the eight-week residential program, women from different ethnic, geographic, and workplace backgrounds took courses in history, English, speech, literature, and economics with the curriculum structured around a theme relevant to the students' own economic situations. Physical hygiene, creative movement, and astronomy rounded out a program that sought to "offer young women in industry opportunities to study liberal subjects and train themselves in clear thinking. . . ."

Beyond the immediate aim of increasing the "happiness and usefulness" of the students' lives, the school had more ambitious goals. The Bryn Mawr Summer School hoped "to offer young women of character and ability . . . the opportunity to study liberal subjects in order that they might widen their influence in the industrial world and help in the coming social reconstruction." It aimed to give women workers in industry some parity in educational opportunity with more privileged university students, living in "academic surroundings of beauty" with "complete freedom from economic anxiety and domestic care." [40]

To train students in the skills of democratic participation, the school involved them in field projects, forums, discussion workshops, and self-governing activities—techniques that became standard procedures for later workers' education programs. Smith's contribution to this curriculum was supplemented by the administrative work of the school's executive secretary, Ernestine Friedmann, a Smith College graduate, former staff member of the YWCA Industrial Department, and a future administrator, with Smith, of the New Deal's workers' education projects. Together, Smith and Friedmann developed an administrative committee at the Bryn Mawr summer program that drew half of its representatives from the college and half from the women students, a pattern that subsequent government-sponsored and university workers' education programs adopted in later years for their advisory committees. The net result was a program that inspired wide acclaim from liberal educators and progressives. [41]

Eleanor Roosevelt visited the campus one summer when her friend Marian Dickerman was teaching there and later recalled: "I sat with some of the classes and talked with many of the students and was impressed everywhere with the quality of eagerness which comes, I suppose, to minds which are denied the opportunity of studying certain things, and when they find that opportunity within their grasp, they at once respond with great eagerness because their hunger for knowledge and their need for the special kind of knowledge they are trying to acquire is far greater than the average student." [42]

Throughout the 1920s, the Bryn Mawr Summer School for Women Workers provided a model for other residential summer schools that were organized, at least initially, to serve women workers: the Southern School for Women Workers, the Barnard School, and the Wisconsin School for Workers, all started in the mid-1920s. In 1926, these summer residential programs formed the Affiliated Schools for Workers with Smith as chair. [43]

The new organization, created to alleviate growing competition for funds, opened offices in New York City in 1927 with the purpose of coordinating programs to enable the expansion of workers' education through training projects and the publication of suitable teaching materials. Its stated purpose exemplified the Progressive movement's commitment to liberal reform through individual transformation. This commitment implied no rejection of this country's dominant economic structures and no attachment to particular political organizations. The Affiliated Schools for Workers stood for "the type of education . . . which is concerned with the interpretation of the past and the present in order that the individual may become an intelligent participant in shaping the future." [44]

V

Like progressives, socialists saw workers' education as a means of transforming individual consciousness and preparing the ground for social change. But in contrast to liberal reformers, their vision of an anticapitalist society was more thoroughly wedded to strategies that called for collective action. Unlike the "pure and simple" AFL business unionists, socialists were committed to workers' education from the start of their organizations in the 1870s. Both the left-wing socialists who believed in revolutionary direct action and the more dominant right-wing socialists who supported working within existing economic and political institutions advocated workers' education as a crucial prerequisite for achieving a workers' democracy. After the Socialist Party and the Industrial Workers of the World were formed in 1901 and 1905 respectively, and after socialists gained considerable influence among immigrant and organized workers, their educational efforts were institutionalized.

In 1906, the Socialist Party founded the Rand School of Social Sciences in New York City to give workers a better understanding of economic and social forces in order to "help them build a better world." In 1908, the Industrial Workers of the World, a radical labor organization, took over a Lutheran college outside of Duluth, Minnesota, to start the Work People's College, a year-round residential school with classes in English and Finnish that, within a Marxist framework, aimed to sharpen the understanding of the worker-students of their role in society and train them to bring about economic and social change. [45]

World War I and the Russian revolution made the prospects for such change seem all the more favorable. Mark Starr, a British socialist who immigrated to the United States in the 1920s, spoke of the development of workers' education in the context of this "hopeful revolutionary period."

In order to secure labor's cooperation during the war, the various governments had given the trade union movement important concessions. Shop committees had sprung up in the heavy industries both in America and in Europe. This seemed to indicate that a large section of the working class wished to assume responsibility for the processes of production. Guild socialism as a philosophy combining certain features of syndicalism and state socialism was rapidly making converts through the persuasive pens of R.H. Tawney and G.D.H. Cole. The first explosions of the successful Russian Revolution were vibrating through millions of hearts. Even the railway workers and miners in this country were offically advocating schemes for government ownership and working-class control. Workers' education seemed an important adjunct to the efficient and successful assumption of power by the workers themselves.[46]

Hopes for such a transfer of power were dashed after 1918 by the government's campaign to suppress the left in this country and the postwar reaction against organized labor. Chastened by these setbacks and wary of identifying themselves with the fragmented and warring parties of the left, socialist trade unionists led by A. J. Muste, a former Dutch Reformed minister, founded the union-oriented Brookwood Labor College in Katonah, New York, in 1921. Brookwood's goals were articulated in decidedly nonradical terms. Its purpose was "to unite a force of education that will service American labor with trained, responsible, liberally educated men and women from the ranks of labor. The new college is not intended to act as a propagandist institution. Thoroughly in sympathy with the aims and aspirations of labor as a whole, the college will closely cooperate with the national and international labor groups."[47]

The coeducational college offered a two-year, residential curriculum that included a first-year emphasis on the social sciences and a second-year concentration on the skills of organizing, collective bargaining, and union leadership. Students, recruited primarily from AFL unions, were supported through scholarships from their organizations and by monies from the Garland Fund that provided aid to the college in its early years.[48]

Brookwood's year-round programs, described by one labor historian as "the labor movement's most ambitious educational enterprise," ran for sixteen years until 1937. The multiple services included youth programs, an extensive correspondence service, a traveling chautauqua, labor theater, and two official publications, *Labor Age* and *Brookwood Review*. During its existence, the college trained over 500 trade-union and community activists, many of whom played pivotal roles organizing the Congress of Industrial Organizations (CIO) and its constituent unions in the 1930s.[49]

Radical workers' education also expanded in the 1920s with the opening of the Communist Workers' Party School with forty students in New York City in 1923. Dedicated to presenting material from "a clearly defined and intransigent revolutionary standpoint," the school hired "reliable, active Party comrades" to develop and promote "a genuine, Leninist ideology" in the seventy-three courses, most of them in English, on Marxist theory, history and economics that the Workers' School offered to several thousand part-time students who were enrolled by 1929.[50]

In the South, a nonsectarian Highlander Folk School, unaffiliated with any union or political group, opened in 1932 in the Tennessee mountains to train activists, organizers, and workers' educators for the labor movement. Modeled on some of the Scandinavian folk schools, Highlander pioneered in accepting Southern adults of all races. In addition to labor history and labor organizing techniques, its program emphasized folk music and drama.

Despite this range of workers' education projects, one writer noted on the eve of the New Deal that workers' education programs, devastated by the lack of financial support following the 1929 stock market crash, in their totality had become "a very small item in the complex of American education." Although some workers were involved in short-term classes or local projects, the combined enrollments in the residential schools, union-sponsored classes, and radical programs amounted to fewer than two thousand students by 1932.[51]

VI

Considerable cross-fertilization blurred the lines between these seedbeds of the New Deal's workers' education program. In a society permeated by religious sentiment and periodically convulsed by evangelical fervor, it was not unusual to find YWCA group workers, seminary graduates, and Christian socialists participating in all the more secular varieties of workers' education between 1870 and 1930. Some progressives who endorsed trade-union education programs during World War I also supported government campaigns to instill patriotic values in the general public as well as to improve the reading skills of army recruits. In the 1910s and 1920s, the left-wing needle-trade unions simultaneously promoted a social-change curriculum laced with socialist ideology and an Americanization program made up of English classes and citizenship training.

Distinctions between union, religiously oriented, and socialist varieties of workers' education were less evident in the 1910s, and 1920s, since the goals of union organization, individual enlightenment, and social transformation were so frequently merged in the rhetoric of the Progressive era. The several institutions formed at the end of this period in 1921 were born of peculiarly hybrid seed: Brookwood Labor College was initially backed by AFL unions; the first president of the WEB, James Maurer, was a prominent leader of the Socialist Party; and the socialist-led needle-trade unions backed Smith's new program at Bryn Mawr.

Although the mixed pedigrees of these institutions suggested a single family tree in 1921, their distinctive lineages were clarified over the next ten years. By 1928, the Brookwood program was in conflict with the conservative, craft union leadership of the AFL because of Brookwood's advocacy of industrial unionism, aid to organizing campaigns of workers in the basic industries, and criticisms of the craft-oriented policies of the AFL. Despite the school's disavowal of radical propagandizing, the AFL in 1928 alleged that Brookwood was "communistic . . . pro-Soviet . . . anti-religious . . . and a threat to the labor movement." It withdrew its support from Brookwood and urged its affiliates to cancel their approval and aid.[52]

As the open-shop campaigns in the 1920s reinforced the AFL's defensive, craft-oriented posture, similar tensions transformed the Workers' Education Bureau. Although the WEB was technically independent of any one labor union, its independence eroded as it became increasingly dependent on the AFL for financial support. When friction developed between AFL President William Green and WEB President Maurer due to the latter's Socialist affiliations, the AFL assumed control of the WEB in 1929, following Maurer's resignation.[53]

This falling out between socialist and craft-union programs in workers' education found expression in the views articulated by each of the opposing camps. At the AFL's 1928 convention, the Executive Council emphasized that workers needed training for intelligent and efficient union membership and little else. "There are the problems of making the trade union movement more effective, of meeting specific industrial situations, of managing a union most efficiently, of formulating union policies, etc. . . . Such matters are properly within the field of workers' education and the more closely that educational work is connected with union activity and union meetings, the more effective it will be."[54]

To insure that workers' education was compatible with the policies and institutional needs of the AFL, new regulations required that affiliation of any program or institution with the WEB be approved by both the AFL central labor body in its region and the AFL state labor federation. This policy aimed to screen out the teachings of untried intellectuals, reformers, and radical visionaries.[55]

A socialist, J.B.S. Hardman, education director of the ACWA, articulated the opposing concept that workers' education should help prepare participants for changing the social order:

> . . . workers' education is not adult education. It is more than that. It is wider in scope, different and more complicated. A university may offer extension courses in labor subjects and attract a large and purely working-class audience. That would not be workers' education, however.

Workers' unions may engage the teachers and pay the rent for the hall where labor courses are given, and even if such courses are attended by working men and women, it will not be a venture in workers' education. Not quite. Why? Because primarily, the workers see in education not only what others see in it, but also a powerful means toward that end which most concerns them. That end is a change in the conditions of social living. . . . Labor wants "things" changed and the labor ideal of education is one of education for social reconstruction and readjustment.[56]

In contrast to Hardman's radical view of the purposes of workers' education and the AFL's blunt assertion of institutional self–maintenance, progressive adult educators continued to promote a liberal faith in enlightenment and citizenship goals for education programs designed for workers. "The techniques of workers education," Columbia Teachers' College graduate Spencer Miller Jr. stated in the mid-1920s, "bring teachers and students together as friends in an adventure of learning." In answer to the question, "why workers' education?" Miller replied: "democratization . . . to create an ability to influence public opinion . . . to help labor's power to serve rationally. Only trained and widespread intelligence will save the American democratic experiment."[57]

What this "intelligence" consisted of and how it would save American democracy were questions that progressives did not often address. Implicitly, the link they drew between reason and action was conceived of in naturalistic terms: reasonable people would discover a way to organize society and would act accordingly. In the process, they would naturally shed the petty interests and class entanglements that prevented social cooperation. The prerequisite for this happy outcome was not a political program or mobilization for collective action, but education in democratic thinking. "This process," Smith later said of the adult education programs she organized in the 1930s, "carried on in innumerable classrooms, is undoubtedly having its effect on other relationships in family life, in public schools, in community organizations. Perhaps in time, these little experiments in democratic thought and action may have a decided effect on the whole pattern of our national life in government and in politics, directing national planning along democratic lines for the benefit of all."[58]

VII

By 1933, workers' education—church, corporate, union, progressive, and socialist—had produced numerous approaches, programs, and institutions. The New Deal's workers' education program, developed by the EEP of the FERA, benefited from them and formed the basis, over the next ten years, of a continuing movement for federal support of workers' education.[59]

As an extension of the New Deal's programs, in 1945, a coalition of labor educators, university staff, and labor leaders formed the National Committee for the Extension of Labor Education, headed by Smith. This committee aimed to draft and secure passage of federal legislation, the Labor Extension Act, supporting federal funding for university- and college-based labor education. The bill failed to pass Congress in 1950.[60]

Thirty years later, Leonard Woodcock, then president of the United Automobile, Aerospace, and Agricultural Implement Workers' Union (UAW) called for enactment of federal legislation that would support university-based labor education through a new drive to establish a federally funded Labor Extension Service. The renewed interest in labor extension legislation received the support of other labor leaders and labor educators. The University and College Labor Education Association (UCLEA), a professional association of over eighty university and college labor education programs, initiated activities to obtain federally funded labor education programs, and appointed a committee to prepare background materials and draft language for proposed legislation.[61]

This book, then, provides contemporary labor educators and policymakers with a case study from the 1930s of the first, national government-supported workers' education program in this country. By chronicling the national WPA workers' educational activities, it serves as a document, adding to the literature that analyzes and increases our understanding of the contributions and limitations of the New Deal's social programs. To these ends, it is informed by Howard Zinn's message:

> It is for today, then, that we turn to the thinking of the New Deal period. Although the New Deal gave us only fragments of solutions, it did leave us—perhaps because those were desperate years and desperation stimulates innovation—with a public discussion more intense and more sweeping than any we have had before or since. People outside the New Deal entourage, invited or not, joined that discussion and extended the boundaries of political and economic imagination beyond those of the New Dealers—sometimes to the left, sometimes to the right, sometimes in directions hard to pick.

> Their thinking does not give us facile solutions, but if history has uses beyond that of reminiscence, one of them is to nourish lean ideological times with the nectars of other years. And although the present shape of the world was hardly discernible in 1939, certain crucial social issues persist in both eras. Somehow, in the interaction between the ideas of the New Dealers themselves and those of social critics who gathered in various stances and at various distances around the Roosevelt fire, we may find suggestions or approaches that are relevant today.[62]

2

Adult Education in the New Deal 1933–1942

A far greater number of white-collar workers and professionals were unemployed than ever before. Manual labor was not the answer. Common sense told us that it was not only inefficient but wasteful to put an artist to work chopping trees or a teacher to digging ditches.

—Harry Hopkins, May 1937[1]

On November 4, 1930, an estimated 6,000 apple sellers suddenly appeared on the streets of New York City, peddling surplus fruit they had received on credit from the Apple Shippers Association.

Barely a year before, the stock market crash of October 1929 had sent disquieting tremors through the business world. Politicians and economists had thereafter assured an anxious nation that rumors of mass unemployment were unfounded and the economy was basically sound, but now workers, reduced to hawking apples for 5 cents each, gave vocal testimony that something was profoundly wrong.[2]

The Great Depression was in its first full year, and the apple vendors of November 1930 were the advance guard of a rapidly expanding army of unemployed. By 1933, there were an estimated 15 million jobless workers nationwide, representing roughly 25 percent of the country's workforce. In Chicago and Detroit, unemployment surpassed 40 percent of the labor force. All across the country, shuttered factories, abandoned homes, breadlines, and shanty towns became commonplace.

Unemployed workers and dispossessed farmers, cast aside like the surplus fruit in New York, were initially sullen and demoralized. In time, however, some of them responded like the "dangerous classes" of old. Between 1930 and 1932, Unemployed Councils organized by the Communist Party and other left-wing organizations appeared in many cities, where they blocked evictions and demonstrated for emergency relief. Army veterans marched on Washington to demand immediate payment of their war service bonus, and were forcibly dispersed by tanks and cavalry. Farmers barricaded highways in the Midwest to block food shipments and force up prices. In Michigan, thousands of the unemployed marched on Henry Ford's plant in Dearborn to demand jobs and relief, and were gunned down by the police, leaving dozens wounded and four dead.[3]

In the face of this mounting crisis, private charitable organizations and municipal welfare departments were simply overwhelmed. Their meager resources were quickly depleted by escalating demands for relief, and their diminishing income from wealthy contributors and hard-pressed taxpayers forced many agencies to suspend operations. Ethnically based banks, insurance societies, and mutual-aid organizations also floundered as the poor and unemployed liquidated their savings and clamored for assistance.[4]

Like their charitable counterparts, private adult education organizations also had to curtail their activities as wealthy supporters, universities, and trade unions began to husband their dwindling resources and cut back their contributions. At the very time adult educators perceived the greatest need to reorient, retrain, and reinvigorate the unemployed, their institutions began to collapse—among them, Brookwood Labor College and the Bryn Mawr School for Women Workers, both of which closed their doors for lack of funds in the 1930s.[5]

The existing system of public education was in no position to fill the void. In 1932, only eighteen states contributed to the support of adult education in their communities; nineteen states had no communities offering adult classes; four states had one community each providing adult classes; and nine states had between one and fifteen towns sponsoring some form of adult education through public schools. Even this modest commitment was jeopardized by the Depression's impact on local, tax-supported education. Headlines announced in 1932 and 1933 that 11,000 New York City teachers were laid off; the pay of Chicago's teachers was $28,000,000 in arrears. Nationally, between 80,000 and 100,000 out-of-work teachers and other jobless educational personnel were lining up to get government relief checks; 85 percent of Alabama's public schools had closed.[6]

I

On a March evening in 1933, Harry Hopkins and William Hodson met with U.S. Secretary of Labor Frances Perkins to convince her of the need for more intensive federal measures to help the millions of jobless and destitute people in need of food, cash, clothing, useful work, and hope. Hopkins, the head of the New York State Temporary Emergency Relief Administration (TERA), and Hodson, the director of the New York City Welfare Council, had come to the Women's City Club in Washington, D.C. to talk with Perkins about the nationwide economic crisis and report on their experiences with work relief in

New York State. They aimed to enlist her aid in lobbying the newly elected President Roosevelt for a national, federally funded work-relief program that would involve massive public spending.[7]

Hopkins and Hodson's persuasiveness and grasp of the welfare scene so moved Perkins that she immediately arranged for them to meet with the president. A few days following that interview, Roosevelt sent a message to Congress asking that an office of federal relief be established.

The proposed relief agency was part of the New Deal's decisive intervention into previously private spheres of social and economic life. On Franklin Roosevelt's inaugural day in 1933, the nation's banking system had collapsed and thousands of workers across the country, in some cities led by left-wing organizations, started mass strikes against wage cuts and speed-ups. "Free enterprise" principles of laissez-faire capitalism seemed spent and discredited— only the federal government, many believed, could restore order to the economy, feed the hungry, and employ the jobless.

The goal of this intervention as designed by New Deal architects was not to change the system, but to preserve it. "Experimentalism was most frequently limited to means; seldom did it extend to ends." Rather than replace private corporations, charities, and educational programs, the national government would take responsibility for regulating their activities and socializing their costs. Over the next six years, federal grants would refinance municipal relief operations; federal job programs would reemploy the jobless; federal agencies would regulate business; federal administrators would distribute old-age insurance; and federal offices would coordinate adult education.[8]

One of the first bricks in this reform edifice was the Federal Emergency Relief Act. Acting on President Roosevelt's initiative, Senators Costigan, LaFollette, and Wagner introduced Senate Bill 812 in March 1933, "to provide for cooperation by the federal government with the states in relieving the hardship and suffering caused by unemployment." Three days later, the Senate passed the bill, which received House approval in early April. Half of the allocation of $500 million was to be distributed among the states to meet their welfare needs. The other half was to be used by a new agency, called the U.S. Federal Emergency Relief Administration (FERA), as the head of that agency deemed fit. President Roosevelt immediately put Harry Hopkins in charge of FERA's unprecedented relief effort.[9]

A graduate of Grinnell College, this Iowa-born "son of a harness maker," as he called himself, began his long career in social work on New York's lower East Side, where he first worked in the Christadora settlement house. After becoming assistant director of the privately funded Association for Improving the Condition of the Poor, Hopkins had been appointed head of New York State's relief efforts in 1931 and 1932 by then Governor Franklin Roosevelt. In cooperation with New York State's Department of Education, Hopkins had experimented with a work relief program that paid jobless white-collar workers to teach various subjects to thousands of that state's unemployed, a successful project that was later expanded to a national scale when President Roosevelt brought him to the capitol the following year.[10]

The forty-two-year-old social worker came to Washington in May 1933 to begin a remarkable career in federal service, starting as the chief of FERA, continuing as director of the Civil Works Administration (CWA) and the WPA and finally serving as U.S. Secretary of Commerce from 1939 to 1944. He informed his work with a distaste for direct relief and paternalistic charity, a sensitivity to the needs of jobless professionals and white-collar workers, a zest for creating millions of temporary jobs, and a courage and daring in administering innovative New Deal agencies that created and maintained, among many other projects, new networks of health, recreation, and education programs.

Education was Hopkins's first priority when the nationwide relief program started in 1933. "I think," he later explained, "we as a nation had wakened to the fact that unemployment means more than physical want and physical idleness . . . . The conservation and development of human resources [is] most important."[11]

The EEP Hopkins launched in the late summer of 1933 focused primarily on putting unemployed teachers back to work. Concerned with the morale and rehabilitation of those jobless professionals, Hopkins felt that "direct relief is a bad thing." Trained persons, he believed, should be used to meet national needs that were not being filled by existing institutions. One of these needs was to help public school systems expand their services and provide new educational opportunities for adults and youths.[12]

"We did not want to duplicate or supplant the regular school system," Hopkins later stated. "We wanted our program to supplement what the schools were not providing. The job of the schools has been considered primarily one of training children. It offers educational opportunities to only part of the many people who need education services. Yet, many adults have not had the chance for this elementary schooling. . . . We have tried to make a beginning in the development of a broad program of social education which would meet the interests and needs of adults and which would aim to fit the needs of our industrial democracy."[13]

To implement the agenda, Hopkins wrote governors and state FERA administrators in mid-August 1933, authorizing them to spend relief funds to hire jobless teachers and reopen rural elementary schools closed for lack of funds. He also authorized the employment of needy, jobless persons—not necessarily certified teachers—who could teach adults to read and write English. He delegated the supervision of these activities to each state's education authority, following the mandates of Senate Bill 812 to work through state education agencies.[14]

As stipulated by federal regulations, the EEP was to enlist state and local cooperation whenever possible. The pattern throughout the New Deal was that a local sponsor, such as a state or local school board or public agency, would submit a plan for a desired program to the national FERA or WPA office, find facilities and materials, and cooperate in supervising and maintaining classes. FERA (and later WPA) funds would pay for teachers and special emergency education administrators. In general, the EEP absorbed approximately 75 percent of the costs of operating the emergency education program.[15]

In September, Hopkins appointed Dr. Lewis R. Alderman director of the FERA Emergency Education Program. Alderman brought his interests in adult basic education and literacy training to his work in the EEP. A specialist in adult education in the U.S. Office of Education, Alderman had been a public school teacher and a principal in Oregon, a school superintendent and a professor of education before serving in the U.S. Army Education Corps during World War I and as education director of the U.S. Navy in the postwar years. Alderman headed the EEP until the WPA ended, and he retired in 1942.[16]

In an effort to avoid conflict with state and local school officials, Hopkins and Alderman repeatedly stressed that work-relief for destitute teachers would result indirectly in greater community benefit. Over the next few years, bulletins from their offices reiterated that emergency funds were not to be used for regular school programs. They deliberately attempted to avoid undercutting local initiatives in education programming and to prevent the replacement of public school teachers with lower-paid, work-relief personnel.[17]

Hopkins and Alderman shared the conviction that the emergency education programs were temporary and that, in the long run, education was essentially the responsibility of state and local communities to be offered through public schools. Understanding the strong traditions of state and local administrative control in this country, both men anticipated that federal programs would be viewed as government interference. Therefore, they concentrated on developing new programs that did not compete with existing school services.[18]

As construed by Hopkins, Alderman, and other New Deal administrators, the initial objectives of this federal initiative in adult education were: (1) to increase understanding of economic, social, and political problems; (2) to provide citizenship training for aliens; (3) to reduce adult illiteracy; (4) to strengthen home and family life; (5) to provide vocational training and counseling; (6) to help adults use leisure time more constructively; and (7) to provide continuing education opportunities to people who had left school early or whose schooling was cut short by the Depression.[19]

These objectives borrowed heavily from the pre-1933 agendas of progressive and corporate educators, combining Americanization and social-engineering goals with a liberal commitment to self-improvement. EEP leaders equated education with good citizenship and increased participation in government affairs. They subscribed to the progressive philosophy that education prepared citizens to help preserve a democracy which, as it became ever more urbanized, mechanized, and centralized, also lost its sense of community and common purpose.[20]

Hopkins articulated the importance of an education in which "the student is encouraged to appreciate the benefits and freedoms of democracy." He was concerned about economic malfunctioning in this society. Fearing that low-earning power and poverty made large numbers of educationally handicapped foreign and native-born residents susceptible to becoming public charges and open to radical influences from abroad, he felt that the solution to these problems lay in expanded educational opportunities rather than in restructuring the economic system.[21]

Education would foster language literacy and social literacy, both of which were needed by functioning citizens in the process of preserving a democratic heritage. "Illiterates," said Hopkins, "are dangerous to a democracy. . . . They are easy prey to propaganda and exploitation." He and the other New Deal leaders also distrusted idleness that came from the shorter workday, or from no work at all. They infused their concerns with moral messages: constructive leisure-time activities were preferable to the aimless pastimes that might lead to radical activities and result in social disorganization. "From [ages] six to sixty," two authors of the period wrote, "Americans seem to get into trouble with their spare time."[22]

This patronizing perspective on adult education was partially balanced by the parallel focus on individual enlightenment, which encouraged adults to examine social issues. In the context of the Depression's nationwide poverty and suffering, and particularly in the context of the militant strikes that eventually produced the CIO, widespread fear of such inquiry would invoke a public backlash. However, the EEP's emphasis on relief and job creation tended to overshadow the program's educational goals, progressive or otherwise. In practice, the EEP's educational activities, like many New Deal projects, were a programmatic collage with no clear-cut philosophy or coherent approach. Created to provide short-term relief for jobless adults to aid in their rehabilitation, the education programs reflected an unhappy marriage between relief goals and education reforms.

Despite these contradictions, the imperatives of relief needs lent force and momentum to the development of new educational methods and programs. The EEP created a context in which educational innovations were amplified and broadcast to large numbers of people. The concept of adult education took on new meaning and vigor during these years, and a related area, workers' education, gained credence with the public.

"We were evangelists," one state EEP supervisor recalled, "spreading the gospel of adult education. We were salesmen of a new type of merchandise so necessary in our rapidly changing society. We were rehabilitators of individuals overburdened with leisure time used for destructive worry rather than for constructive self improvement. Above all, we were pioneers in the wilderness of the education of the future." [23]

The EEP programs reached out to include new populations that had been denied educational opportunities: farmers, immigrants, women, minorities, industrial workers, and out-of-school youth. And they offered new meaning to individuals who felt they were falling through the cracks of a shattered economy. Throughout the New Deal decade, learners and teachers testified to the role the education programs played in helping them get through hard times.

One adult participant wrote: "Attending this class has served to open up new vistas of thought, study and interest. It gives many of us a feeling of poise due to the fact that we become more sure of ourselves. It awakens other avenues of curiosity. . . . I mean that sense of wanting to know, to dig deeper into subjects, to become more aware, more alert, to be more comprehending." [24]

A New Deal instructor summarized his experience as a teacher for the EEP: "I was not feeling well and was mentally downcast. The school for which I had applied I had been unable to get. I was down to my last ten dollars and wondered what I should do. . . . Then I got an offer [from the EEP] to go to work at Cheyney and get paid for it, the school from which I had graduated just twenty years ago. . . . It all has been an uplift to me and of a helpfulness I shall long remember. I certainly hope and shall try to repay Uncle Sam for his bet on me." [25]

This man's heightened loyalty to the nation and its political institutions fulfilled a key goal of the EEP. To preserve as well as to reform America's social fabric, this patchwork program sought to boost morale, provide jobs, teach new skills, and produce an "informed" citizenry.

II

In "Back to School Desks Millions Go," a feature article of the Sunday *New York Times Magazine*, the author wrote that "the whole outlook for adult education has brightened," and cited the large numbers of adults who were "activated by the need as keen as hunger and thirst" to attend classes that they felt would bring them "more security and happiness." The EEP responded to needs and requests from many groups in the population who "had a white-hot urge to find out straight how they could handle their daily lives." [26]

In 1936, approximately ten years after the founding of the American Association for Adult Education, a quarter of the U.S. population was enrolled each year in some form of adult education. Approximately two million were engaged in projects or classes sponsored by the EEP. Early in 1936, Hopkins noted that there were more adults enrolled in New Deal classes than would graduate from all the high schools and colleges of the United States that June. [27]

Across the nation, farmers met in crossroads school houses for night forums on national and international affairs; black sharecroppers congregated in rural churches to learn to read and figure; workers met in union halls and factories, sometimes after midnight at the end of their shifts; young women cued up to register for evening clerical courses taught in high schools or in community centers. The astonishing number and variety of free classes and programs were unprecedented in adult education history. [28]

The largest number of adults was enrolled in New Deal classes that were administratively designated "general adult education." They were called by one observer "the encyclopedia open for all who would read as they run." Most of the classes taught social sciences and humanities: history, economics, civics, psychology, foreign languages, and literature. In addition, "general adult education" in some locales was the catch-all division for classes in public affairs, real estate, public speaking, parliamentary procedure, everyday law, and a range of cultural and arts programs. By 1937, 200,000 adults a year were enrolled in some 20,000 general adult education classes that employed from 4,000 to 20,000 instructors a year, plus administrators and clerical personnel. [29]

One education writer termed the state of Michigan "a huge laboratory" because of the diversity of New Deal-sponsored classes and programs that included ninety-nine one-year college programs and aviation ground schools. In New York City where efforts were made to satisfy requests from ten or more people for any type of class, general adult education included field trips, a truancy elimination program, and education clubs for out-of-school youth. Three hundred teachers in fifteen states carried on correspondence courses for those persons who were unable to get to New Deal classes. [30]

In order to encourage participation in community affairs, there were forums, panel discussions, study groups, and lectures used in a widespread program of social civics. Radio stations, colleges and universities, and government agencies such as the Tennessee Valley Authority and the Agricultural Extension Service received support from the EEP to carry out successful public affairs programs. For many mountain communities or rural towns, the local study groups, community forums, and debates were a new form of adult education. They were reminiscent, the President's Advisory Committee on Education wrote, of the "experience of the New England town meeting, the cracker barrel sessions of the rural store, and the Chautauqua movement"— all traditional ways Americans in small towns had participated in the life of their communities in what was viewed as happier times.[31]

The President's Advisory Committee on Education later enthused about this use of traditional means of communication: "If democratic procedures are to persist, this type of educational activity will have to become one of the most important in the field of adult education."[32]

Literacy training was the first type of emergency instruction authorized by Hopkins. It was aimed at the 8 to 10 percent of the U.S. population that could not read or write. According to the 1930 census, four and a quarter million adults in this country were classified as illiterate, and the U.S. Office of Education estimated that there were thirty million who had never completed elementary school. Although public schools, especially those in large cities, had long incorporated basic education and naturalization training into their regular night school programs, the innovations of the EEP literacy and citizenship classes led to massive achievements.[33]

The literacy classes aimed to teach participants to read a newspaper with understanding and to write an intelligent letter. They included approximately a quarter of all enrollees in the EEP. Day and night classes met in a range of sites from community centers to mountain shacks. Teachers drove to the homes of adult learners, bringing class supplies and materials they devised to relate basic education to the participants' daily lives. Instead of Dick and Jane primers, relief instructors prepared readers on nutrition, child care, basic health and safety, consumer issues, and homemaking skills.[34]

Dramatic gains in literacy rates were publicized and celebrated across the country during the New Deal decade. Although figures are not available as to the exact number of persons who were taught to read and write in New Deal classes, in the South where the literacy problem was especially severe, Alabama's program announced in 1935 that 5,000 whites and 7,000 Blacks had been taught to read and write through EEP classes in the preceding year. By the mid-1930s, Mississippi claimed to have moved its literacy rate from forty-fourth in the nation to well over the midway mark. In the North, New York City—with more functional illiterates than in any other state except Texas—mounted an extensive literacy campaign.[35]

In 1937, the U.S. Commissioner of Immigration and Naturalization officially recognized the completion of a WPA class as fulfilling the education requirements for citizenship. Although no data are available on the number of enrollees in naturalization classes since they were frequently combined with literacy programs, it was estimated that hundreds of thousands of aliens passed their citizenship tests after completing a New Deal program. By the early 1940s, a WPA progress report estimated that approximately 1,300,000 persons had been taught to read and write in the New Deal classes and that literacy in the country had been increased by more than one-sixth.[36]

The President's Advisory Committee report lauded the flexible scheduling, small classes held in informal settings, and the preparation of adult-oriented materials that led to the outstanding success of these classes and their praise by public school officials and relief administrators. "This program is the one most likely to be adopted as part of the local program of many states," the Advisory Committee report stated in projecting adult education needs for the post-New Deal period when funds for emergency education programs would be withdrawn.[37]

The New Deal's parenting and homemaking classes constituted 13 percent of all enrollments in WPA classes by 1937. The parenting programs illustrated a successful collaboration of the U.S. Office of Education, the National Council on Parent Education (a private organization), and the New Deal's emergency programs. Most of the participants were mothers on relief. They took classes on home and community health care, first aid, food buying and preparation, family dynamics, home sewing, and crafts. In some states, the EEP added square dancing and other recreation opportunities to the programs on family-life.[38]

Although private organizations had conducted preschool as well as parent education prior to the 1930s, this was the first attempt on so wide a scale to carry out a publicly supported national program in these fields. Classes were taught by human service professionals from relief rolls. An impressive list of national private agencies and organizations cooperated to recruit and train volunteer discussion leaders; to supply books and class materials; to arrange field trips to hospitals, preschools, and health centers; and to interpret the program to the public. An effective national advisory board contributed to the high quality of the projects and laid the groundwork for potential long-term programs that the President's Advisory Committee anticipated might continue as an essential part of the public education program after the emergency period had ended.[39]

Although vocational education was one of the four largest EEP adult education programs, reflecting the acute needs for training and retraining skills, it was one of the least successful of the basic EEP projects. In 1934, the FERA allotted funds to states to supplement rather than duplicate existing vocational education programs and to be used solely for relief work developed locally and supervised by local school officials. No specialist in vocational education was hired for the national EEP staff and the resulting confusion in the administration and execution of the program were its major failings.[40]

Five content areas were included in vocational education classes: trade and industrial education, home economics, agriculture, commercial training, and vocational counseling services. Administration varied in different locations, and the duplication of services was widespread. Agricultural education, for example, was conducted by the EEP, the Rural Rehabilitation and Subsistence Homesteads Program, the Tennessee Valley Authority, the Farm Credit Administration, the Agricultural Adjustment Administration, extension divisions of land-grant colleges and universities, public school agricultural programs, and country agricultural agents.[41]

Efforts to coordinate the multitude of federal, state, and local vocational programs were only partially successful. In 1935, the government organized a Federal Committee on Apprentice Training in response to employer complaints about a shortage of skilled metal workers. To establish standardized curricula, promote state and local programs, and avoid duplication of effort, the Federal Committee brought together representatives from the U.S. Department of Labor, the National Youth Administration, the Office of Education, and the National Industrial Recovery Board. But even if these agencies had successfully coordinated their own efforts and linked them to local programs, the EEP's emphasis on hiring unemployed workers as teachers made it difficult to anticipate the program's educational impact and avoid duplication.[42]

Vocational education instructors drawn from the relief rolls were deemed qualified to teach their trade if they had prior work experience in the subject to be taught. An effort was made to train students for fields in which there might be job openings, to avoid trades that were overcrowded or becoming obsolete, and to anticipate state and local manpower needs. This goal was hard to accomplish. Compounding the difficulties of the vocational training programs were problems of securing appropriate, up-to-date equipment. Materials supplied by sponsoring agencies were often not suitable for adult use. Stoves used in high school classes, for example, were inadequate for training professional cooks.[43]

Classes were usually held in public schools and lacked the flexibility and innovative methods and materials used in the other emergency adult education programs. The duplication in programming and the lack of close supervision of training methods and outcomes led the President's Advisory Committee to state in 1940 that better coordination was needed between the regular state-sponsored public school vocational programs and those initiated by the New Deal's EEP.[44]

The workers' education program was one of the smallest of the EEP programs, involving a fraction of its total budget. One of the nation's leading specialists in workers' education, Smith was appointed to the staff of the EEP soon after it was initiated. Her primary role was to act as a liaison with school officials and state welfare administrators in helping to make emergency government services available to workers' groups.[45]

In a "Memorandum of Policies to Guide the Organization and Instruction of Workers' Education under the FERA," workers' education was defined as "a program to give industrial, clerical, domestic, and agricultural workers an opportunity to train themselves through the study of those issues that were related to their daily lives as workers and as citizens." Following the EEP pattern, requests for services were initiated at state level and workers' education classes were administered on a state basis. By 1936, twenty-five state supervisors of workers' education had been hired to help plan, publicize and administer local workers' education classes. During the New Deal decade, thirty-five states conducted workers' education; seventeen of them maintained ongoing activities.

Response to workers' education programs was highest in midwestern and western states, in New York City, and in Pennsylvania. New England lagged behind in instituting government-sponsored workers' education classes, and in the South, where there was some confusion as to the meaning of the term workers' education, relief efforts concentrated on meeting the overriding needs for literacy and basic education. The greatest demand for the New Deal workers' education classes came from communities where workers were actively organizing into collective bargaining units. In these areas, the emergency workers' education program frequently served as the educational arm for the fledgling unions.[46]

A smaller but vital area of New Deal adult education services was the program offered to disabled persons on relief, providing them with retraining and rehabilitation. Emergency funds were allocated to serve unemployed handicapped adults through a program jointly administered by state relief administrations, the U.S. Office of Education, and the New Deal's EEP.

Forty-five states participated in the program, which benefited approximately 65,000 permanently disabled adults. Emergency funds were used to supplement monies allotted by the regular vocational rehabilitation program started in 1920 with the passage of the Vocational Rehabilitation Act. Emergency funds were also allocated to pay for artificial limbs, instructional supplies, equipment for trainees, and their travel, maintenance, and tuition while taking classes. A three-step program of counseling, vocational training, and job placement was conducted by persons hired from relief rolls. Vocational training was provided in approximately a hundred different occupations and on all employment levels.[47]

A wide range of miscellaneous education activities for adults was also initiated and administered by the EEP. These included classes in safety and health; first aid; instruction for the deaf, lip-reading and Braille; handicrafts; education services to adults in prisons, reformatories and industrial schools; preparation of books, bibliographies, study courses, and other instructional aids;

education tours to community resources; and classes for adults employed in New Deal work camps and in other educational projects administered by federal agencies.[48]

Without a doubt, the EEP activities helped revolutionize the methods and attitudes toward dealing with the unemployed. Despite multiple problems and philosophical contradictions, its educational programs had value for participants in the classes as well as for those who were engaged in administration and teaching.

Reflecting in his autobiography about his WPA job in the 1930s as Workers' Program Service supervisor for Minnesota's twin cities, Hubert H. Humphrey recalled: "In a sense our program was an instance of massive group therapy, providing people with a feeling of hope and worth and personal improvement at the same time they prepared themselves for jobs." Humphrey credited his WPA work with providing him with strong labor support and contacts during his successful political campaigns for mayor, congressman, and senator in the decades following the New Deal years.[49]

III

How effective was the EEP? If the primary aim of the New Deal's education programs was to provide work relief rather than the dole for jobless persons, this goal was effectively met. From 1933 to 1942, more than 200,000 persons a year were employed by the EEP, with an average of 40,000 employed in any one month. Work-relief enabled them to maintain at least a minimum standard of living, preserve their skills and develop new ones, and gain self-confidence and hope.[50]

As an education program organized on a work-relief basis, however, the EEP encountered many difficulties. The list of problems was long and varied. The temporary nature of the program and the insecure tenure of emergency personnel made it hard to build upon initial successes. The lack of a coherent education policy, together with administrative confusion, increased paperwork, and the poorly defined roles of newly hired state and local emergency personnel, all made planning difficult. Inadequate funds for supervision and conflicts between public school administrators and those hired on New Deal projects undermined coordination of parallel efforts. Encroachment on professional prerogatives in areas such as hiring and program planning also proved troublesome, and, in a number of cases, the teaching in emergency education classes was patently substandard.

Opinion within the education profession was split on the value of the emergency education projects. On the one hand, praise came from the General Education Board that noted "broad movements were started and policies laid down for a well-planned advance in educational work for which, in the normal course of events, it might have been necessary to wait for decades." On the other hand, critics within the organized education profession challenged alleged federal control of state and local education activities. They questioned whether programs that were supposed to develop local initiatives in education for adults should be federally based. They claimed that the federal program did not foster integration of adult education into the public schools and was leading to a dual system of educational administration.[51]

Professional educators questioned and, at times, attacked the selection of emergency teachers from relief rolls, claiming that few certified teachers were actually unemployed long enough to qualify for relief. They thus challenged Hopkins's statements that FERA and WPA programs were aimed at work relief for jobless professionals. Professional educators were also provoked by the assumption that college courses and the certification process were not necessary requirements for good teaching. They were especially irked by a statement in a 1937 WPA teachers' manual: "We have learned that people can be taught by people not far advanced beyond them in education but who possess an understanding of the lives and problems of their students."[52]

Critics of the emergency education programs also pointed to the high rate of teacher turnover, resulting in poor quality programming and instruction. They criticized the practice, prevalent in some areas, of New Deal instructors actively recruiting students in order to form a class. Although it was not openly verbalized in articles attacking the New Deal education programs, many opponents assumed that political patronage helped some persons attain teaching jobs in the emergency programs.[53]

Without a doubt, relief employment practices did intensify problems of long-term planning and quality teaching. Uncertainty from month to month about continued federal emergency funding reduced the program's effectiveness in numerous areas. Although many New Deal teachers infused their work with creativity and commitment, others participated without conviction. Faced with tenuous relief status, low pay and lack of opportunities for promotion, many New Deal instructors treated their relief assignments casually, as a temporary, part-time job with no future. Inadequate allocations for on-the-job supervision in a number of states meant that careful hiring and preservice and inservice training were shortchanged.

Professional educators correctly recognized that most emergency instructors were inexperienced or unqualified for their relief jobs. FERA and WPA regulations stipulated that EEP instructors be unemployed and experienced in the field to be taught but not necessarily in teaching that subject. Those teachers who were unemployed were often the younger, less experienced individuals who had been laid off in school system cutbacks in the early 1930s. Thus, emergency instructors included those who had been dropped by public school systems, young college graduates who could not find jobs, or persons who had worked in the labor force but had never taught.[54]

In March 1935, for example, there were 31,000 persons teaching for the EEP. Most of these were not certified teachers. Indeed, only 6,900 had a high school education. Those with college and university degrees or course work numbered 238. The instructors hired to teach emergency classes were paid approximately $1.00 per class hour plus $1.00 for class preparation with a maximum number of weekly hours that they were allowed to work. This pay rate was a third to a half of salaries made by certified teachers in public school systems.[55]

Tension continued to surface between New Deal administrators and the public school profession because of the experimental nature of the New Deal education programs and their nontraditional formats, contents, and settings. Educators also felt that established channels for curriculum development and personnel hiring were being bypassed.

An ideal scenario was developed by the National Educational Association (NEA), whose legislative chair, Sidney Hall, wrote President Roosevelt in 1939. Hall suggested that emergency education activities be transferred to the U.S. Office of Education, which would then transfer them to the states. Federal monies should then be forthcoming through the U.S. Office of Education to states that would develop and administer their own programs through regular public school system channels. In response to this proposal, President Roosevelt stressed that the current temporary unemployment-relief program did not impose additional administrative burdens on state bodies, and minimized conflict with the existing policies and procedures of the regular education agencies. Thus, the short-term, work-relief emphasis of the emergency education programs prevailed.[56]

In response to educators' criticisms about ambiguous standards and transient personnel, New Deal administrators turned their attention to teacher training. Not only were residential teacher-training workshops run by the WPA to meet the needs of inexperienced teachers, but some states conducted additional crash courses in teaching methods that helped overcome some of the difficulties of hiring instructors from relief rolls.

The teacher-training programs also served to disseminate information about adult education and to foster an attitude of experimentation among educators. As one person wrote, "[the EEP] had taken education somewhat out of the hands of the educators who were in danger of becoming a sort of priesthood and has secularized it once more by transferring some of the initiative and the control to the people who are to be educated." As another person stated, "The teacher training program was possibly the most valuable contribution of the Works Progress Administration. . . . It took thousands of teachers and professionals who were literally on the scrap heap of life and not only trained them to do a job well but also to perform a service to the community." [57]

Smith initiated the teacher-training programs in the EEP. In 1934, as a result of her persuasion, the EEP authorized a six-weeks residential training for instructors of workers' classes. Encouraged by the effectiveness of the 1934 workers' education training sessions, the EEP allocated monies for residential teacher training for instructors in other EEP adult education divisions to be held in each state in 1935. Using WPA funding, a number of states continued these residential programs throughout the 1930s. [58]

Most of the New Deal residential teacher-training institutes were held on college campuses. Sessions included courses on the social foundations of education, adult education philosophy and history, adult education methods, and the development and utilization of materials and visual aids for adult learners. Discussion-leading techniques and the skills of planning conferences and workshops for adults were included in all the institutes.

The teacher-training programs served to disseminate some of the philosophy of the progressive education movement, which peaked in the late 1920s and early 1930s. Discussions at these sessions included examination of Kilpatrick's work on the project method in adult learning, Thorndike's research on adult development and learning abilities, Dewey's books on education and experience, Counts's challenge to educators to build a new social order, Beard's interpretation of history and current socioeconomic structures, and Rugg's analysis of economic and social milieus. Concepts such as "the whole person," "experiential learning," "planned social change," "education as an instrument of social reform," "individual potential," "democratic participation," were articulated and taught. The residential institutes attempted to become education laboratories that modeled group living, informality, discussion techniques, participation of trainees in decision-making, graphics workshops, forums and debates, and field trips that made use of community resources.

The New Deal teacher-training institutes influenced public school administrators and teachers as well as emergency education personnel. WPA-written bulletins and manuals on the philosophy, methods, and materials in adult education were sent to public school employees as well as to those on emergency projects. Course outlines, instructional materials, visual aids, and bibliographies were available to public school systems as well as to classes run by the EEP.

Teacher training continued to receive attention throughout the New Deal period. State emergency education supervisors met annually in two-to-five week residential sessions. Some colleges and universities offered credits for this training and some state departments of education accredited participants for their state teaching certificates. Summer school courses in adult education were initiated at a number of universities for regularly enrolled students as well as for part-time emergency education personnel.

The relief aspects of the emergency program, therefore, although hampering effectiveness and quality by the limitations they imposed, helped turn a liability into an asset through creating a need to train new practitioners in adult education. The program offered professional opportunities to some jobless teachers who discovered a shift in direction for their future work. New Deal instructors who subsequently found jobs in the public school systems went back to classrooms with an expanded understanding of community problems and the willingness to experiment with new teaching techniques.

The New Deal adult education programs, engaging about two million persons a year in classes and projects, brought to light the desire for education among adults and a range of their interests that had been latent before the federal program. Several of the EEP programs were cited by the President's Advisory Committee for special commendation. The literacy and naturalization classes were a model that "might serve as a key to the education of the masses." The nationwide scope of the program, the actual numbers who learned to read and write, and the innovative incorporation of homemaking, parenting, and public affairs information were praised for their role in training aliens and native-born individuals in citizenship responsibilities and giving them some language skills that, it was hoped, would keep them off future welfare rolls.[59]

Public affairs education, designed to enhance the practice of democratic government, especially in southern and rural areas, was commended as a needed community response to current affairs. The parenting and homemaking classes, noteworthy for their educational innovations, were recommended for expansion and continuation beyond the New Deal period.[60]

Meeting at the New School for Social Research in October 1935, a New York City Council on Adult Education panel unanimously held that the emergency programs had vitalized education by reaching new populations of students, utilizing staff who were not professional teachers, creating some full-time adult education jobs, and developing an adult education-minded public. In addition, panelists pointed out that, for the first time, adult education "has been visibly and directly connected to the bread and butter problems of living."[61]

The emergency education programs prodded public schools into a new conception of their responsibility in offering educational opportunities for all community groups. Public school personnel made new and long-term contacts with adult citizens and with civic and social organizations—a relationship that had been developed only to a slight degree before the 1930s—and laid the basis for public and private cooperation in adult education programs for the future.

The New Deal EEP national and local advisory committees linked emergency programs to community organizations and agencies and included community people in a process of decision-making and program planning that had never been done before. Participation on these advisory and planning boards helped create an awareness of adult education in the community, helped sensitize local leaders to the education and welfare needs of diverse groups in their locale, and developed a network of government and community practitioners who continued to work together on various education and community projects. Adult education councils, existing in only a few communities before 1933, were established and strengthened. Settlement houses, parent-teacher associations, libraries, farmers' organizations, trade unions, prisons, civic associations, churches, and community centers developed ongoing adult education projects.

The New Deal emergency education activities alerted school administrators to new kinds of programming and the need for flexible scheduling. They learned about the inadequacies of school buildings for adult use, and the need for informal classrooms and workshop space. New Deal teacher-training activities increased the awareness of special methods used in teaching adults. The emergency programs linked adult education with New Deal projects in art, music, drama, literature, and writing, instead of confining class content to basic education, naturalization, and vocational training. They increased the demand for more community resources and the utilization of public school buildings at night.

A number of states testified about the effects of the WPA programs on state education departments. "The experiments and demonstrations made possible by the Works Progress Administration have advanced the [adult education] program of California by twenty years," wrote Dr. Mann, director of that state's division of adult education, in one evaluation. Across the country in New Hampshire, W. M. May, a state education official, predicted: "There will be more adult education than ever before as a result of the WPA program. . . . The farsightedness will eventuate in a wider extension of opportunities when we no longer have federal aid for adult education." [62]

The New Deal projects prompted colleges and universities to develop research projects that would yield data about adult learning. They pointed to the need, still not adequately met, for more appropriate instructional materials for adult classes and for more skillful use of community resources in the adult learning process.

As the President's Advisory Committee report summarized, the EEP was "an educational offering of major significance made available to the poor and the needy. . . . That there was and is a demand for services rendered is manifest in the persistence and growth of enrollments. What the regular education agencies have failed to provide, the people have found in a relief program. . . . It is not improbable that by thus beginning with underprivileged groups, the need for and advantages of this program will become more obvious and take deeper and stronger root." [63]

3

Workers' Education in the Federal Emergency Relief Administration 1933–1935

I would like to write a poem,
But I have no words
My grammar was ladies' waists
And my schooling skirts.

—By a Student in a
Workers' School, 1934[1]

Workers' education was the smallest and most controversial of the New Deal's emergency education programs. It was awarded only 1 percent of the EEP budget and was constantly threatened by tensions in federal-state relations and lack of strong national and local support. Suspicious of the term "workers' education," critics of the Roosevelt Administration's labor and education policies attacked the program for alleged anti-American content and left-wing influences. Even within some circles of the labor movement, the federal program met with apprehension and distrust. It survived the nine-year period—at times, just barely—because of the single-mindedness of its director, Hilda Smith, the interventions of Eleanor Roosevelt, and the lobbying zeal of some of its labor allies.

The New Deal workers' education program developed at a time in the history of this country when economic, political, and social conflict underscored the importance of special programming for adult wage earners. New Deal leaders were confronted with the need to preserve a capitalist economy and a political democracy in the face of deepening depression in the United States and revolutionary political and economic change in Europe. In this context, it was seen as imperative to preserve the loyalty of jobless workers to the U.S. system of government and to our capitalist economic structure. Mass education was viewed as one way to maintain morale, give jobless workers some constructive activity to occupy their time, and demonstrate the concern of the federal government for expanding educational opportunities for the less privileged groups in the nation.

The small program had a large impact because it helped fill a need for classes and instructors created by the growth of the labor movement during the Roosevelt Administration. The sudden emergence of unions in the mass production industries, the passage of the National Industrial Recovery Act, and the rise of the CIO all created an enormous constituency of organized workers and local leaders with no experience or training in collective bargaining. There was no guarantee that these newly organized workers and leaders would not be overwhelmed, as the Knights of Labor had been fifty years before, by the difficult task of consolidating their movement. Left to their own devices, they might also look to the radical left for guidance. In either case, the New Deal's reformist program would lose a significant base of organized support. Liberals, therefore, believed it was imperative to train local union activists in union administration, labor law, parliamentary procedure, contract negotiations, and community services.

In addition, the New Deal workers' education program developed the first broad-scale project to systematically train teachers with pedagogical skills appropriate for working-class adults. These trained instructors became teachers in classes sponsored by the government, unions, and public schools across the country.

Although the program continued in one form or another until the end of 1942, many of the programmatic approaches and problems of the program's decade-long existence were rooted in its first two years under the FERA.

I

Smith, the director of the EEP's workers' education program, was the first of four education specialists to be hired in the national FERA offices. With her background in social work, education, and college administration, she was to have a large impact on the workers' education projects of the New Deal administration as well as on the philosophy and methods used in other emergency education programs.

As outlined in chapter one, Smith was a leading representative of the Progressive movement's commitment to workers' education in the 1920s. As founder and director of Bryn Mawr Summer School for Women Workers, she had established a residential program, curricula, and teaching methods that other workers' education programs copied between 1921 and 1927 and were models for other workers' education programs in future decades. Her educational views found a ready audience in the Roosevelt Administration, where like-minded reformers held sway. Eleanor Roosevelt—like Smith, a former settlement house teacher—had long-standing contacts with Rose Schneiderman, Maude Nathan, and other leaders of the national WTUL. Mrs. Roosevelt's intense relationship with Marian Dickerman, the Vassar-educated Democratic

Party activist and educator who had taught one summer at the Bryn Mawr school, and her own visit to the Bryn Mawr summer program in 1925 had convinced her of the need to educate workers to participate more fully in the workings of a democracy. Secretary of Labor Perkins had worked in the slums of Chicago with Jane Addams at Hull House. Hopkins had also worked in the settlement house movement and was a long-time advocate of Progressive reform.[2]

In the summer of 1933, Clinch Calkins, a labor writer, visited the Bryn Mawr Summer School for Women Workers struggling to survive its thirteenth summer on Depression-depleted funds. On returning to Washington, she arranged for Smith to meet with government administrators to seek federal money for the residential workers' education programs at Bryn Mawr College and on other college campuses. Smith's quest to Washington led to a nine-year venture that marked the first time the U.S. federal government supported a non-vocational program of workers' education.

Together with Miller, the director of the WEB, Smith made the rounds of Washington offices in August 1933, attempting to persuade officials in the U.S. Department of Labor, the U.S. Office of Education, the Women's Bureau, the AFL, and the newly formed FERA to start a national, government-sponsored education program for unemployed workers. She hoped through this means to also channel monies to the financially ailing network of residential programs coordinated through the Affiliated Schools for Workers.[3]

Smith and Miller compiled a list of recommendations that included a national advisory service in workers' education classes; plans for schools and camps for unemployed women; a program of teacher training for workers' classes; and a list of community and union groups that would cooperate with a government-sponsored program. They left their memos on the desks of government officials during their August visit. Neither received a reply.[4]

In mid-August 1933, the FERA issued its first authorization of relief funds, allocating money for unemployed teachers to be hired through relief agencies to teach unemployed adult illiterates. Smith and Miller prepared two more memos: one on the need for the FERA to educate adult workers beyond the literacy programs being planned, and the other on the education needs of young adults displaced from their jobs through NRA regulations. The first memo outlined a plan of action:

> In cooperation with state educational institutions to coordinate the existing programs of organizations concerned with this field of education; to organize new schools and classes where necessary of various types (including evening and daytime classes, weekend schools, summer institutes, summer and winter resident and non-resident schools); to train unemployed teachers in a new method of experimental education for these

groups; to conduct a department on educational methods and research in teaching problems; to prepare and distribute suitable pamphlet material; to institute a placement service in cooperation with various community organizations, enabling workers to meet their new responsibilities through intelligent action.[5]

Smith and Miller suggested that a national director of workers' education be based in the U.S. Office of Education and that a $10,000,000 appropriation from the FERA finance these activities.[6]

It became evident that Hopkins had the final word on FERA program directions. Smith was advised to see him directly and had succeeded on at least one occasion in early September in getting Eleanor Roosevelt to talk with him about the importance of workers' education. A brief meeting in New York was finally arranged by their mutual friend and colleague Walter Pettit, the director of the New York School of Social Work. Although Smith's prime purpose was to raise funds for the Bryn Mawr Summer School for Women Workers and the other residential workers' education programs, their twenty-minute interview culminated in Hopkins offering Smith an FERA job. Their discussion also broadened Hopkins' concept of using jobless teachers to instruct "unemployed and other adults who are in need of further general education activities to make them well-informed, responsible, and self-supporting citizens."[7]

Smith recalled in her autobiography that Hopkins told her that workers' education must not be propaganda for the New Deal. Smith replied that she "knew nothing of the New Deal and was interested in 'straight education.'" Two weeks later, Hopkins wired: "Please report to work on Monday."[8]

Smith reported for work in Washington on Monday, September 25, 1933, in the midst of the hustle and bustle of early New Deal activity. She was assigned to the office of Dr. Alderman, newly hired as director of the EEP. Hopkins gave her the title "Specialist in Workers' Education" and sent a memo to school and relief administrators announcing that workers' education was to be established as an emergency relief effort to put jobless teachers to work. The program would be organized on a federal-state basis that was in no way to compete with or eclipse existing public education activities.[9]

The memo included a definition of workers' education, no doubt written by Smith:

Workers' education offers men and women workers in industry, business, domestic service and other occupations an opportunity to train themselves in clear thinking through the study of those questions closely related to their daily lives as workers and as citizens. The instruction program is based on an attitude of scientific inquiry in the light of all the facts and implies complete freedom of teaching and discussion. Its purpose is to stimulate an active and continuous interest in the economic problems of our times and to develop a sense of responsibility for their solution. . . . The plan of instruction is as broad as the interests of the workers themselves . . . to develop ability to think clearly, to analyze facts, and to learn a method which will lead to more independent study are important to keep in mind as classroom purposes.[10]

The definition was probably the first public statement of the distinction between workers' education and adult education. Included in many New Deal publications and quoted in speeches, it attempted to justify the use of public funds for the education of wage earners as workers rather than as a part of the general adult population. The definition, which drew heavily on the philosophy and goals developed by the Bryn Mawr Summer School for Women Workers, reflected Smith's values and program concepts based on her education during the progressive-minded decades of the early twentieth century and her formative experiences in helping develop the philosophy and curricula of other summer schools for working women during the preceding twelve years.[11]

Smith viewed workers' education as a separate and distinct branch of adult education, with a specialized purpose: to meet the needs of persons handicapped by a lack of formal schooling, and to help them develop leaders within their own ranks. She was concerned with the intellectual and citizenship skills needed by workers. She felt they needed information, practice in analytical thinking, and experience in democratic decision-making so that they could deal more intelligently with economic and social issues that needed to be solved if the democratic nation was to be preserved.

Her concept of workers' education had remedial overtones. It aimed to use public school facilities for people who lacked elementary schooling. She anticipated that workers' education was a transitional activity that might potentially be merged with adult education when workers overcame their resistance to classroom work and when changes were made in the methods used in adult education classes. "Until then," Smith wrote, "special consideration should be given those workers who cannot profit from the usual lecture course or adult forum and whose first concern is with the problems of labor and industry."[12]

For the next six weeks, Smith waited for Hopkins to spell out the specifics of the work he expected her to initiate. In November, she presented him with a one-page memo outlining her concepts of policies in workers' education. It highlighted a goal of independent thinking to be attained through freedom of teaching and discussion and based on a full knowledge of facts. Classes would be organized as "democratic groups with the teacher as leader and one of the group, not as an authority figure."[13]

The memo reflected Smith's belief that "education leads directly from the classroom to the community." It supported the right of workers to organize and bargain collectively. Although Smith had only marginal contacts with labor unions and there is no evidence that she understood the power politics of unionism, her experience with organized women workers at the residential summer schools led her to anticipate that workers would request classes in labor history, labor law, consumer problems, parliamentary procedure, public speaking, and current events.[14]

Hopkins read the memo, Smith later reported, took up a blue pencil, and initialed the top. He said: "This is just what I brought you to Washington to do."[15]

II

In the first flush of excitement over the start-up of FERA activities, the workers' education program moved quickly after Hopkins approved Smith's memo. Smith wrote to school officials, FERA state administrators, unions, and community groups, announcing the program, spelling out the procedures for obtaining instructors for workers' classes, and recommending a series of policies. Local groups such as unions needed to request classes through a state or local community sponsor such as a state department of education, a state department of labor, or state-supported colleges and universities. Jobless teachers were to be hired from relief rolls. The program needed supervision by the state or local superintendent of education.[16]

The "Memorandum of Policies to Guide the Organization and Instruction of Workers' Education Classes under Point 3 of the Federal Emergency Relief for Unemployed Teachers" that Smith wrote and sent to school and relief officials around the country linked the need for workers' education to workers' new civic responsibilities and to the shorter work week in industry assured by National Recovery Act codes. It stressed the need for content immediately applicable to workers' lives; recommended an informal setting, using "hands-on" graphics workshops, visual materials, dramatic skits, and field trips; and advocated building the curriculum and study plan on the interests, needs, and experiences of the worker-student participants.[17]

The policy memorandum recommended that workers take part in designing the curriculum and study plan based on an integrated social studies program. It recommended the use of discussions led by teachers who were informal resources and guides rather than reservoirs of total knowledge. In short, Smith basically transferred her experiences at the Bryn Mawr Summer School for Women Workers to her concepts for a workers' education project in the national emergency relief program.[18]

Spurred to more intensive workplace activity by their interpretation of New Deal labor policies, a number of workers' groups wrote immediately to request classes. The chair of the Central Labor Council in Worcester, Massachusetts, replied to Smith's communication: "The delegates were interested in practically all the subjects mentioned in your announcement but particularly in those subjects pertaining to the interpretation and other details concerning NRA codes." [19]

In New Orleans, taxicab drivers scheduled classes late evenings after work. Night-shift workers in North Carolina cotton mills met at 5:00 a.m. to talk about current events before they went home for breakfast. In Kansas, a rural town closed all the stores on Friday afternoons so that shop clerks and their employers could attend FERA-sponsored economic forums. In Texas, the mayor and township officials, all former members of the boilermakers' union, took the initiative in forming workers' classes. [20]

In Michigan, the state supervisor of emergency education reported: "For the past several months, it has been utterly impossible to answer requests for teachers in local unions. There has been an influx of [union] membership in Detroit and there is great need for the development of new leadership. My office is flooded with requests." In Colorado, the organizer of sugar-beet workers wired for classes in rural economics, labor history, and current events. A group of members from the Southern Tenant Farmers' Union hitch-hiked to Smith's Washington office to ask for classes in arithmetic. "The planters down our way won't hear to arithmetic," they told her. "They don't want we should know too much about our share of the crops and the wages." [21]

For many teachers as well as participants in these early classes, the programs were a unique and challenging experience. Jobless instructors welcomed the opportunity for paid work, and many responded positively to the new clientele. Caught up in the ferment and hopefulness of the emergency education programs, many instructors exhibited innovation and flexibility in working with the new program. Although most classes were held in schools or in union halls, many instructors met their worker-students in community buildings or in their homes, especially in rural areas. One instructor in Arkansas reported:

> I met my first class last evening. I drove ten miles over a rough country road through a dreary rain to a poor, three-room farm house. There in the kitchen, I found a half circle of chairs placed around a crackling wood fire. A kerosene lamp on the mantle lighted the bare walls. By 7 o'clock, the chairs were filled with work-hardened men, their faces brown and worn from sun and dust, their eyes anxiously searching mine for some explanation or sign of hope. At first suspicious of the "schooling," fearful of showing their ignorance, and self-conscious in expressing their ideas, they soon thawed and we were deep in discussion of the Bankhead Act. [22]

It was a unique experience for teachers and worker-students accustomed to traditional classroom content and methods. Many felt liberated by the opportunities to discuss issues close to home and heart. In a government-sponsored class in Wisconsin, Mary Regenboog, a worker-student, wrote "An Ernest Plea."

> Let our school system
> Teach us about ourselves.
>
> We learn about Egypt,
> Her tombs and treasures;
> We're taught the philosophy of Greeks.
> The wars that have been
> Inflict us with dates
> To memorize and learn for weeks and weeks.
> I know now what has been;
> The things that were done;
> But now, the present, the future,
> How is everything now?
> Please tell me. Teach me to know
> My fellow workers, thinker,
> My living people.
>
> So many things, important ones
> Are a question mark only.
>
> Please teach me *now*.[23]

Despite the positive response from many areas of the rank-and-file movement, many public school administrators questioned Smith about the need for separate workers' education classes. They argued that evening high schools, citizenship programs, vocational training, and university extension services, all traditional forms of adult education before the 1930s, were open to adults of all social classes. They expressed fear that a special program for workers would separate them from other adults, create class consciousness, and lead to agitation. They predicted that "propaganda of a highly dangerous character would be inherent in such a specialized program for one group in the population."[24]

Smith and her small Washington staff countered these charges with letters to school officials that traced the rationale for separate programs: (1) workers were not reached through regular community channels; (2) their limited education background necessitated special teaching methods to link their everyday experiences to the learning process; (3) familiar, informal learning settings were needed to help workers overcome resistance to learning in more formal school classrooms; and (4) workers needed information on new federal regulations and an opportunity to discuss topics not usually covered in general adult education programs.[25]

Moreover, Smith emphasized, workers needed classes scheduled at convenient times and places because of the nature of their work, and they needed to be contacted through a major national channel they could trust: the labor movement. To answer the charges that workers' education would lead to class consciousness and conflict, Smith stressed the transitional nature of workers' education, the importance of a well-educated citizenry, and the need for independent thinking and free discussion that is "considered essential to the process of educating workers and other groups in a democracy." [26]

These issues were addressed again in February 1934, when Smith convened a meeting of approximately seventy national leaders of education, government, workers' education and community organizations in response to an official call from U.S. Secretary of Labor Perkins and U.S. Commissioner of Education George Zook. The one-day meeting in Washington focused on issues of teacher training, supervision, contacts with the labor movement, and materials for use in workers' classes. Perkins chaired the meeting and Zook gave the opening address, lending status to the gathering and the official support of the U.S. Office of Education.

Zook underscored the need to "offer adults the opportunity to improve themselves during enforced idleness," as well as the need "to preserve the fundamental character of American Government." "Education is important," he claimed, "because democracy is failing in other countries and being replaced by centralized government through lack of popular knowledge and unity of action." [27]

The conference, which included an address by Harold Rugg of the Progressive Education Association and remarks by George Counts of Columbia University's Teachers' College, recommended that educational objectives be sustained in spite of the difficulties of working within a relief administration. It suggested that rural as well as urban workers be included in the program, that trade union representation on local advisory boards was essential, and that residential teacher training as well as on-the-job training be initiated for instructors of FERA classes. [28]

At the sessions, Smith attempted to clarify and limit the federal government's role in workers' education, stating that "the U.S. Government is not trying to conduct workers' education; it is not prepared to conduct such a program. We are hoping that workers' education groups will conduct their own programs. The Government will offer to such groups the facilities of Government agencies and will cooperate in trying to provide materials, in getting experienced people to supervise and teach, and in securing space for classes." [29]

This statement and Smith's success in involving Zook and Perkins in the conference are indications of her efforts to clarify the tenuous balance between federal government and local initiatives in developing and carrying out a nationwide workers' education program. She recognized the longstanding tradition of state and local control of public education and the need to diversify the sponsorship of workers' education programs. And she knew the political importance on a national level of working closely with the U.S. Office of Education where she had originally hoped to base a national workers' education program.

In the fall of 1933, Smith lobbied Zook to contact the director of the General Education Board of the Rockefeller Foundation to award special grants to the Affiliated Schools for Workers and to the WEB to enable these organizations to implement the FERA workers' education activities. The resulting grants of $70,000 to each of the organizations over the next two and a half years enabled them to add field staff, prepare special workers' education materials, develop labor institutes and conferences, and do intensive work in teacher training. Their efforts helped to decentralize the federal program and develop classes in communities not reached by Smith's small Washington office staff.[30]

For the Affiliated Schools, the grant marked a new beginning. It enabled the organization to enlarge its program and to shift its focus from meeting the education needs of working women to providing services to the male and female members of newly organized unions. The Affiliated Schools' network, comprised mainly of women educators who had worked on the staffs of women's colleges, YWCAs, settlement houses, and other reform organizations in the 1920s, had helped develop a methodology for workers' education at the residential schools. Over a period of years, they had experimented with methods of teaching adult workers in their desire to help adult students analyze economic forces that affected their lives and to give them the tools to continue their participation in union and community affairs.

The Affiliated Schools' executive committee decided to work only in communities where there was enough interest to maintain workers' education activities beyond the time of the grant. They concentrated on developing advisory committees, expanding a publications program, establishing a traveling library of labor-oriented material, conducting in-service teachers' training, and setting up correspondence services for union groups unable to be reached by field visits.[31]

Affiliated Schools' staff initiated these activities in eighteen communities in the East and Midwest from 1934 to 1936. Experienced workers' educators, many of whom had taught at the residential schools for women workers, moved to an area for two to six months to work intensively with labor, community, and government representatives to help develop classes and conduct inservice teacher training in cooperation with the emergency program.[32]

In Philadelphia, Affiliated Schools' staff helped develop a well-functioning advisory board that planned an extensive program cosponsored by the board of education in public schools, Ys, and union halls. In Pennsylvania's anthracite region, Affiliated Schools' staff organized and taught classes in union

administration, labor drama, and labor leadership to miners, garment workers, and textile workers. For domestic workers in Columbus, Ohio, twice-a-
week classes in English, economics, and household arts were arranged by the
Affiliated Schools' staff member. At Howard University in the nation's capital,
a series of economic forums were planned to help develop leaders and instructors for workers' education in the black communities.

Classes in union administration, leadership skills, labor history, and government were requested more frequently than could be provided by the Affiliated Schools' staff member in Detroit. At their own offices on Second Avenue
in New York City, the Affiliated Schools' staff carried on a full program of
classes for students recruited mainly through the New York WTUL. In Atlanta, Georgia, a staff member for the project attempted to set up interracial
classes, which culminated after months of tension in a meeting of workers at
the Atlanta Labor Temple, the first interracial labor meeting in that city.[33]

The grant helped the Affiliated Schools expand its publications, which
were used extensively by the FERA workers' education classes. In 1934 and
1935, newly written and widely circulated titles included: *Education and the
Worker Student*; *Labor and the NRA*; *Unemployment and Problems*; *Introduc-
tion to American Trade Unionism*; and the *Worker and the Government*. In
addition, manuals on teaching methods and bibliographies for teachers of
workers were developed. Two special studies were conducted: one on how
participants at the 1934 Wisconsin Summer School for Workers used their
summer experiences in back-home community settings; the other on patterns
of government support of workers' education in Europe.[34]

Two staff members from the Affiliated Schools, Helen Hermann and Louise
McLaren, spent periods of time in Washington working with the national
office of the emergency workers' education program. McLaren, who directed
the Southern Summer School for Women Workers, helped set up some programs in the South; Hermann served as administrative and research assistant
from 1934 to 1940. In addition, Smith hired Ernestine Friedmann, an Affiliated Schools' staff member, as assistant in charge of teacher training and field
work from 1934 to 1942.[35]

When the grant ended in 1936, the Affiliated Schools reduced its involvement in New Deal-sponsored projects. However, it continued to maintain its
traveling library and its correspondence service started under the General
Education Board grant. To the end of the decade, running on the momentum
gained in its collaboration with the emergency program, it expanded services
to union groups, conferences on workers' education, publications and activities in behalf of white-collar workers, although no longer in such close contact
with the federally sponsored workers' education programs.[36]

Smith drew into the FERA project some of the people from the Affiliated
Schools' network to help staff the national office. She also recommended a

number of these experienced workers' educators as state supervisors of workers' education in the emergency program and as directors of the teacher training centers and the schools and camps for unemployed women. She helped the organization obtain financial aid to continue and expand its work in a broader setting. Affiliated Schools' staff members attempted to develop in these communities integrated mechanisms for sustaining ongoing workers' education programs. The effect of these efforts was a widespread seeding of ideas, attitudes, and information into diverse communities and groups.

Several years after this field program ended, Affiliated Schools' director, Eleanor Coit, recalled a letter that she received from a participant in one of the programs: "I never did have a chance to express my gratitude for what the school did for me. People here at home keep asking me 'Just what did you learn there?' And how can I tell them that I learned more than say, the provisions of the National Labor Relations' Act; that I learned a new outlook on this world and my relation to it; and that the labor movement has emerged for me as something with dignity and power, something that someday will have the force of an avalanche and that I must be part of it." [37]

III

Smith's program had a much more problematic relationship with the Workers' Education Bureau and with the conservative leaders of the American Federation of Labor who dominated WEB policy. Conflicts surfaced over different concepts of the purpose of workers' education and whether or not programs could be controlled by the AFL. There were objections to appointments of personnel, the political orientation of relief instructors who taught emergency classes, and the content of some of the classes.

As described in chapter one, the WEB, organized in 1921, was a confederation that included local unions, city central labor bodies, state federations of labor, and international unions. Of all the workers' education organizations that emerged from the 1920s, the WEB had closest ties to the AFL, which gradually became its principal source of funding. In turn, it functioned as the AFL's education arm in the 1930s and 1940s and formally became the AFL education department in 1954.

In contrast to those workers' educators who wanted to prepare workers for building a new social order, AFL leaders emphasized the functional role of workers' education in enhancing the effectiveness of trade unions and maintaining orderly industrial relations. AFL President William Green was specific about the role of workers' education: "Workers' educational work falls into three divisions: (1) discovering how the union can carry on its work more intelligently and efficiently; (2) developing the best technique for making collective bargaining successful and maintaining constructive and mutually beneficial relations with industry; and (3) helping wage earners to take part in community and national issues. The first two divisions of our problem must be worked out under union supervision and control." [38]

The New Deal workers' education program was initiated during a period of turmoil within the organized labor movement. The main issues involved the philosophical and structural response of the traditionalist, craft-oriented AFL to the stirrings among industrial workers for union organization. Industrial unions had gained in membership under Section 7A of the National Industrial Relations Act and were aggressively campaigning to change the AFL's membership, organizational structure and methods of organizing in the mass production industries. By 1934, it was obvious to reformers within organized labor that traditional craft-union structures were unable to cope with the large numbers of unskilled and semiskilled workers who were clamoring for union protection. At the 1935 AFL Convention, John L. Lewis, president of the United Mineworkers' Union, led the fight against the craft-union forces and, supported by the presidents of eight powerful unions, formed the Committee for Industrial Organizations (CIO). The following year, the AFL suspended the rebel unions, and, in 1938, the CIO reconstituted itself as a separate federation, the Congress of Industrial Organizations.

From 1934 until the end of the decade, bitterness and factional warfare divided craft unionists from industrial unionists as they battled each other for control of the nation's labor movement. Against this backdrop, AFL officials became increasingly suspicious of agencies other than the WEB that were carrying on workers' education. The AFL's leaders feared that instructors in the New Deal workers' education program might advocate structural change in the economy and new leadership in the labor movement.

Smith and Miller, the WEB director, had collaborated in contacting government administrators in the summer of 1933 to urge them to develop a nationwide workers' education program. It appeared that Miller was initially supportive of the government-sponsored program. He called it an important "folk movement" and, at the 1934 AFL convention, claimed that "nothing in the entire history of American workers' education can compare with the rapidity and extent to which this movement has been developed in the last ten months." As time went on, however, Miller became less supportive as AFL leaders pressured him to promote only AFL–approved programs. [39]

With funds that Smith helped the WEB obtain from the General Education Board and with an additional small grant from the Carnegie Foundation, the WEB expanded its staff in 1934 and 1935, adding three regional directors and a staff person to aid Miller in the Washington office. The WEB concentrated on interpreting newly passed legislation to groups of workers throughout the country. It developed a series of one-day institutes in thirty-three states, worked closely with AFL labor councils to include workers' education in regular membership meetings, and arranged for community radio programs on labor topics.

WEB staff and leaders viewed their mission as setting up effective machinery within the ranks of organized labor so that "workers' educational interests might be conserved and developed on its own initiatives." They supported programs developed and controlled by AFL officials on state and local levels.

Disagreements surfaced about the staff members that Smith recommended or hired. Although Smith had attempted to secure the support of top AFL leaders from the beginning of the New Deal program, she did not consult them in hiring staff for her Washington office or in recommending state supervisors of workers' education who were hired by the states' emergency education divisions. AFL leaders distrusted "outside intellectuals" and were chary of independent workers' education staff that they could not control.

Smith and the staff of the WEB had different goals for workers' education. Smith emphasized the importance of freedom of discussion and critical thinking about economic and political issues so that workers could be more knowledgeable when they participated in their unions and communities. The WEB stressed the importance of workers' education in building strong unions and conserving the gains that labor was making under the Roosevelt Administration.

A symposium on workers' education in the October 1934 issue of the *Journal of Adult Education* reflected these differences. Edited by Miller and his assistant, Mollie Ray Carroll, articles by WEB staff took the view that workers' education should "contribute to the smoother functioning of labor." They supported the need for "orderly relationships between labor and management" and viewed workers' education as important to the process of enhancing the competencies of union leaders and activists so that they could improve their organizations.[40]

Distrust of outside, radical influences was evident in one of the articles. Harry Russell, the WEB regional director for New England, expressed apprehension about the new "college educated members in some of the unions [who] evince an enthusiasm to do things unheard of in the old-line trade unions." He feared that "terrible mistakes can be made, resulting in tragedy for the labor movement and for the community where industrial mass movements do not realize the responsibility attendant upon organized labor's activities."[41]

Throughout the New Deal decade, AFL leaders were explicit about wanting Smith and other New Deal administrators to appoint staff who came from the Federation. In May 1934, President Green wrote to U.S. Commissioner Zook asking that state supervisors of workers' education be cleared by AFL state labor federations and by the WEB. Zook responded that the U.S. Office of

Education did not control New Deal appointments and warned that states might resent indication of any federal control of appointments.[42]

The issue of appointments came up again at the 1935 AFL convention. AFL leaders declared that "state supervisors of workers' education should have close contact with and understanding of the American labor movement. . . . Otherwise, they are prone to confuse labor's ideas with dogmas of class conflict or to fail to appreciate the importance of integrating education with labor's life work."[43]

Throughout the balance of the decade, differences continued to surface between the New Deal and the AFL over the administration of the worker's education program. From time to time, Smith attempted to reconcile these differences by meeting with AFL representatives to work out better cooperation. At one such meeting in June 1935, AFL representatives complained about the low-relief wages paid to emergency instructors, the strict relief requirements determining utilization of teachers, and the failure to consult the AFL on instructors, supervisors, and class content. Perhaps reacting to Smith's recommendations for the appointment of a number of women as field representatives and state supervisors of workers' education, WEB staff member Paul Vogt recommended that "field representatives should be men."[44]

In practice, many AFL unions did make use of the New Deal workers' education services, for the most part through the work of local projects cosponsored with the WEB. At one point, the AFL's leaders acknowledged that "where there is an effective workers' organization [to sponsor workers' education] the gains have been substantial; without [organized unions] the results have been meager."[45]

IV

Despite these problems with AFL leaders, the first two years of the workers' education program were marked by important accomplishments. Smith had successfully introduced the concept of workers' education as a specialized branch of adult education. By emphasizing its importance as a preparation for citizenship, she had infused workers' education with a purpose that New Deal liberals could support. To Hopkins's focus on relief and rehabilitation, Smith had added the concept of educational remediation. Special programs for workers could and should amend their lack of formal schooling and give them the information, skills, and opportunities to work together to help heal the ailing democratic nation.

Smith had tapped into her network of allies within the New Deal to hold a national conference on workers' education and another national conference on the special needs of unemployed women (see chapter 5). As a relief effort under the FERA and the CWA, the workers' education program was able to muster at least nominal support from Hopkins, Perkins, Aubrey Williams, and other New Deal administrators. Smith maintained her access to the White House through memos to and meetings with Eleanor Roosevelt. She solicited the first lady's support for both the broad program of workers' education and for specific projects such as educational camps for unemployed women.[46]

In the spring of 1935, approximately 45,000 men and women were enrolled in 1,800 classes taught by 480 instructors in 570 communities, an enrollment that had increased four-fold since the program started in the winter of 1934. Typical classes enrolled about twenty-seven students; an average of eighteen attended weekly classes over a one-to-five month period. Social sciences, economics, and labor history were the classes most often requested.

Approximately half the classes were held in public schools and nearly all of the remaining ones were held in union halls. The occupational background of the worker-students ranged from factory workers and farmers to stenographers and retail clerks. About a third of the participants were women. Most of the students had left public school after eighth grade.[47]

Organized and unorganized workers were recruited through existing organizations such as unions, Ys, and settlement houses. The sponsoring organization formed the class, provided the meeting place, and arranged for an FERA instructor. In some cases, relief instructors recruited their own classes through talking before interested groups and posting announcements on union and settlement house bulletin boards.[48]

For most of the participants, the FERA classes were their first experience with adult education. Many enrolled in several classes and combined a program in workers' education with courses in literacy, citizenship, or leisure time activities sponsored by other divisions of the EEP. Public schools and union halls became lively centers of adult and workers' education, for the first time accessible to a large working-class population.

Despite the negative reaction from some school officials, AFL leaders, and critics of the New Deal, the program was tangible evidence for jobless workers and teachers around the country that the Roosevelt Administration cared about their plight. The free classes reinforced the image of a federal government that was providing new kinds of services to meet the issues affecting working-class lives. After hearing an FERA-sponsored talk on decent workplace conditions, a stitcher in a garment factory remarked: "This is all news to me. I never knew anyone cared what happened to us in the shop." [49]

In city and country areas, those who had been denied schooling responded warmly to the chance to share in educational benefits. Smith cherished and frequently quoted the responses of individuals in her evaluations of the program's success. She published actively in magazines and journals, promoting what she felt was the substantive significance of the workers' education programs. She tried to evoke for other educators and policymakers some of the discussions she had with individual workers. In one article, Smith included a poem she had written based on a conversation with a young southern mill hand, which symbolized for her the response to the new FERA-sponsored educational opportunities.

No, ma'am, I never got to go to school.
There was a raft of young'uns there at home
In that old cabin up on Hickory Creek.
But nary a school on all the mountain side,
So none of us has ever got to go.
Yes, ma'am, I'd awful like to go to school,
For I ain't had no schooling much at all.
Seems like if I could get to go to school
I'd maybe see some sense in goin' on,
Or even fix some way to help at home.
But now, seems like I can't make head or tail
Of anything, I get so awful tired.
Seems like with schooling, I'd larn how to live.

Could all them girls in the tobacco mill
Larn something too, and maybe get a chance?[50]

4

Teacher Training
1934–1935

Let's dress academic words in overalls before we use them in workers' classes.

—University of Tennessee Teacher
Training Center Pamphlet, 1934[1]

When the FERA started in the fall of 1933, its architects did not intend to establish a federally funded national teacher-training program to further the FERA emergency education activities. For Smith, however, teacher training was a high priority. She viewed the FERA as a context in which to train workers' education practitioners and as a base from which to gain support for the work on education methods that had been pioneered at the residential schools for workers in the 1920s. She took the leadership in pointing out the need for teacher training to New Deal administrators and government officials, and obtained emergency funds to finance forty residential centers in the summers of 1934 and 1935. Held for approximately six weeks on college and university campuses in twenty-seven states, they were the first federally funded teacher-training program in this country.[2]

Approximately 1,700 trainees and 200 staff were involved in sixteen centers in 1934 and twenty-four centers in 1935. The centers, which were administered by Smith and her Washington staff, served as models for resident teacher training centers started in 1935 for instructors in all of the New Deal's emergency education divisions. Despite many administrative problems that developed from merging a pedagogical experiment with a relief effort, the teacher-training program was one of the most valuable contributions Smith and her colleagues made to the New Deal education projects during the FERA and WPA years. They engaged school and relief officials, trainees, and community supporters in a program that consciously attempted to break with traditional philosophies and practices of classroom teaching. The centers involved several thousand persons in an intense learning experience that helped prepare them to teach new adult clienteles in emergency classes and in non-relief settings. The centers helped sensitize participants to labor issues, inform them about new government legislation, and expose them to nonformal, experiential teaching techniques.[3]

The concept of systematic teacher training for workers' education programs was not new by the 1930s. However, Smith showed great foresight in seizing the opportunity presented by the national emergency education program to promote a federally funded national approach to meet these needs.

I

Throughout the 1920s, the need to train teachers for workers' classes was discussed at meetings of the WEB, the Affiliated Schools for Workers, and Local 189 of the American Federation of Teachers, the local union of workers' educators started at Brookwood Labor College in 1924. Leaders of the workers' education movement were confronted with the shortage of instructors sympathetic to the labor movement and committed to the goals of social reform. It was also difficult to find teachers who were experienced with the informal classroom practices that were proving effective with groups of working-class adults.[4]

Smith viewed herself as a promoter of these earlier progressive efforts within the FERA education activities. A nationwide teacher-training program modeled on some of the work she had done at the Bryn Mawr Summer School for Women Workers might disseminate the philosophy of progressive educators and group workers that had burgeoned during the 1920s. It might also help finance the staff and economically floundering programs of the Affiliated Schools for Workers, which was consciously experimenting with new learning modes for adult workers. Thus Smith, in promoting teacher training, was also promoting a continuation of the work she and her colleagues in workers' education had begun prior to the New Deal programming.[5]

The memo that Smith and Miller circulated to government administrators in August 1933, before she was hired for her New Deal job, recommended a nationwide program "to train unemployed teachers in a new method of experimental education . . . to conduct a department of educational method and research in teaching problems [and] to prepare and distribute suitable pamphlet material." Once she came to Washington, she lobbied Alderman, Hopkins, Zook, Eleanor Roosevelt, and Aubrey Williams, with memos, and in meetings with them presented the case for federally financed teacher training.[6]

In November 1933, Smith wrote to U.S. Commissioner of Education Zook and recommended a six-week pilot program to train teachers for workers' classes. She suggested that the project be based at the Bryn Mawr College and run in conjunction with the summer school for women workers. "This course,"

Smith wrote to Zook, "would include the study of economic history as related to the current economic problems of adult workers, the relation of the worker to the government under NRA, use of materials and classroom procedures." This outline for a curriculum of a teacher training center became the basic pattern for the centers that were set up in 1934 and 1935.[7]

The need for persons trained to lead workers' courses became more urgent in the winter of 1934 when requests accelerated for instructors to teach FERA-sponsored workers' classes. Relief instructors included industrial, white-collar, and professional workers whose educational backgrounds ranged from high-school dropouts to Ph.D.s. New Deal regulations did not require them to have college degrees, only to be unemployed, eligible for relief, and to have worked in the field to be taught. Few were familiar with workers' lives or workplace conditions or were experienced in teaching adults with little formal schooling.[8]

Adult education and workers' education were new fields in the early 1930s. Even among the thousands of unemployed certified teachers there were few who had previous experience in adult classes. For the most part, adult education in the school system was limited to classes in Americanization and vocational education, and few community groups, except some unions, YWCAs, and settlement houses, engaged in any systematic adult education projects. Even in those settings traditional teaching techniques were used.

The constant turnover of New Deal instructors compounded the problem of finding appropriate teachers for workers' classes. Changing relief regulations and congressional appropriations meant that most were assigned for three to six months at best. Regulations required instructors to leave their emergency classes if they found regular employment and were thus disqualified for relief.[9]

Many white-collar workers and professionals, jobless for the first time in their careers, were anxious about their own protracted periods of unemployment. Many felt the stigma of being on relief, needing to report to a neighborhood relief office, and passing a financial means test. Some became despondent in the struggle to piece together a living and look for long-term employment. Others needed further education and training for their personal rehabilitation, as well as to enhance their potential to find nonrelief jobs.[10]

The special needs of workers' education, according to Smith, called for instructors with "the courage to experiment, belief in the ability of workers to learn, and an open-minded attitude regarding the rights of workers to organize and bargain collectively." Most teachers of workers' classes needed guidance and aid to meet these goals. Most also lacked training in social sciences, the field that workers' education and adult education leaders in the 1920s had deemed crucial to prepare teachers for their important role in building a new society. Many depended on traditional lectures and textbook readings to instruct their worker-students, despite the fact that these methods were often difficult for workers to comprehend.[11]

Smith's goals for the teacher-training centers were clearly pedagogical rather than rehabilitative. They reflected her liberal political views and her moral commitment to use the education process to involve more people in taking an active role in bettering social and economic conditions. To this end, she wanted to broaden teachers' social vision. "Teachers as a whole have a narrow outlook on social questions," she wrote, "centering their attention upon classroom duties, job holding, and requirements for promotion; they often do not see themselves or their work in the social setting. Not until the depression . . . did teachers as a group realize that they were involved."[12]

Smith's expectations for the teacher-training centers were both ambitious and vague. The training centers, she held, should help participants work out their philosophy of education, become proficient in the use of methods and materials for adult worker-students, and orient them in studying the life experiences of wage earners. She viewed the training centers as educational laboratories where trainees would experience the process of learning to cooperate with other participants, work as a group, and take action on issues that would enable a democratic society to work more effectively. Through these experiences, trainees would be better able to help worker-students think analytically about their lives and participate with more understanding in group action.[13]

Smith never specified what issues were important to address through group action. Although she supported workers' rights to join unions, it is not clear whether the group action she advocated was through wage earners' collective role in their unions or in their communities. Her focus was the relationship between educational democracy in the classroom and social democracy in the country. To facilitate this participatory process, she advocated specific teaching methods: participant-centered learning in small, informal groups with instructors serving as discussion leaders rather than as authorities.[14]

For Smith, the classroom was a microcosm of the larger society, a democracy writ small. The interactions between classroom citizens, their ability to be partners in solving social problems, and the development of a classroom environment that fostered free, critical thinking and maximum participation mirrored Smith's vision of an ideal, a democratic society where such a classroom was an important part of the democratic process. In the future, Smith held, "the control of the society [would be determined] through the participation of all those affected by plans for economic and social patterns," a type of social control that could be obtained in the United States through an education process that would lead to "new ways of living, a new conception of freedom, social standards unrelated to material success, and a new understanding among nations."[15]

Central to this process was the teacher. Smith aimed high in her profile of a successful instructor of workers' classes. A workers' teacher should possess: "a sympathetic understanding of the labor movement; experience in trade union or workplace groups; knowledge of economics; knowledge of his/her subject; communication skills; good teaching techniques; willingness to learn from students; ability to relate teaching to their experiences; intellectual integrity; a broad cultural perspective free from prejudice; interest in the students as individuals; a belief in their desire to learn; a warm attractive and sympathetic personality; and a sense of humor." [16]

In Smith's view, teacher trainees would acquire these personal characteristics through their experiences in a democratic education process. They then would adopt this philosophy and these methods in their own classroom settings, continuing a process that would prepare worker-students to participate in the changes necessary to make a democratic nation function more effectively.

The 1934 Report on the Teacher Training Centers included as a frontispiece a poem Smith had written to give shape to some of her ideas:

Give us new tools for teaching those who build
The structure of their lives in industry;
Those men with minds alert, whose hands are skilled
To speed machines in mill and factory.
For knowledge of their world the workers reach.
They call us daily. Give us skill to teach.

We are the teachers, struggling too to live;
Uncertain of the future, stripped of pride;
Still with our schooling and our skill to give
To those for whom long schooling was denied.
Give us the tools that we may understand
The need of those who work with mind and hand
That in a world of turmoil, worn and racked,
Those whom we teach may courage gain anew;
In every class hew to the heart of fact
Marking new lines of action, straight and true.
We are the teachers. Show us then the ways
To build foundations for the better days. [17]

II

Smith's strategy to develop a national teacher-training program was to promote and support existing programs within the workers' education movement, obtain the necessary approval from FERA director Hopkins, and draw on the expertise of her network of experienced workers' educators from the Affiliated Schools for Workers. It is apparent from the idealistic tone in her memos and lobbying efforts that she did not fully anticipate the organizational problems involved in setting up this unique and specialized project within the context of a national relief program.

Her memos and meetings with New Deal administrators continued throughout the winter of 1934. They were finally given support at a Conference on Workers' Education that she convened in Washington, D.C. in February 1934, which recommended a national program of teacher training.[18]

Her proposal for a teacher-training project took a positive turn in an April 1934 meeting with Hopkins. She convinced him that such a project might rehabilitate the jobless white-collar workers and professionals who were his special concern, and might also serve a need not being met by existing educational agencies, which was his prime operating principle.

Hopkins and Aubrey Williams, his assistant director, supported Smith's plan to train 500 teachers for workers' education in sixteen centers, organized on an interstate basis, that would bring relief-eligible trainees from each state to the closest teacher-training project. Hopkins allocated an average of $5,600 for each of the centers and, on May 31, informed state relief administrators that FERA funds were authorized to support this program. State directors of emergency education, working with state and local public school officials, would have responsibility for organizing and supervising the projects. States needed to submit a plan to the national FERA office of emergency education, ·outlining the proposed location, budget, and organization of the center in their locale.[19]

Although the centers were officially the responsibility of the state directors of emergency education, Smith's office was responsible for outlining policies, recommending curricula, hiring center directors, writing publicity, and preparing manuals, bibliographies, and other materials to be used in the programs. In hiring center directors and other related personnel, she drew on her old network of teachers and administrators who had been connected with the resident schools for workers in the 1920s. Many of these were well-educated, middle-class women who had worked for YWCAs or other social reform organizations and who shared Smith's views of the role of workers' education and adult education.[20]

The energy and commitment of Smith's allies derived from their own motivations to work for social progress; they frequently performed nearly impossible tasks with missionary zeal. Their personal status and education helped give them credibility and acceptance from public school administrators and gained them entrance into the education establishment and relief bureaucracy whose cooperation was necessary in organizing the training centers. Most important, they helped articulate the values and philosophy of what they viewed as an education movement designed to integrate educational practice with democratic socialization and to meet some of the educational needs of working-class adults.

To organize and administer the teacher-training program from the national FERA office of the Specialist in Workers' Education, Smith picked her colleague Ernestine Friedmann who had been her able assistant in the 1920s in organizing and directing the Bryn Mawr Summer School for Women Workers. An important figure in Smith's former network from the Affiliated Schools for Workers, Friedmann was instrumental in carrying the liberal reform concepts of workers' education developments from the 1920s into the New Deal period. Friedmann came from the same educational and career background as many of the women who, in the first two decades of the century, viewed jobs in the workers' education field as a route to professional mobility—an arena where they could use their education, social position, and energy to do social good.

After graduating from Smith College in 1907, Friedmann had worked with the YWCA Industrial Department for about ten years, organizing and teaching classes for young working women and developing education and recreation centers for women war workers during World War I. She completed her course work for a Ph.D in economics from Columbia University while organizing and directing the summer programs for women workers at Bryn Mawr College, Barnard, and at Vineyard Shores in New York State. A fellowship from the Scandinavian Foundation permitted her to spend 1925 in Sweden studying workers' schools. She then taught economics at Wheaton College in Massachusetts and at Rockford College in Illinois before joining the New Deal workers' education project in 1934.[21]

In 1935, Smith also requested funding to hire eight field staff for three summer months to help organize the teacher-training centers and the educational camps for unemployed women (see chapter five). She called them her "roving ambassadors." Their charge was to confer with state authorities on the need for teacher training, help organize the centers, and advise state supervisors of emergency education on fall classes in workers' education. In some areas, they attempted to organize advisory committees of educators, social workers, community activists and union leaders. Along with the center directors, the special field staff zealously accomplished a prodigious amount of organizational work in a very short time.[22]

In both 1934 and 1935, the teacher training centers were hastily set up in approximately two weeks time because federal authorization and financial allocations for the program were delayed until late spring. Within this time period, center directors, aided by Friedmann and in some areas by the field staff, worked out housing details, office organization, schedules, curriculum, staffing, and recruitment of trainees. In addition, before the centers opened, the directors needed to enlist the cooperation of state and local public school officials who, if they felt bypassed by the New Deal emergency education program, would not help recruit teacher trainees.[23]

In a number of areas, public school officials were hostile to teacher training for workers' classes that would be financed by FERA and held in school buildings. Some felt that economic and social issues were too controversial to be discussed in such public settings. Even the more supportive school officials were puzzled by the new departures in subject matter and teaching methods planned for the centers. Smith and Friedmann used the opportunity to distribute hundreds of copies of official government news releases and memoranda to local school superintendents and relief administrators. Most of the materials underscored the need to train practitioners who could teach worker-students about current issues and motivate them to participate in citizenship responsibilities.[24]

Much of the work of the center directors necessitated close cooperation with relief offices that were still in the process of expansion, coordination, and standardization of procedures. The teacher trainees had to be certified as eligible for relief. In some states, they needed to pass a reading test or an IQ test given at relief offices by social case workers. Auditors needed to be consulted since they were responsible for methods of disbursement of earmarked funds. This proved to be a major undertaking since, as the 1934 report later stated, "daily, authority shifted and one had to search patiently for the persons [within the relief organization] to share responsibility for organizing the centers."[25]

In order to utilize the expertise developed at the residential schools for workers and to give teacher trainees the opportunity to observe workers' classes, centers were set up in connection with residential workers' schools at Bryn Mawr College in Pennsylvania, Weaver College in North Carolina, Barnard College in New York City, the University of Wisconsin at Madison, and Occidental College in Los Angeles. In addition, state universities in Georgia, Iowa, Massachusetts, New York, Tennessee, and Texas were used. Harvard, Yale, the University of Chicago, and Gulfport Military Academy in Mississippi were also among the sites chosen.[26]

Intricate financial and administrative procedures were involved in setting up the interstate centers, ordering materials and supplies, and arranging for trainees to travel to a center in another state. Frequently, as Smith noted, "a tired teacher on the way to a training center sat for hours in a railway station at a state border waiting for someone to arrive with an authorization to purchase a ticket across a state line. [Center administrators] could congratulate themselves if on the opening day . . . most of the enrollees were on hand or on the way, if the office and classroom space had been authorized, and if the financial situation was not so acute that everyone was too anxious to concentrate on the work."[27]

Teacher trainees were recruited on short notice in a variety of ways: through state and local school superintendents, relief offices, union groups that had used FERA instructors, and in a few cases, through the social science programs of some colleges and universities. Only about half of the trainees in 1934 and 1935 had college credentials. Of these, about 10 percent had M.A.s and 4 percent had Ph.D.s. The rest had not finished college or had no higher education beyond high school or eighth grade. Many, however, had worked in industry and a number were union members. Some had already taught the previous winter in FERA classes for workers' groups. Less than half had the industrial experience and social science knowledge that Smith recommended.[28]

The problem of recruiting and selecting able candidates proved difficult in both years. Handicapped by the late decision to hold the training centers in 1934 and 1935, center directors often found it hard to locate qualified recruits. Emergency classes had ended for the season; many instructors had been dropped from the relief rolls. In 1935, when the WPA replaced the FERA, many needy persons who had been instructing emergency workers' education classes under FERA were disqualified for the teacher training programs. Under the WPA, the unemployed were classified by trades, and it was impossible in most states to use jobless workers who might have made excellent workers' educators but who did not have academic background to give them teachers' status under the new WPA classification system.[29]

Smith and Friedmann hoped that trainees would be selected by locally formed advisory committees and interviewed by training center directors before the centers opened. However, that process proved impossible in most cases because of the short time available to organize the program in both years. As a result, most trainees arrived at the centers with little advance knowledge of workers' education or adult education or awareness about what their training would involve.

III

In retrospect, Smith and Friedmann expressed disappointment that the 1934 and 1935 teacher-training centers were "three-fourths a relief program and only one-fourth teacher training." The relief aspects of the program complicated the recruitment of trainees and faculty and led to some burdensome and frustrating administrative problems that affected the quality of center programming. Nevertheless, despite these complications and the overriding tensions and anxieties generated by the Depression, a number of innovative activities were undertaken to involve trainees in new teaching practices and unique community experiences.[30]

Some of the trainees enrolled in the centers because they were assured of six weeks' relief pay of $18.00 per week and three meals a day. Some of the centers had hundreds of applicants for the maximum of fifty openings in each program. In Puerto Rico, over 2,000 jobless people applied. In a few states, applicants were told by relief administrators that the training would lead to jobs as emergency education administrators at a pay scale higher than what they would make as temporary relief instructors.[31]

A number of the trainees arrived at the centers ill and needed medical care. Despite the instructions to come alone, some brought their families hoping to provide spouses and children with a summer's room and board.

Several of the center directors described the problems of starting the program with participants who were ill-informed about industrial workers, labor unions, and workers' education. After visiting the center in southeast Pennsylvania, Eleanor Coit, the director of the Affiliated Schools for Workers, noted that not more than ten of the fifty trainees understood or were interested in workers' education at the beginning of the sessions. Florence Nelson, a staff member at the Arkansas center, wrote that only four of the forty-eight trainees had previously heard of workers' education and that "the psychology of looking down on the worker as an inferior being was instilled in their thinking."[32]

Constance Williams, the director of the Connecticut center at Yale University, reported: "The students wanted jobs and were willing to do almost anything to prepare themselves for work that would offer economic security. Their first reactions to the training center was one of bewilderment. Few of them had any comprehension of the labor movement. Many, however, did become interested in the work. To put it bluntly, their attitude was 'If the government will pay us to learn, we will learn it.' During the third and fourth weeks, the students seemed to gain an understanding of what we were trying to do."[33]

Relief aspects of the program led to daily problems. The 1934 report vividly summarizes these difficulties:

> If the center was located elsewhere than in the locality of a State Emergency Relief Office, instructions came to the [center] director through the State Education Office or through the local relief office. . . . In one center before salaries or teachers' relief allowances could be paid or even stamps bought, the requisition had to go to the City Director of Adult Education, the Director of the Works' Division of the FERA of that city, then on to the State Education Office, and finally to the State Emergency Relief Office. . . . The teachers arrived with money enough for one day and immediately had to pay for their meals in the university cafeteria. . . . Requisition forms were misplaced in several relief offices because the system of accounts made no provision for any resident place or special funds. . . . All supplies had to be requisitioned in many cases through the Relief Office and in three centers, these necessary supplies did not arrive despite daily inquiries, until the fourth week of the school.[34]

In contrast to this reality, Smith idealistically anticipated that "all class-rooms in the training centers, if well conducted, would be laboratories where new teachers experimented with making analyses of economic and social situations and in using different teaching techniques." She sent a policy memo to all center administrators and staff indicating that the main objective of the centers was to help trainees discover and practice methods of teaching social sciences to workers. She stipulated that the centers be run as nondidactic learning experiences and, to that end, recommended the following proce-dures: (1) basing the center's program on the needs and interests of the train-ees; (2) involving the trainees in developing curriculum and participating in the governance of each center; (3) incorporating adult education methods in all center classes and group work; (4) using trainees as discussion leaders and the center's staff as resources and guides; and (5) developing contacts with workers and their organizations.[35]

Her policy memorandum listed three main goals for the centers' programs and recommended the courses to implement them. To help trainees under-stand the issues in the American economy, she advocated classes and discus-sions on labor and government, labor and economics, and current events. To help the trainees understand workers' lives and workplace conditions, she counseled visits to factories and farms, reading workers' autobiographies, and discussions with workers from various industrial and rural backgrounds. To help trainees understand workers' education, she suggested visits to workers' education classes at the summer resident programs, a review of organizations in the field of workers' education, guest speakers, and reading materials issued by the Affiliated Schools for Workers and the WEB.[36]

A number of these recommendations proved unrealistic given the back-ground of the trainees as well as the limitations of the faculty who had been hastily recruited to staff the centers. In many of the projects, the faculty did not have the experience with adult education methods and did not understand the needs and problems of the trainees or their potential worker-students. About 10 percent of the faculty were academics. Others had served on govern-ment labor boards, had researched labor problems, or were industrial work-ers. Most faculty had little time to prepare their courses or become familiar with the center's goals. Most of the faculty members, accustomed to tradi-tional classes, found it difficult to create an informal classroom atmosphere and involve the participants in a process of self-learning. Thus, only a few of the centers were able to consistently carry out Smith and Friedmann's goals.[37]

Among the 200 faculty members in 1934 and 1935, however, about a third had taught in residential workers' schools or in evening classes. They included Lillian Herstein, active in the WTUL and in the teachers' union, and a former teacher at the Bryn Mawr Summer School for Women Workers; Colston

Warne, an economist from Amherst College with a number of years of teaching at workers' summer schools; Amy Hewes, an economist from Mount Holyoke College and an experienced teacher in programs coordinated by the Affiliated Schools for Workers; Susan Shepard, experienced in teaching drama to women workers at Bryn Mawr College; Nelson Cruikshank, a minister who worked closely with the labor movement in New York State and New England; Arthur Calhoun, who had been on the staff of Brookwood Labor College; and Mercer Evans, a professor at Emory College who was a specialist in southern economics and labor.[38]

It took a great deal of flexibility to staff the intensive, residential training centers. For those faculty who understood the centers' goals and were committed to creating an experiential learning process, it was a rewarding experience. Nelson, a teacher from the Arkansas center and of YWCA classes for industrial women, reported on the process that she used:

> I was kept very busy the first two weeks trying to maneuver and steer the discussion to enable the group to find out for themselves what a worker is and what it meant to be a worker. During the third week, we turned to the study of how to lead a discussion. . . . I purposely did not give them this material on discussion techniques in the beginning because the ideal of group discussion as a teaching technique was new to all of them and they would not have been able to detect the qualities, whether good or bad, in discussion groups. After having developed a background for effective and serious thinking in the group on worthwhile topics, it is more than encouraging to note how conscious they became of themselves and others in the group and demanded worthwhile thinking of the group. It was then that we began our cooperative education in class and in seminar meetings.[39]

Most of the centers had similar schedules with daily classes from Monday through Saturday on labor and economics, labor and government, and basic methods in workers' education, the three topics suggested by Smith in her policy memorandum. She also suggested specific teaching methods that center staff attempted to follow with varying degrees of success: classroom presentations, independent study, group discussions, tutorials, observation of workers' classes, practice teaching, workshops to develop graphics, panel discussions, report writing, and labor drama.[40]

Reports from the 1934 and 1935 centers indicate that an attempt was made to include the following information in each of the programs:

—The economics classes included information on the development of business organizations, state and local economic problems, theories of the business cycle, problems of unemployment, coordination of production and consumption, economic policies, alternative economic systems, and the cooperative movement.

—The labor and government courses included discussion of New Deal policies and programs, new legislation such as the National Recovery Act, social security, and the relationship of government programs to workplace conditions.

—The courses on workers' education included material on continuing education needs of wage earners, cultural heritages of foreign-born workers, methods in workers' education, reading material recommended for workers' classes, workers' biographies and autobiographies, and the importance of discussion techniques.[41]

In addition to the classroom work, field trips were an important part of each center's activities, planned to meet the goal of familiarizing trainees with working-class life styles, workplace and community conditions, and workers' organizations. Trainees attended meetings of local unions and central labor councils. The Pennsylvania participants bused to the national AFL Convention held in Philadelphia in the summer of 1934. Colorado trainees drove to Denver from Colorado Springs to march in the 1934 Labor Day parade. Trainees visited unionized factories, public-housing projects, newspaper offices, cooperative enterprises, and community resources such as shelters for the unemployed.[42]

In an attempt to have the centers become education laboratories, a number of the programs involved trainees in group activities. Some centers compiled bibliographies and manuals for teachers of workers' classes on parliamentary procedure, labor drama, and workers' writing. Trainees in some of the programs conducted surveys and studies of work and living conditions in nearby communities. At the Occidental College center in California, participants produced studies on racial conflict in Southern California, the causes of strikes on the Pacific Coast since the start of the National Recovery Administration, the growth of union membership in California during the Roosevelt Administration, and the content of labor plays. In Gulfport, Mississippi, teacher trainees helped jobless workers organize an Unemployed League.[43]

About half the centers in 1934 and 1935 used labor drama to demonstrate a technique useful in workers' education and to provide a recreation for center participants. Trainees wrote plays about sharecroppers, household workers, prostitution, and conditions in textile, coal mining, and other industries. They frequently wrote and presented skits based on their own experiences: a scene in an employment bureau, a job interview, the first meeting of a workers' education class. At the Michigan center at Olivet College in 1935, trainees scheduled public readings of the Depression-era plays *Stevedore* and *Free Tom Mooney*, and put on a mock *Trial of the Machine*. In Madison, a skilled drama teacher used trainees to stage plays in the campus auditorium for the college and community audience.[44]

Evenings at the centers were usually spent in group activities: singing labor songs, putting together a center newspaper, holding mock forums and panel discussions, folk dancing, and working in teams on class reports. Guest speakers from nearby community organizations or from Washington spoke on topics that presented an idealized vision of America: the League of Nations, the cooperative movement, technological advances in industry, the role of the artist in society, ethical business practices, and progressive education.[45]

Thus, despite the inadequacies implied by Smith and Friedmann's evaluation of the program as three-quarters relief, the program did generate substantial innovations in developing a democratic educational framework for adult students that had relevance to their lives. Although teacher trainees and center staffs gave the 1934 and 1935 teacher-training program a mixed evaluation, citing multiple organizational and administrative problems, on balance, many primary accomplishments could make the national and local center staffs proud.

Workers' education had been presented in the context of adult education philosophy and methods. Many trainees were involved for the first time with informal, experiential learning techniques. In some centers, trainees read and discussed the work of educational philosophers and adult educators, and became familiar with the aims and practices in adult education. Trainees learned how workers' education related to the expanding organizational needs of the labor movement. They became aware of the role of unions in workplaces and communities. They were encouraged to develop "a social philosophy in harmony with labor's goals," and in some centers, they implemented that philosophy through "self-governing student councils" that focused on curriculum, field activities, and community contacts.[46]

Smith and Friedmann could claim with justification that at least some of the teacher-training goals for the centers had been fulfilled.

On the other hand, criticisms of the centers focused on the paramount administrative difficulties. Evaluations of the programs from individual center reports and the overall reports from the national office cited the need for earlier appropriations and authorizations, and for more cooperation from state school and relief officials. There was also a clearcut need to establish functioning advisory committees, and careful recruitment of trainees and staff, as well as closer cooperation with the labor movement. Finally, measures had to be taken to provide specific information about community conditions in the cities and towns where trainees might be teaching following the training period.[47]

IV

One of the most basic problems that surfaced in a number of the centers was the relationship of the summer programs to emergency education classes in the fall. The choice of instructors for training, the curriculum, and the planning during the summer months were greatly hampered by the lack of information about where the trainees would be placed and what they would teach after the centers closed. As the 1935 report stated, "the constant changes in supervision and the new policies in relief had made any relationship between training and program almost impossible. If decisions on fall plans could be known before the teacher training is undertaken, the efficiency with which this training could be carried out would be greatly increased." [48]

Many of the trainees were unclear and uneasy about how the summer's experiences would translate into their future work lives. Having received the intensive training in the government-sponsored centers, some trainees wondered what responsibility the government would take to find them relief or regular employment. In Connecticut, a trainee questioned his future in a poem published in that center's newspaper:

"Where To, Mr. Hopkins?"

Well equipped with federal pencils and notebooks
Our first interest was in unemployment
Resulting from the "impact of this crisis."
Kultur and culture assumed new meaning
Economically speaking. In labor relations
The chair flourished under Cohen. [an instructor]
Solidarity became reality on a country estate.

Elsewhere, we pantomimed and playacted
Dramatically for Miss Shepard.
Union men expounded theses.
Communists presented desperate dreams.
Adult education was clarified
By Connecticut's dispenser of federal education funds.
Turkish, Japanese and Polish delegates
At the ILO conference
Added color and accents.
Overall, genial Miss Williams, our director, presided.
Now we ask, "Where to, Mr. Hopkins?" [49]

Some trainees were confused about future action in their home communities and questioned the risks involved. Constance Williams, the Connecticut center director, reported that some trainees asked: "If we go home and discuss these things, won't we lose our jobs?" Williams wrote: "It became increasingly clear that there is no reassuring answer. The center could not give its students confidence that there were people in the community who wanted their services. The unemployed teachers left the center last week feeling frustrated and stranded. The opportunity to learn to develop workers' education played a less active role in shaping their attitudes and efforts . . . than the desire of getting a job." Williams concluded in her report to the national office, "In some way, the responsibility for workers' problems must be made more real." [50]

Some of the trainees, however, did find a way to apply their learning. Some were motivated to take initiatives to develop workers' classes in their home communities. In rural Columbus, Mississippi, Dorsie Dowdle, a participant in the 1934 Mississippi training center, wrote to another trainee about her fall experiences. Although the county school superintendent asked her to teach emergency shorthand classes, she was so determined to teach workers that she organized an evening class in her family home:

> That night they came flocking in until the little living room was packed to overflowing, mattress workers, factory workers, home visitors, and then the white-collar class—two aristocratic old ladies wanting nursing, and others with far more education than I have. . . . In fact, I've never seen such a mixed group. Everything went along fine until I got to current events. . . . The strike question came into the discussion. Two of the women got into a hot argument. . . . Words grew hotter and hotter. Mama turned pale. Lovie was shaking her head at me wanting me to stop. Dovie was motioning from the door to come into the kitchen so she could tell me to stop. Perhaps I should have stopped, but I was so interested I just kept going. Finally, Lovie rose up and said she thought we had enough of current events and about that time the clock struck 9. After that, Mama and them forbade me teaching anything like that to cause a row. Mama said that she had never been so embarrassed in her life. So I didn't until the night all the family went to church and then I put over one of the best lessons yet in workers' education. . . . And since that time I have been continuing it and they don't know it is workers' education or rather there has been no disputes so of course it is all right. [51]

Approximately 60 percent of the trainees in 1934 and 1935 were subsequently hired as emergency teachers in New Deal workers' education and adult education classes. In some areas, they were assigned to teach literacy classes or vocational courses. In some cities, they were placed in emergency classes held at Ys and settlement houses. Several of the trainees were appointed state supervisors of workers' education or city/county administrators in the emergency education program. Trainees such as Sam Berger, Frank

Fernbach, Hal Gibbons, Chris Jorgensen, Roy Reuther, Mike Rider, and Nat Weinberg went on to long-term careers on union staffs or in related organizations. In some areas, trainees formed an alumni group to spur interest in workers' education and organize classes in that locale.[52]

Smith's advocacy of teacher training and the response to the centers in 1934 made New Deal administrators aware of the need to train instructors for all areas of the emergency education program. In summer 1935, a nationwide WPA teacher training program was authorized; its administration came directly under EEP Director Alderman. Centers that trained teachers for workers' classes were absorbed into the EEP training centers after 1935. These projects were supervised by state directors of emergency education working closely with state and local school officials. Unlike Smith's centers, however, there were no federally hired field staff or other Washington personnel.[53]

By and large, the centers that Smith and Friedmann initiated in 1934 served as models for the six weeks' EEP teacher training projects. Held on college and university campuses, they focused on teaching methods for adult classes and on New Deal legislation and social programs. However, there was no potentially controversial material on labor unions, workplace conditions, or working-class life styles.

Some of the centers were fairly successful; others fell short of their goals. Some faculty hired for the summer programs were knowledgeable about their content areas but had no background developing adult learning experiences. Many of the centers also faced administrative problems of reimbursing participants for their travel expenses and obtaining material and supplies.

In the fall of 1935, when the WPA started, federal funding was no longer available to pay a weekly relief allowance to unemployed persons while they attended a teacher training center. Nevertheless, some states continued some form of teacher training throughout the New Deal period and paid for these projects from state emergency funds. As the Advisory Committee Report noted, "This training has been so effective that some states have expressed their willingness to accept training and experience on the emergency program in partial credit toward state certification as teachers. Some of the cooperating universities and colleges grant college credit for work completed at summer school conferences."[54]

In the summer of 1938, for example, a four-week residential workshop was held on the campus of the University of Michigan to help teachers develop a better understanding of the philosophy, principles, scope, and implications of adult education. The curriculum stressed the teachers' role in the New Deal emergency education program, promoted democratic classroom procedures, and encouraged extensive reading and study about current education, economic and civic problems. Trainees also learned how to adapt current printed materials for use in adult classes, and how to prepare their own written units of instruction. These workshops were a direct outgrowth of the program initiated by Smith and Friedmann and carried on their work of disseminating information about adult learning and the need for new kinds of teaching techniques.[55]

Throughout the remaining years of the WPA, teacher training was continued in a variety of forms under state rather than federal direction. Some areas organized statewide one- and two-day conferences for emergency education personnel, while others established two- to five-week programs such as the one at the University of Michigan, using college faculty as teachers and consultants. One- to two-week workshops trained state supervisors of emergency education how to help instructors improve their teaching techniques, and as colleges and universities began to offer degree programs in adult education, they also organized regular summer courses that emergency teachers could attend for credit.[56]

Smith, however, persisted in her vision of a teacher-training center devoted solely to the needs of instructors of workers' classes. In 1937, she proposed using her family estate at West Park, New York for a six-weeks' residential teachers' training center. She submitted a plan to Alderman for an ongoing training center "to build an adult education program under the WPA . . . to enable teachers of workers' classes through group work to analyze their experiences . . . to meet their own growing and changing needs in methods, content, and administrative problems [and] to see the relation between their individual work and the local and national adult education movement." Smith felt that such a center was needed "so that learning and life may be joined to purposeful ends, resulting in better understanding and utilization of all the educational resources of the community."[57]

As the President's Advisory Committee report later observed, "It is probable that every teacher in the emergency program has received some form of in-service training." That accomplishment can be directly attributed to Smith. Her vision and persistence led to thousands of persons experiencing new ways that they and other adult students could learn. She had flagged for New Deal administrators the need to conduct federally funded teacher training in a massive, government-sponsored, public education program. Her advocacy in lobbying to initiate such a nationwide project and her determination to base the training on the goals of democratic liberalism made a contribution to the workers' education and adult education fields that carried far beyond the New Deal period.[58]

Many of the trainees who participated in these programs acquired new skills in organizing and teaching adult classes. They became familiar with the techniques, new at the time, of leading discussions, using visual aids, and involving community resources to aid adults apply their learning to their lives. Many of them gained confidence through the experience of being part of a novel, social experiment. For some, it was a needed time for physical and mental rehabilitation that aided in improving their health and morale.

For most of the trainees, the involvement with their peers in the teacher-training centers was their first experience with an educational democracy where they were given some opportunities to plan programs, express opinions, and assume responsibility for group activity. Long before the term "group dynamics" became familiar, trainees in these New Deal programs were engaged in a peer-oriented process that was unique for that time.

In areas where there had been time to develop an advisory committee, members of labor unions, community organizations, and educational institutions became familiar with the aims and techniques of workers' education and laid the basis for working together in their communities to develop workers' education projects.

The training centers had an impact on many colleges and universities, which became aware of their possible roles in developing credit and degree programs in adult education and noncredit extension programs in workers' education. Many of the university faculty who staffed the teacher-training centers enriched their own teaching skills as a result of their summer's experiences.

Despite limitations and administrative frustrations of working within an emergency relief context, Smith made significant advances in linking important concepts in adult education to the New Deal's pragmatic programs for ameliorating the effects of the Depression on the unemployed. In the process, the lives of many participants and staff in the teacher-training centers were changed. "Whatever kind of teaching I do," one trainee wrote, "I will never be the same person. I feel as though I have been living in a new world and I don't want to lose touch with it again." [59]

Figure 1. Learning To Read and Write in a WPA Adult Education Literacy Class. Courtesy of the National Archives and Records Service.

Figure 2. A WPA Workers' Education Class in Illinois Teaches English through Analyzing Workers' Paychecks. Courtesy of the National Archives and Records Service.

Figure 3. A WPA Workers' Education Class with Sugar Beet Workers in Colorado. Courtesy of the National Archives and Records Service.

Figure 4. A WPA Workers' Education Class just outside Chicago Learns English through the Study of Social Security. Courtesy of the National Archives and Records Service.

Figure 5. A Labor Play, *Mill Shadow,* Performed by a WPA Workers' Education Class in New York City. Courtesy of the National Archives and Records Service.

Figure 6. Finnish Lumberjacks Learn to Read English at a WPA Workers' Education Class in the YMCA, Duluth, Minnesota. Courtesy of the National Archives and Records Service.

Figure 7. A WPA Class in Creative Writing Taught by Author Meridel Le Sueur at the Minneapolis Labor School. Courtesy of the National Archives and Records Service.

Figure 8. A Workers' Education Class Taught by a WPA Instructor at the State Fair Grounds in Pueblo, Colorado. Courtesy of the National Archives and Records Service.

Figure 9. A WPA Workers' Education Class in Mimeographing Leaflets, Allegheny County, Pennsylvania. Courtesy of the National Archives and Records Service.

Figure 10. A Workers' Education Class in Akron, Ohio. Courtesy of the National Archives and Records Service.

Figure 11. A WPA Workers' Service Program Workshop at Hull House, Chicago, September 1942, Teaching Workers How to Make Visual Aid Materials. Courtesy of the Archives of Labor and Urban Affairs, Wayne State University.

Figure 12. Library in Union Hall of the United Electrical, Radio and Machine Workers in Chicago, September 1942, Set Up by the WPA Workers' Service Program. Courtesy of the Archives of Labor and Urban Affairs, Wayne State University.

Figure 13. Shop Stewards in the United Automobile Workers Union in Chicago Learn about Labor Legislation in a WPA Workers' Education Class. Courtesy of the Archives of Labor and Urban Affairs, Wayne State University.

Figure 14. A WPA Workers' Education Class on Pictorial Economics, North Carolina. Courtesy of the Archives of Labor and Urban Affairs, Wayne State University.

Figure 15. Learning Skills in Millinery at a WPA Adult Education Class in New York City. Courtesy of the National Archives and Records Service.

Figure 16. A WPA Workers' Education Class Held in a Home in Louisiana. Courtesy of the National Archives and Records Service.

Figure 17. An Outdoor Discussion Group at a WPA Workers' Education Teacher Training Center in Indiana, 1935. Courtesy of the National Archives and Records Service.

Figure 18. Palmers' Lodge, Idaho, an Educational Camp for Unemployed Women, c. 1935. Courtesy of the Schlesinger Library, Radcliffe College.

Figure 19. Household Workers in Cleveland, Ohio, Rehearse an Operetta about Household Labor in a WPA Workers' Education Class. The Operetta *Belle O'Hara* Was an Original Work by the Class Teacher, Florence Nelson, Who also Headed the Residential Camp for Unemployed Women in Arkansas, Summer 1935. Courtesy of the National Archives and Records Service.

Figure 20. FERA Educational Camps for Women, 1934 and 1935. Courtesy of the Schlesinger Library, Radcliffe College.

Figure 21. Training Unemployed Women to Be Household Workers in a Michigan WPA Workers' Education Program. Courtesy of the Archives of Labor and Urban Affairs, Wayne State University.

Figure 22. Unemployed Women at WPA Camp Eleanor Roosevelt Perform a Puppet Show. Courtesy of the National Archives and Records Service.

5

The She-She-She Camps:
An Experiment in Living
and Learning
1934–1937

I came filled with thoughts of myself and my family. I'm going with interest in
each and everyone of you. I didn't know I could do what I've done here. I'm
taking home more than I brought. I'm taking thoughts of beauty and kindness
which will help me when the clothes that I made here have been used up.

> —Participant in a 1934 Camp
> for Unemployed Women[1]

Soon after Smith arrived in Washington in September 1933 to start her job as
Specialist in Workers Education in the FERA, she was asked by Director
Hopkins and his assistant, Clarence Bookman, to "do something" to meet the
needs of jobless women. The program that she initiated and developed promoted educational camps in a nationwide New Deal experiment for women
on relief. Nicknamed the "she-she-she camps" by their detractors, these
projects were frequently compared to the successful Civilian Conservation
Corps (CCC) camps in which unemployed men were put to work on highly
visible public service projects in order to develop practical skills. The she-
she-she camps were considerably less successful, however, and much less extensive than their counterparts for men.[2]

The camps' program for women was short-lived. From 1934 to 1937, 8,000
to 10,000 women enrolled in seventy-five centers, for six-week to two-month
periods. In the summers of 1934 and 1935, the camps' program was administered nationally by the FERA workers' education project. In late 1935, the
project was transferred to the National Youth Administration (NYA); it lasted
until the fall of 1937, when federal funding for the project was cut and most of
the camps were closed.[3]

Smith's project highlighted the limited place of women workers in the New
Deal. Hopkins hired her as a workers' education specialist but her position
was vague and controversial, and her efforts to promote and fuse education

and relief programs for women were treated for the most part with benign neglect. Although women's organizations around the country, aware of the plight of jobless women, pressured New Deal administrators to handle the problems of female unemployment, the inequities in women's receipt of public relief increased and their list of economic grievances grew longer throughout the Depression decade.

I

By 1932, two million women in all occupations felt the financial, physical, and mental effects of being without paid work. A new and alarming phenomenon developed in the country—bands of young, homeless women roaming the streets, reluctant to seek aid, frequently sleeping in train stations or behind heating ducts in subway bathrooms. "It's one of the great mysteries of the city where women go when they are out of work and hungry," Meridel Le Sueur wrote in 1932. "A woman will shut herself up in a room until it is taken away from her and eat a cracker a day and be quiet as a mouse so there are no social statistics concerning her." "Men thronged the breadlines," National Women's Party activist Helena Weed observed at the height of the Depression, while "women hid their plight." [4]

Private charities exhausted their resources for those women who did seek help, and New Deal agencies concentrated on ameliorating the lot of male heads of households, still regarding women as peripheral workers. They remained antagonistic toward hiring women while men were out of work. Many of the New Deal projects discriminated against women in their hiring practices, regulations, and wage scales. Women were denied access to higher paying public service jobs, were paid lower wages, and, if married, were subject to layoffs from their public and private sector employment. Women made up only a small percentage of the total recipients of federal work relief jobs. By the end of 1934, only 142,000 women had received emergency work relief, in contrast to approximately nine times that number of men. [5]

In the spring of 1933, during his frantic first Hundred Days, FDR developed a national work conservation program for young, jobless males, a concept that he had put forward in his acceptance speech at the 1932 Democratic National Convention. The idea of work camps for unemployed youth, foreshadowed in the writings of social philosophers Thomas Carlyle, John Ruskin, and William James, had been tested in a number of European countries in the 1920s, where young people were conscripted or volunteered for public service for periods of six to eighteen months. It is probable, although Franklin Roosevelt denied it, that he was influenced in his thinking by William James, his Harvard professor in 1912, who had called for "youth armies" working on national service projects in a "moral equivalent of war." [6]

The Civilian Conservation Corps Bill (Senate Bill 598), signed by Roosevelt on April 1, 1933, was the first New Deal measure designed to deal directly with the unemployment problems of young men. It enrolled 2.5 million males during its ten-year period, paid them $1.00 a day, and maintained them for an average of a year. The CCC was one of the most publicized and successful of the New Deal experiments, reflecting the president's lifelong commitment to forest conservation, his romance with rural life, and his assessment that the "tree armies" of jobless males that he had started as a relief measure while governor of New York State were a sound investment of public funds since they employed a hard-hit age group in work not ordinarily performed by private industry.[7]

Meeting in March 1933, a month before the CCC bill was passed by Congress, the national WTUL called for a parallel network of schools and camps for jobless women to be financed by the Costigan-LaFollette-Wagner relief bill, housed on public property, and modeled on the YWCA residential camps for young women in industry. Smith incorporated this recommendation in a memo that she circulated to New Deal administrators in August 1933 to solicit their aid for workers' education schools and activities, and she expanded it two months later in her response to Hopkins and Bookman's request that she "do something" for unemployed women.[8]

The network of educational camps for jobless women would not have developed, however, without the leadership and active intervention of Eleanor Roosevelt. The first lady, in the center of the New Deal's political sisterhood, used her contacts, influence, and prestigious White House facilities to advocate aid for the forgotten women of the Depression and New Deal years. Aware of the WTUL proposal through her close connections with leaders of that organization, Eleanor Roosevelt had also been influenced by the concept of a young workers' corps of eighteen to twenty-five year olds, an ideal advanced in a slim 1932 volume, *Prohibiting Poverty* by Prestonia Mann Martin, the granddaughter of educational philosopher Horace Mann. The book, which went through eight editions between 1932 and 1934, drew heavily on Edward Bellamy's bestseller *Looking Backward* for its vision of a utopia in which youth would be organized industrially to produce needed goods and services for the whole society. "It may be possible to try out some of these ideas under emergency relief," Eleanor Roosevelt replied to a correspondent who had written enthusiastically to her about Martin's book.[9]

Prodded by the continuing destitution of jobless women and inspired by this "utopia drafted by a woman," Eleanor Roosevelt did initiate such a project in the spring of 1933. She asked FDR for funds to "provide healthful employment and useful instruction amid wholesome surroundings for needy young women." The president sent her proposal on to Hopkins who agreed to the plan, allocated monies from the national relief appropriations, and instructed the New York director of emergency relief to comply with Mrs. Roosevelt's requests for a model camp for unemployed women to be started in her home state.[10]

Camp TERA (Temporary Emergency Relief Administration) opened June 10, 1933, in a Depression-closed employee vacation facility owned by the New York Life Insurance Company in Bear Mountain State Park, not far from the Roosevelt home in Hyde Park. For the next four years it was identified by the press, the public, and its personnel as Mrs. Roosevelt's special project since she and her daughter served on the advisory board, sent holiday presents, corresponded with staff and participants, and made occasional visits.[11]

At the start, Camp TERA benefited from the sponsorship of two powerful and highly visible public figures, Mrs. Roosevelt and her ally, Secretary of Labor Perkins, who helped preside at the camp's opening. But TERA soon generated public confusion as to how this experiment compared with the CCC program and whether females would be paid to perform public service. From 1933 to 1937, when the New Deal camp program folded, the purpose of TERA—later renamed Camp Jane Addams—and the other camp projects for women continued to be misunderstood. Camp administrators were confused about how to synthesize educational goals and relief objectives, and relief agency personnel were never clear about how the program's administration should be divided among the national, state, and county levels.

The needs of jobless women, however, were so acute and the response of the recovery program was so inadequate that Camp TERA stirred the public imagination and sparked headlines across the country in the days immediately following its opening. Letters and telegrams received at the White House pledged facilities owned by individuals and organizations for similar projects. Young women wrote to Mrs. President and Madam Secretary to apply. The YWCA director in Macon, Georgia, offered the government its fully equipped, eighty-seven acre camp; the president of Temple University's Women's Club volunteered her family estate in Maine; and the welfare director in Cincinnati, Ohio, promised that if Camp TERA was successful, his city would initiate a camp for needy girls.[12]

Twenty-year-old Marie Ether, the oldest of thirteen children in an Idaho farm family, was one of the many who wrote her congressman asking to attend such a program. "We haven't had no crops for three years and the prospects look bad for this year. As their [sic] is no job in sight around here and as I do not have a high school education, I thought it would be educational to go."[13]

Smith also thought it would be educational if numbers of young women like Ether could attend federally funded residential programs where they could take classes, develop group skills, exercise critical thinking, and experience personal growth. Modeling these schools on her experience at Bryn Mawr, she anticipated a program where unemployed women could learn about the economic conditions that affected their lives and be able to translate that knowledge into community action.

Her proposal to Hopkins called for federally financed, experimental residential schools where, in two-month sessions, jobless females could develop a sense of "social responsibility." Hopkins's immediate response to Smith's proposal was favorable. But in contrast to the speed with which other New Deal projects were being launched, he did nothing for a number of months to expedite her recommendations.[14]

Social workers, the network of progressive women in national government positions, and women's organizations stepped up their campaign to lobby New Deal administrators to develop more adequate work relief policies and programs for women. At a White House Conference on Women's Needs, engineered by Eleanor Roosevelt and FERA Women's Director Ellen Woodward in November 1933, Hopkins admitted that "the government has not done what it should [about jobless women] and feels pretty humble about it." He pledged government monies and determination to "care for unemployed women" and asked the hundred or so conferees for advice on how to extend that relief. Conference participants suggested establishing special public works jobs for women, earmarking 20 percent of federal funds for state-initiated women's work relief, and developing a network of schools and camps for jobless girls and women, a project that was being discussed by Smith, Mrs. Roosevelt, and members of the WTUL.[15]

As time passed with no further action on her plan or on any other women's work relief projects, Smith requested to speak at a conference of FERA field representatives held in Washington in February 1934. A number of the FERA staff opposed her proposal, anticipating "serious discipline problems if women were brought together to live." Undaunted by these reactions, Smith launched a publicity campaign through the publication of a widely distributed pamphlet, "The Woman with the Worn Out Shoes," which outlined the plight of jobless females and the problems of destitute transients and summarized the recommendations for a network of schools and camps that might keep these women constructively occupied and off the streets.[16]

Together with Eleanor Roosevelt and Woodward, two of her most vocal and influential advocates in the support system of social feminists in the national government, Smith orchestrated a White House conference in April 1934 that convened eighty women from national community and social welfare organizations, public agencies, and New Deal offices. The participants expressed a range of suggestions for a schools and camps program, including the need for health and morale-building activities and a curriculum that would educate jobless women for more intelligent participation in a democratic society.[17]

One government staff member cautioned that in a recent national survey of FERA administrators, over half had indicated that they had no interest in such a proposal and that there was no need in their states for such a program. Assistant FERA administrator Aubrey Williams, who was pinch-hitting for Hopkins at the conference, pledged "limited funds" to carry out the plan, while making clear his displeasure with the term "workers' education"—a component of the recommended curriculum that he felt "smacked of class distinctions." [18]

Despite precarious support, Smith moved quickly after the conference to set up a national advisory committee to consult with her office and to advise the states in curriculum development, the selection of teachers and students, and budgetary allocations. The national advisory committee included many national and New Deal leaders during the next few years. [19]

A comprehensive "Memorandum on Standards and Procedures in Establishing Resident Schools and Educational Camps for Unemployed Women," which Smith sent to Hopkins in May, reflected her vision of a well–rounded educational program that integrated workers' education, social sciences, and English. The "Memorandum" also recommended vocational guidance, health education, and opportunities for cultural and recreational activities. It advocated the discussion method of teaching to help students analyze their economic and social worlds, and a system of self-government to enhance their skills for problem-solving and community participation. [20]

Hopkins approved the proposal as a relief measure and wrote to state relief administrators in May 1934 that limited funds were available for resident programs for jobless women. He asked states to telegraph detailed plans and budgets within the week for proposed projects to open that summer. His memo stipulated that states would be responsible for obtaining rent-free facilities, appointing local advisory committees, and supervising each program. He gave no role to Smith's national office in the hiring of personnel and ignored the national advisory committee's proposal that it supervise budgets and consult on program development. Twenty state relief administrators wired within a few days that they were ready to apply.

The program would be confined to on-site education and group activities. CCC administrators had vetoed the national advisory committee's recommendations that young women in the resident programs be used, as men were, in reforestation and community service projects since "work outside the camps [for women] was not practicable," they claimed, "and the supervision and transportation costs would be greatly increased." Thus, significant work and training opportunities for women in the program were curtailed from the start. [21]

Less than a month after Hopkins's approval, Smith and Mrs. Roosevelt used a White House press conference to publicize the start of a national program "intended to serve as social and educational laboratories [from which] women will go forth to cope more intelligently and with renewed strength and courage for their special problems." They estimated that each school would cost $6,000 for approximately sixty students drawn from relief rolls for an eight-week term.[22]

Within a few weeks, twenty-eight schools and camps were operating within twenty-six states and the District of Columbia. Smith drafted and distributed "Suggestions for Organization, Curriculum and Teaching in Residential Schools and Educational Camps" to all project personnel and to state relief administrators. The manual succinctly summarized much of progressive education philosophy regarding education for democratic living. It recommended a system of participant self-management and group decision-making about the administration and content of each project. It included a statement of Smith's long-standing desire to help workers help themselves through workers' education, and her definition of workers' education, which she included in all of her publications: a curriculum that "offers men and women workers . . . an opportunity to train themselves in clear thinking through the study of those questions closely related to their daily lives as workers and as citizens." [23]

Noble though Smith's ideals were, they contributed greatly to the confusion of purpose that quickly swamped the program. They implied a long-range, far-reaching approach to problems that, in the press of the New Deal's focus on economic recovery, received only short-term, stop-gap solutions.

II

The schools and camps for women were organized by state relief agencies in cooperation with local YWCAs, some ongoing workers' education programs, women's clubs, churches, and settlement houses. Federal funds covered food and maintenance, which averaged $8.00 a week per enrollee, staff salaries, and the upkeep of buildings used in the programs. In addition, in 1935, the women participants received spending money of $.50 a week. State or private funds were solicited for equipment and other organizational costs.

Smith's role was to administer the program as part of her job in the FERA Emergency Education Program. She was aided by a small Washington staff that included Friedmann, who was also spending time on the teacher training projects. In 1935, Smith received permission and funds to hire eight field staff for three months; like Friedmann, they split their time between the residential teacher training centers and the women's educational camps. The state supervisors of workers' education, hired by the emergency relief program in twenty-four states by 1934, also aided the organization of the programs. The mix of state, local, and national direction, however, subjected the program in many areas to cross purposes and confusion.[24]

Hasty and haphazard recruiting, pressures to fill quotas, lack of advance publicity, and poorly informed county relief and welfare workers meant that most of the women participants arrived at the residential programs ill-informed about what to expect. Although local advisory committees and camp directors in some states had time to interview some applicants, for the most part enrollees were sent to the projects directly from the relief offices. Most of the women were under twenty-five and single; a third had never worked or had held only relief project jobs. Approximately 90 percent were Caucasian, and many came from small towns and rural areas, a pattern that continued through 1937. "I was told to be ready to leave in three days. I didn't know what the course of study would be or in what line of work," one woman later wrote to Smith.[25]

Many had anticipated vocational training and thought they would be assured of jobs following the program. "I attended with the idea that the school, being a government school, would mean a lot in securing a job," one participant complained following her summer's experience. "The school was a good idea but if you can't get a job after you return home, the government school can't mean very much." A group of young women who had been to TERA wrote to Mrs. Roosevelt that they had gained health and an interest in life during their stay, but could not find paid work on their return to the city. "Now, after four weeks of tramping through the streets, more than one girl says there is nothing left except suicide or tramping on the roads." Smith estimated later that only one-fifth of the enrollees in 1934 and 1935 found paid work on their return home, many in New Deal-sponsored relief projects.[26]

Despite Smith's emphasis on educational activities, it was the harsh realities of the times that determined the real focus of the camps. Most county agents sent women who needed food and shelter first and foremost. After visiting a number of sites, a Washington staff person from Smith's office reported: "To see a group of girls assemble on the first night was to receive an immediate and tragic impression of the results of unemployment. Thin, emaciated girls . . . they were overcome by the sight of a simple supper. Many showed symptoms of long fatigue, exhausted nerves and mental strain. Many expressed anxiety in leaving husband, father or brothers unemployed, thankful, however, to relieve them of the burden of another person to feed for the summer. All were bewildered in trying to understand what was happening in their own lives."[27]

Frequently, there was a discrepancy between the expectations of what "should" happen and the actual camp experience. A camp director reported, "The first week the girls would not sing in the dining room as I, who had been brought up on private camp traditions expected them to do. . . . I realized that they were there to eat. Singing marred the flavor of corn bread dripping in butter . . . and made questionable the assurance of a second helping." Staff, too, did not always match Smith's vision. Many of them, also hired from relief rolls, looked on their subsidized stay in the residential programs as a chance to escape their own desperate family and community conditions and to live and eat well for a few months in a supportive and healthy environment.[28]

Despite material issued from Smith's office, the seventy-five educational camps reflected regional cultural differences and varying goals and educational perspectives. In Arkansas, black sharecroppers' daughters lived on the campus of a Negro agricultural college. In New Jersey, a project was run for jobless professional women, the only one of its kind in the country. In Philadelphia, forty women lived and studied in a midtown YWCA. In Ohio, unemployed clericals spent six weeks on the Oberlin campus, packed into a small frame house run by the Affiliated School for Workers and its Summer School for Office Workers. In the Ozarks, women from mountain families took part in a project developed collaboratively with the Opportunity School, an ongoing program for illiterates. In New York City, trade-union women, now jobless, lived in a Barnard College dormitory. In North Dakota, young women left Indian reservations for the first time to go to a camp in a nearby town. In Michigan, small groups of jobless women were taught domestic service skills in houses rented for the purpose.

Nine of the projects in the summer of 1934 were connected with ongoing, university-based workers' education programs in Wisconsin, California, and Ohio. Despite Smith's recommendation that workers' education be included in each project's curriculum, these were the only centers to include union-oriented materials and discussions. In most of the camps, participants did not have enough experience in the workforce or in workplace organizations to discuss labor history and labor problems. Because some of the camp participants and many people in surrounding communities were so openly antagonistic to unions, Smith recommended in late 1935 that the term "social civics" replace the term "workers' education," and that discussions focus on current events and community problems instead of on workplace issues.[29]

In all of the projects, participants divided their time between site maintenance, study, and recreation. Food preparation, house cleaning, and curtain sewing were considered laboratory work in some places, since the staff assumed that the participants would be homemakers. A number of the projects ran beauty shops; some trained the young women to sew simple dresses. Some held sessions on table setting, home cleanliness, and personal hygiene. Commenting on the "she-she-she" focus of her experience, one young woman wrote Smith that "most of us got the impression that they wanted to teach us something useful if we got married immediately and that that was the only proper thing to do."[30]

The scope and quality of the education classes varied among the projects, although the teaching methods recommended by the national office were based on progressive education ideals. Many of the camps scheduled three or four morning classes daily. Reports from the individual projects indicate that there was an attempt to discuss different social systems, the new social security legislation, the cooperative movement, war and peace, and simple economic trends. Participants supplemented class work with trips to local businesses, public-housing projects, cooperative stores, union meetings, museums, and education centers.

Two-thirds of the camps scheduled classes in English grammar, composition, reading, and public speaking. Poor library facilities hindered reading programs in a number of the sites, but staff encouraged the women to read daily newspapers and current magazines, and a number of the projects dramatized current events through student-developed skits based on the WPA "living newspaper" model. Almost every camp published a newspaper, many with superficial social notes and gossip but some with book reports, poems, and short essays on personal experiences. In one project, enrollees sent weekly reports to their home-town newspapers; in a number of centers, the women took part in mock forums and debates. Some of the centers ran small co-op stores for refreshments and toilet articles; a few set up a simple "credit union" that made modest loans. In an attempt to broaden the social vision of the participants, guest speakers from Washington, nearby community groups, and local educational institutions spoke on topics such as good business practices, the League of Nations, the cooperative movement, and the artist in a democracy.[31]

Smith's 1935 report pointed out that an attempt was made "to develop a professional interest in some type of work for which the student was fitted and in which she might have a genuine professional pride. Very few of the girls had thought of work from the point of view of a life interest and quite naturally, their immediate concern was to earn a few dollars." Many of the projects included sessions on personal and job counseling and group discussions on practical employment problems. In some camps, the women practiced filling out job applications, studied community job-referral facilities, and rehearsed job interviews. Although vocational training was not an original purpose of the program, several of the camps trained the young women for office or domestic work. Some of the projects attempted to organize follow-up programs to help the women find jobs and to continue to develop the interests and skills cultivated in the summer programs.[32]

Recreational activities, nature study, organized sports, and student government formed a part of the daily schedule. However, in a number of the projects, social life became an issue. Harry Gersh, a teacher at Camp Jane Addams in the mid-1930s, recalls that for many of the girls from New York City, evenings were a problem:

These campers were neither Girl Scouts nor YW girls. . . . They were, for the most part, slum-raised, street-wise women translated from teeming neighborhoods and crowded city apartments into the clean, brisk and totally foreign air of a state park. . . . Camp Jane Addams was fenced and campers were not permitted outside the fence. Inside, there were 153 female campers, 18 female staff, one old man hidden in the kitchen, one married man with wife present and two young male teachers. . . . It was a most unnatural environment for these young women. . . . The above is reported only because it illustrates a basic flaw; the planners and directors of the camps didn't really understand with whom they were dealing and, therefore, how to deal with them. No one had thought that sexual isolation would be a problem.[33]

Eventually at Camp Jane Addams and at many of the other projects, there were weekly dances to which young men from nearby CCC camps were invited. In addition, through the student government process, some of the young women negotiated a periodic weekend during the summer to return to their homes.

Across the country, community reactions varied in response to the program. In some areas, residents donated furniture for the facilities and volunteered to help clean the camps, fix appliances, and help with daily chores. In other areas, projects were viewed suspiciously. In July 1936, in Rockland County, New York, for example, the American Legion accused Camp Jane Addams of using public funds to promote communism, citing as evidence that the camp was gated and restricted to outsiders, that the enrollees sang the "Internationale" and other labor songs, and the staff provided a forum for anti-American speakers. Similar attacks were mounted in other communities by the American Legion and the Hearst newspapers against the WPA emergency education programs and the camp projects throughout the period, adding to the accumulation of negative reactions that eventually led to their demise.[34]

Despite many problems and shortcomings, the program's paramount contribution was to help restore health and self-confidence to the thousands of young women who had come to the resident projects emaciated and exhausted by their long struggles with Depression problems. Eye glasses, dental work, and in some cases minor operations were negotiated for the women in a number of communities. Seventy-five percent of the women reported weight gains, and many attested to "a new outlook on life."[35]

On their evaluation surveys, which were part of a follow-up research project recommended by the national advisory board for the 1934 and 1935 sessions, participants testified to their positive experiences:

It seemed like someone did have an interest in whether we lived or starved and was trying to help.

It was a blessing for me to have the opportunity of spending eight weeks in a school building up my physical and mental strength, being sure of food, shelter and above all companionship. Since returning home, things have been much brighter even tho I am still unemployed.

After going to the FERA school, I felt that while conditions might be bad, they are not hopeless.

It's not only that I am getting enough to eat for the first time in three years, but I am beginning to think of myself as a real person again.[36]

III

Late in 1935, after the FERA was transformed into the WPA, the program for jobless women was transferred for administrative convenience to the NYA, which provided women between eighteen and twenty-five years of age with paid work as an alternative to relief. Changes in the program, however, were not significant enough to revitalize the project, since there was still a lack of serious commitment on the part of the New Deal administrators to provide enough funds and support staff to put the camps program for women on a firmer foundation.[37]

Smith remained chair of the national advisory committee and was a major influence in the program's continuation. Administration however, was assigned to a five-person staff at the NYA headed by Dorothea de Schweinitz, a national advisory committee member who had previously worked for the U.S. Department of Labor. Smith and de Schweinitz hoped that the NYA would create 150 camps and schools to serve 15,000 young women, but funds were never made available for more than a third of that number.[38]

Under the NYA, the project shifted its focus to give young women under the age of twenty-five who had never held a job some rudimentary vocational skills in addition to group living, education, and physical rehabilitation. Seventy-five percent of the enrollees in 1936 and 1937 were under the age of twenty; most were Caucasian and came from rural areas or small towns where there were no jobs, no job training, and no other NYA project.

As in former years, the camps were housed in donated or low-rent college or school buildings, YWCA camps, or on private estates. From January 1936 through the fall of 1937, when the program was eliminated, approximately 5,000 young women were enrolled in about fifty projects; exact figures are hard to obtain, since some of the women enrolled in several sessions and some of the camps were open year-round and included several terms. Most of the projects, however, folded after a single four- to eight-week session because of administrative problems, difficulties in recruiting participants, and failure to obtain financial and political backing from federal and state agencies.

Under NYA regulations, the women worked approximately three hours a day for maximum wages of $25.00 a month, from which they paid approximately $15.00 for room and board. The NYA required that participants have $5.00 a month after their expenses were paid. Work projects for the women's camps aimed to be socially useful and to prepare the enrollees for their future homes, workplaces, and communities. Most of the work, however, was sex-stereotyped, emphasizing physical dexterity, good work habits, and training in homemaking and child care. Girls prepared hospital dressings, sewed for institutions and for families on relief, painted signs, repaired books and toys, produced Braille materials, and did simple clerical tasks and mimeographing for other WPA projects. In some camps, they worked in nearby communities as playground and nursery school aides.

Many of the camps lacked equipment and supplies for serious work. Production of even simple objects was hindered by poor administration, cumbersome procedures for ordering and obtaining materials, and an uneven flow of supplies to the camps. But despite the limitations of the work projects, a number of camps did undertake imaginative learning projects and incorporated some self-government into their programs.[39]

In 1936, Smith still viewed the program as "a social laboratory in which it is hoped that the girls will acquire the skills, poise, a knowledge of resources, and experience in self-government and democratic procedures." A staff report highlighted the programs' objectives in 1936: "to develop an understanding of the obligations of citizenship . . . to develop qualities of initiative and cooperation for solving social problems . . . to develop attitudes and abilities for community service."[40]

Opposition to the work-camp programs for women, however, continued to be a problem. Although there is no documentation, the national advisory committee reports imply that many NYA administrators attempted to scuttle the projects by claiming that they did not understand their objectives and, if they did, by questioning their necessity. Although NYA deputy director Richard Brown admitted that the national staff and national advisory committee had done a good job of interpreting the program, he told a national advisory committee meeting in September 1936 that other New Deal agencies needed to see "eye-to-eye" with them about the program and that other government agencies needed a better understanding of its concept and objectives.[41]

In alerting the national advisory committee to the continued confusion about the program's objectives, Brown was communicating an administrative message that the program was in trouble. Some government officials complained that the costs of the program for women were higher than the costs of nonresidential NYA programs; that it was difficult to plan useful public work for inexperienced young women; and that the quality of the articles made in the women's camps was spotty. They cited problems in filling the camp quotas of approximately eighty enrollees because, they claimed, parents were reluctant to let young women live away from home even during the Depression. They cited cases where camps were attacked by local community members or by the American Legion as sponsoring leftist discussions and programs.

Some of the issues raised pointed to real problems. Recruitment for the women's schools and camps had grown more difficult under the NYA because wages for the young women were so low after room and board were paid that the girls could not send money home to their families and could scarcely buy toilet articles or pay for other personal needs. Complaints had been lodged by some communities fearful of the forums and free discussions and suspicious that radical, anti-American ideas were being taught by federally paid staff who were outsiders to the community. Some camp staff were left-wingers, reflecting the variety of political affiliations current in the 1930s.[42]

Transportation to and from the residential projects remained a major problem throughout the four years since the federal government never appropriated travel funds for enrollees who had to depend on the National Guard, public school buses, camp staff, or private individuals to drive them to the camps.

Finding qualified staff was also a continuing difficulty. During the FERA years, regulations required that teachers be hired from relief rolls. For the most part, teaching staff during the WPA period were borrowed from other WPA divisions. Many interested persons were discouraged from accepting jobs with the program because of changing government regulations and procedures, the hasty organization of many of the camps, low-wage scales, uncertain job tenure, limited free time, and no vacation pay. Although a 1937 study of close to 500 staff members of the women's camps program indicates that about 60 percent had attended some college and 30 percent had a college degree, it was hard to find teachers competent in their fields who could also function effectively with young adults in an intense residential experience.[43]

Early in 1937, government appropriations for emergency education were reduced and, alarmed at the implications of this move for the women's camps project, Smith again called on Eleanor Roosevelt's help through a memo to the White House. She suggested that $500,000 be allocated for twelve to fifteen demonstration projects in 1937–1938, which would serve 3,500 to 4,500 young women in a work and study program of vocational counseling, follow-up job training, and placement when the women returned to their homes. The national advisory committee met on August 3 and endorsed this proposal. It recommended that the NYA concentrate on spring and summer residential programs to reduce the costs of heating the facilities. It suggested more on-the-job training opportunities where enrollees could earn higher wages and obtain valuable vocational experience. It also underscored the need for residential projects for older women under the auspices of the WPA Adult Education Division.[44]

The August 1937 meeting was the last for the national advisory committee. On August 16, Mrs. Roosevelt paid a surprise visit to the 130 campers and staff at Camp Jane Addams and meeting with them on the dock overlooking Lake Titorati, shared her "unofficial opinion" that the camp would be closed the following month for lack of funds. The following day, the *New York Times* announced that the women's camps would close as of October 1, 1937. The reason given was the "relatively high cost of the camps as compared with other NYA residential work projects which will be continued and expanded." The article stated that costs of $45.00 per enrollee per month had been planned for the women's work camp projects, while the actual costs ranged from $38.00 to $58.00 per month (an average of $48.00—$3.00 more than the budgeted amount). The article also assured the public that this move would have no effect on the men in NYA work camps or in the CCC.[45]

The *Final Report of the National Youth Administration, 1936–1943* claimed that the work camps for women were the forerunners of a highly successful NYA network of residential programs developed from 1937 until the war years, and that they helped prepare NYA administrators for problems in coordinating and organizing work and living situations involving large numbers of people. The report concluded: "Consequently, the final abandonment of the old program did not constitute a complete loss, although some of the best characteristics of that program, namely self-government, cooperative management, personal guidance, and workers' education were now relegated to a less important role." What the official report failed to point out was that shutting down the program meant abandoning significant efforts to help unemployed women.[46]

IV

Smith persisted in her advocacy of the schools and camps program for women and attempted to revive the concept in 1940 in connection with war defense. Writing to Mrs. Roosevelt about the need for programs aimed at jobless women between the ages of twenty-five and forty who were too old for eligibility in NYA projects, she explained that "the CCC camps with their millions of dollars for wages, education work, travel and supervision constantly remind me of what we might do for women from the same families. As so often is the case, the boys get the breaks; the girls are neglected."[47]

Her friendship with Mrs. Roosevelt had given her carte blanche in bringing her visions and problems to the White House and, through the first lady's intervention, had secured the attention of FDR and the limited support at the program's start of a few New Deal administrators. Smith and Mrs. Roosevelt shared a heartfelt belief in the equal rights of women who, if given the proper intellectual "tools," could "work out their salvations wisely and well." But neither Smith, nor Mrs. Roosevelt, nor their cohort of liberal women in New Deal government had the power to mount a long-term, comprehensive, federally supported national education program for jobless women.

Their campaign to establish such a program floundered because of external pressures and internal contradictions. Externally, the she-she-she camps were seen as a social aberration by a country that had rarely used public resources to meet work-related, educational needs of adult women or, for that matter, of men. Indeed, the concept of the camps challenged the status quo by suggesting that women might go beyond their roles in the home and undertake extended, or different, roles in the labor force, and in public life. In the crisis atmosphere in which the EEP was first established, criticism of the women's camps was muted by the pressing need to feed and house the unemployed. But as the nadir of the Depression passed, conservative critics singled out the EEP's most controversial aspects, and the she-she-she camps were high on their list.

Internally, contradictions sprang from a mixing of goals and personnel. On the national level, the program was promoted by progressive educators and reformers, led by Smith. Her educational goals focused on long-term changes: education, by producing an informed citizenry, would ultimately preserve democracy and save the existing economic system. With respect to women, the only institutional models for such an education were the elite, private colleges from which Smith and her cohorts had graduated, and the residential schools for women workers that she and other progressives subsequently established.

At Bryn Mawr College and the other institutions that made up the Affiliated Schools for Workers, the curriculum had addressed the mind, body, and spirit of adult women, and the she-she-she camps were supposed to reflect these same philosophical commitments. But in practice, this was an emergency relief program administered at the local level by people who often had no attachment to the high principles of progressive reform. Smith's long-term agenda was too broad in its concept and too diffuse in its impact to take root in such a crisis-oriented context. Progressive educators, with their gaze fixed on distant horizons, could not easily transverse the New Deal's maze of quixotically shifting personnel, varying congressional appropriations, and changing regulations.

What, then, had the young women gained in these residential projects? Certainly, mental and physical health improved; self–confidence quickened; and group skills improved. Young women broadened their life experience, confronted new social and intellectual stimuli, and tasted the first freedoms of moving away from family households and home-town communities. The program also gave young women some control over their lives at a time when the United States had lost control over its economy.

On balance, however, the she-she-she camps left neither long-term programs for the education or job training of women, nor reforestation projects that would make a nation proud. They were limited by the Progressive movement's emphasis on educating individual women rather than on shifting their relationships to family, workplace, and society. But they did represent a significant social experiment on behalf of a controversial principle—that government has a responsibility in meeting women's education and job-related needs. They linked the programming of some of the New Deal education projects to the philosophical and moral concepts of earlier progressive philosophers and educators. In so doing, they underscored the need for women to be an educated and active citizenry and promoted the use of public resources for those who had been America's forgotten people.

6

Workers' Education in the
Works Progress Administration
1935–1942

It has always seemed to me that this particular phase of education is important especially at this time when people seem to be beset by fears of socialism and communism. It seems particularly vital that the workers of our country should have an opportunity to study the labor movement and the economic problems of the day.

—Eleanor Roosevelt, "My Day,"
January 29, 1936[1]

From 1935 to 1942, New Deal workers' education activities crested and then declined, following the pattern of expansion and retrenchment of most of the WPA programs. In those seven years, however, new programs were initiated that reached workers in thirty-four states, new program formats were developed, and new labor advisory committees were organized—in some communities quite successfully—that broadened the base of labor planning and participation in the New Deal workers' education program.

When the Committee of Industrial Organizations began to galvanize the energies and commitments of workers in 1935 and 1936, it found itself active on a dozen different fronts. Hundreds of thousands of workers were joining sitdown strikes, signing union cards, and asserting their rights to engage in collective bargaining, political action, and community affairs. John L. Lewis told workers: "The President wants you to join a union," and many associated the New Deal with their new-found workplace victories. Accordingly, newly organized workers named their lodges and local unions "Blue Eagle" and "NRA."[2]

President Roosevelt "was somewhat perturbed at being cast in the role of midwife of industrial unionism." Indeed, although accepting labor support and financial contributions in his victorious 1936 campaign, Roosevelt attempted to remain neutral during the height of the sitdown strikes. Not so his Democratic Vice-President John Nance Garner who denounced Lewis as "a traitor to his country." Other political leaders in both parties articulated—and voted—their alarm at the perceived threat to private property, traditional management prerogatives, and the country's free enterprise system.[3]

The attempt in the second half of the 1930s to quell the New Deal and scuttle its innovative cultural, arts, and workers' education activities derived from at least two additional factors. The cutback of WPA activities in these years reflected the growing conviction in Congress that the emergency period of the Depression had ended and that the Roosevelt Administration, therefore, should ease up on economic and social reforms. Despite the passage of the Fair Labor Standards Act in the second half of the decade, by and large the years after 1936 were a different kind of New Deal, one characterized by stalemate and retrenchment.[4]

Congress and the public were also alarmed by the involvement in the new CIO unions of some Communist Party activists; at the same time, some radicals who wished to express their idealism and ideology in action did so by becoming instructors and participants in New Deal workers' education projects. As a result, the WPA workers' education program was damned for its political implications rather than praised for its educational intent. Pressured by lack of support within the WPA administration during the second half of the decade, the program changed its concept and course, a direction that both broadened and marginalized its scope and effect.[5]

I

The WPA was created by the Emergency Relief Appropriations Act of 1935 to provide employment on public projects instead of dispensing direct relief funds. The rationale behind the WPA was to preserve workers' self-respect and to conserve their skills. WPA guidelines stipulated that projects must have authorized local sponsors and general public usefulness, that they not compete with private employment, that they be conducted on public property and be completed by the end of each fiscal year.[6]

The WPA began to provide jobs in August 1935, after a hiatus of seven months following the end of the emergency relief program. In order to receive WPA funds, workers' education projects and personnel needed to meet requirements set by three major government divisions: the state education department, the federal WPA administration within each state, and the division of emergency education programs within each state's WPA. Further limitations were imposed. Only those persons classified as teachers on WPA rolls could be assigned to workers' classes or activities. This shut out many individuals whose past experiences with unions, workplaces, or adult groups might help them to be more effective as teachers of WPA workers' classes. In addition, WPA instructors on workers' projects were ranked as "skilled" rather than as "professional," and their WPA wage rates—already much lower than public school salaries—reflected this discrepancy.[7]

Despite these bureaucratic limitations, which eventually had a devastating effect on the workers' education program, Smith was hopeful when the WPA was established in 1935. She was beginning to make some inroads into gaining official support from unions, and she believed that it would be possible to garner support for a long-term, permanent workers' education program under federal sponsorship.[8]

Enrollments in all emergency education programs continued to expand across the nation. From 1935 to 1937, the impetus given labor by the National Labor Relations Act (NLRA) and the rise of the militant Committee of Industrial Organizations, which spearheaded organizing drives and sitdown strikes in the mass production industries, prompted an upsurge of activity in New Deal workers' education programming. Between January 1935 and February 1936, Smith claimed that her national office received over 100,000 letters, most seeking information about new legislation, government regulations, and WPA employment procedures. A large number requested classes on labor problems, social security legislation, and consumer issues.[9]

Within the AFL, the New Deal workers' education activities were slowly being publicized. However, although twelve state federations of labor passed resolutions supporting the program, and AFL union members in a number of states participated in the classes and activities, on a national level Smith experienced suspicion and resistance from AFL leaders.

Smith attended the 1935 AFL Convention, where factional fights between advocates of craft unionism and industrial unionism dominated the proceedings. Although WPA workers' education materials were displayed and distributed, Smith noted that the whole tone of the convention "was decidedly critical of the New Deal in connection with the ending of the NRA, inadequate social security legislation, and the relief program." She decided not to address the convention and reported that "If the cooperation of Labor is to be gained for workers' education, something active and intense will have to be done very soon, otherwise state federations of labor will continue to be either indifferent or openly antagonistic. Our workers' education state supervisors have not, apparently, succeeded in winning their support in many states."[10]

Smith attempted to improve relations with the AFL's leaders by organizing a Washington meeting to solicit their ideas on policies and programs. Very few of the invited participants attended. WEB staff member Paul Vogt later wrote to WEB Director Miller who had missed the meeting: "Suspicion surfaced that the Emergency Education Program is propagandizing for things that the long experience of organized labor leaders has shown to be inimical to the organized labor movement." It was necessary to guard the interests of the craft-oriented AFL, Vogt reported, by having its leaders determine the content of WPA workers' classes and choose personnel for the program.[11]

In December 1936, WPA workers' activities reached a peak with an enrollment of over 65,000 workers in 3,000 classes, using about 1,000 instructors drawn from relief rolls in thirty-three states. The diversity of the programs is indicated in Smith's 1936 report: six- to eight-week classes in current events, labor law, labor economics, labor history, and union administration held in public schools and union halls; week-long institutes on New Deal legislation; forums on current events co-sponsored in rural areas with the WPA Forum and Lecture Division; small co-op stores and buying clubs, outgrowths of classes on consumer problems; use of WPA instructors to staff the residential Wisconsin School for Workers on the campus of the state university in Madison; labor libraries developed in some union halls and labor temples; two labor colleges in Minnesota's twin cities, staffed by instructors from WPA rolls; a WPA-prepared history of the ILGWU; a labor play presented by a WPA class to a convention of the Ohio State Federation of Labor; classes for workers in settlement houses in New York City and Chicago; a marionette project for Philadelphia's trade-union groups; and active citywide advisory committees in a number of locales.[12]

Smith viewed the acceleration of classes and programs as an affirmation of the need for a long-term federal workers' education program. Her 1936 report recommended a permanent federal office or bureau that would use nonrelief personnel for supervision and teacher training, promote statewide labor advisory committees, and give grants to ongoing organizations such as the Affiliated Schools for Workers and the WEB.[13]

Attempting to strengthen the WPA workers' education program through close working relations with other federal agencies and to thus lay the groundwork for a permanent program, Smith organized the interdepartmental Technical Committee on Workers' Education. Headed by Josephine Roche, the chair of the president's interdepartmental Committee on Health and Welfare, the committee included representatives from a number of divisions in the U.S. Department of Labor, the U.S. Department of Agriculture, the Social Security Board, and the WPA. The committee met two or three times before Roche's resignation from her federal job and 1937 WPA staff reductions caused it to disband.[14]

Smith attempted to carry this campaign to Congress. Early in 1937, the *New York Times* reported: "A campaign for a permanent workers' education program as a nonrelief project is being launched by American labor forces. A $4,000,000 bill for a four-year experiment is being drafted for introduction into the next session of Congress." The aim of the bill, the *New York Times* reported, would be to guarantee workers' education as a recognized, permanent activity of the government, to remove it from WPA jurisdiction, and to place it under a separate government department or commission. It would also serve to extend existing emergency workers' education projects and make possible the expansion of enrollment in workers' programs. The bill died in Congress that year.[15]

Smith's efforts came at the very time that the WPA as a whole was under intense attack and when many employers and their allies were mobilizing to stop the acceleration of workplace organization. Linked as it was in individuals' minds with the burgeoning militancy of labor and to economic changes and instability, the WPA workers' education program suffered mounting attacks in the press, in Congress, and in state capitals. Not even the efforts of well-meaning supporters, such as Eleanor Roosevelt, could save WPA workers' education projects from becoming the focus of those who feared or who hated the political and economic changes that the nation was experiencing in those years.

II

From 1933 on, newspaper headlines and articles challenged the content, teaching methods, materials, and personnel in the New Deal workers' projects. Under headlines that proclaimed "Reds Rule FERA Schools," "Red Theories Taught Free by Uncle Sam," "Little Red School House," "WPA Institute Had Socialist for Director," dailies from the *New York Times* to small-town newspapers charged that partisan, class-conscious subjects were taught in these programs. The articles claimed that anti-capitalist, pro-Soviet materials were used, that students discussed socialism and communism, that books by radicals were assigned, and that instructors had left-wing leanings.[16]

A full-page advertisement by the Republican Party in western Pennsylvania stated that FERA's workers' education teacher-training center in that state was "designed to make the students scoff at religion, sneer at the Church, jeer at the Supreme Court, and then go forth to stir up workmen against employers . . . and to arouse class hatred whenever possible." An article in the *Cleveland Plain Dealer* charged that students in an FERA school sang "The Internationale," discussed strikes, and wrote skits that satirized the capitalist economy. The *Seattle Post Intelligencer* ran an article accusing the Georgia workers' education center as being "a hotbed of radical propaganda."[17]

The *New York American* reported that the Federal Grand Jury Association, an organization that included New York Governor Herbert Lehman, had protested to the U.S. Senate Appropriations Committee about radical influences in WPA workers' education projects and urged it to take action "to prevent relief allotments being used to support schools for communists, their teachings, or their students." The letter charged that workers in New York City WPA classes were taught to picket, sing leftist songs, and read books such as *The Nigger* by Communist Party secretary Gil Green, pamphlets by Communist Party leader Earl Browder, and life stories such as the autobiography of Big Bill Haywood, the former leader of the Industrial Workers of the World.[18]

The *Washington Times* reported the reaction of the village president of Olivet, Michigan, to the 1935 workers' education teacher training school held in that community: "The people of the village shuddered through six weeks of communistic activity at one of 100 similar schools operated throughout the country by the Raw Deal with tax payers' funds. . . . Men of Olivet wanted to take matters in their own hands and drive the students out of the village but I helped dissuade them. And to add insult to injury, a lot of those crackpots spent the money the government gave them on beer." [19]

A number of the WPA teacher training centers and classes were investigated by national and state WPA administrators as a result of these charges. In all cases, they were cleared. Negative public opinions, however, persisted in many areas of the country and exaggerated the influence of some of the instructors who were affiliated with left-wing groups. Patriotic associations such as Liberty Leagues, American Legions, and Daughters of the American Revolution sent resolutions to Congress calling for an immediate end to the New Deal workers' education activities. Hearings held by the House Un-American Activities Committee in the 1930s stirred up additional controversy by focusing on alleged Communist infiltration of industrial unions and the "traitorous" actions of New Deal politicians who supported—or failed to repress—the CIO.

Smith downplayed the charges brought against her programs. In her press statements she stressed the importance of free speech and inquiry in the education process. "The School is being operated precisely as it was planned by the Government and according to my instructions," she told a reporter from the *New York Daily News* who interviewed her about alleged Communist teachings at the New York City School for the Unemployed, a WPA workers' education project. "The policy is to present every point of view in economics, history and politics—not just one—and to promote and encourage free and full discussion." [20]

Smith enlisted Hopkins's support for a strong public statement defending the workers' education program. He was quoted in the *Baltimore Sun*: "The workers' education program attempts to offer an opportunity for the study and free discussion in classes, but a fundamental of the program is that students must be left free to draw their own conclusions. Anyone who says that any part of the program is carried on for the purpose of destroying the country or spreading foreign propaganda or spreading communism just doesn't know what he is talking about. Anybody who knows me at all knows that I don't operate that way and that I don't let any part of any program operate that way." Hopkins, Smith later reflected, "understood the difficulties of this specialized program, the constant opposition it met, and the need for training personnel if the job were to be done at all." [21]

Smith's staunchest ally in New Deal echelons was Eleanor Roosevelt, who from 1933 on maintained a continued interest in workers' education. Smith kept the first lady informed of her problems and victories, and Mrs. Roosevelt's interest was the main reason FDR and other New Deal leaders agreed to continue this government-sponsored emergency education program. [22]

Mrs. Roosevelt invited Smith, her staff, and support committees to the

White House on at least four occasions between 1936 and 1942 and several of her nationally syndicated "My Day" newspaper columns featured her opinions about workers' education. In 1938, the first lady met with Smith, Alderman, and WPA state supervisors of workers' education in her cottage at Hyde Park, New York. She reflected on this meeting in her daily column:

> There never was a time, I think, when people realize more fully the need for greater knowledge. It is not only because it has a bearing on their own economic situation but because it makes a difference in their understanding of the general conditions in the world. From my point of view, this particular phase of adult education is important to democracy. It develops an ability to read and to reason, to listen to other people's viewpoints, and to discuss questions before making decisions. This is valuable enough in relations between individuals, but in employer and employee relations and in international understandings, it will mean a great step towards reasonable and peaceful settlement of many disputes.[23]

Mrs. Roosevelt's advocacy of workers' education highlighted the essential difference between the liberal's model of personal enlightenment and the radical's doctrine of class consciousness that critics of the New Deal accused the Roosevelt Administration of promoting. Far from advocating class conflict, however, Eleanor Roosevelt held that workers' education would promote "peaceful settlement" of workplace disputes. To solve the economic problems of the day, workers and employers must cooperate, Roosevelt declared in "My Day." "Cooperation with an uninformed group is practically impossible and will not lead to the intelligent solution of the problem." In her view, workers' education should not only communicate information about New Deal accomplishments, but should also promote a form of social self–control, an understanding of "what it is in ourselves, in human nature as a whole, which must be fought down if we want a New Deal. . . . Only through understanding can [workers] be expected to look at questions in a comprehensive way. Our great difficulty in the past has always been that individual groups see only their own point of view and cannot understand the situation as a whole."[24]

By stressing the need for cooperation and understanding, Mrs. Roosevelt voiced her hopes that informed workers would agree with New Deal leaders. She believed that if given the opportunity to question and explore new information, workers could also be brought to cooperate with management, as well as with the New Deal administration. It was a well-intentioned liberal defense of workers' education that, in the face of escalating union militancy and company violence, became increasingly ineffective against conservative critics.

Other obstacles gradually undermined the program's viability. Investigation of relief eligibility of WPA instructors was intensified, resulting in a constant turnover of teaching staff, interruption of classes, and termination of courses and activities. In 1937, WPA regulations included an eighteen-month maximum time period that persons could be employed on WPA projects. This regulation led to further layoffs of instructors, frequently before courses were completed. Although WPA regulations allowed a 10 percent quota on noncertified employees, many states did not follow these guidelines because of pressures to reduce the costs for nonrelief personnel. Supervisors of all WPA emergency education projects became steadily less effective because they spent large amounts of time coping with changing guidelines, replacing instructors, and, with the cutbacks in budget for support staff, doing clerical chores.

Continuing communication problems between WPA national and state offices became a serious obstacle to the effective operation of all WPA programs. Smith's newsletter, "Concerning Workers' Education," which she had published and distributed in 1934 and 1935, was discontinued because of budget cuts. There were no channels through which Smith and other EEP national specialists could send materials or information directly to instructors or to state and local supervisors of their projects. There was no way that Smith could directly contact state supervisors of workers' education. All letters and materials needed to be sent to state WPA directors who then sent them on to the state's chief school officer, who then sent them on to local sponsors of WPA education programs, usually district school boards. Workers' education materials and communications deemed controversial by many state and local school superintendents failed many times to reach the local level of workers' education staff and instructors.[25]

As EEP Director Alderman wrote to Aubrey Williams, "The specialists on the Washington staff are employed primarily to render service to the state programs; but the regulations regarding communication act to defeat the purpose for which they are employed." And as Smith allowed herself to complain, "Better communication was crucial so that differentiation could be made between the needs of WPA construction projects and the needs of an education program."[26]

Responding to threatened Congressional cuts in appropriations and to Smith's requests for their help, AFL and CIO representatives met with Aubrey Williams in separate sessions in August 1937. The CIO representatives made a case for government-supported workers' education based on the existing tradition of publicly supported education for business and farm groups. AFL representatives used their meeting a week later to press for more control over WPA workers' programming. "Educators," the AFL representatives said, "should serve and not dominate this field. . . . Labor's experience shows that to put workers' education in the hands of those not responsible to labor is to invite irresponsible teaching by those advancing their own objectives. The functional necessities of the labor movement require that unions assume responsibility for the direction of workers' education."[27]

By 1938, Smith reported that WPA workers' education programs were weakening even in the face of increased demand for their services. By that point in time, there had been almost a 50 percent reduction in WPA workers' education programs. Throughout the nation, approximately 500 instructors were employed on projects involving approximately 38,000 participants from union and community groups.[28]

Despite this overall decline in program, pockets of important activity were being generated. Friedmann reported from an April 1938 field trip to Georgia:

> The work here is becoming more vital every week. Mrs. Dillard [the state workers' education supervisor] has it well in hand, meeting all threats with great skill. She consults all around before she does a thing and so keeps everyone going with the work. The teachers know their subject matter better than any group I know. They still need help with method but know what they need to know. . . . The auto groups meet three different times a week. Two are groups of shop stewards studying their jobs, labor regulations, and the functions of the union. The third is a general group in history and problems of the labor movement. Three textile groups represent an important start. . . . The conditions are terrible and the workers most discouraged, but what spirit—what canny wisdom. . . . This afternoon, the workers' education program held its first labor forum. The AFL groups have especially cooperated with choosing subjects and speakers. However, both groups [AFL and CIO] were there today and both took part from the floor. Both groups told me that they think our contributions in bringing them together on neutral ground to be very important. The discussions of labor relations was thorough and all felt it was a good beginning. Tomorrow night, Mrs. Roosevelt will speak to 5000 rural and urban women who are trying to bring city and farm into direct contact. If only we had enough trained teachers to offer education classes along this line, we could begin rural work. . . . Mr. Lassiter [the WPA state supervisor] is very conscious of this as an experiment for the whole South and as co-partners in an enterprise they all believe in.[29]

Smith attempted at this time to develop a national labor advisory committee to consult with her small Washington staff and to encourage states to continue and expand the program. Twenty-five members were appointed, serving as individuals rather than as official labor representatives; they elected Mark Starr, education director of the ILGWU, as chair. The national committee met only once, a four-day meeting in 1938 that included sessions with WPA and other government officials, and a White House meeting with Mrs. Roosevelt. The reason given for discontinuing the committee was that WPA funds were not available to bring members together.[30]

Smith's mood at this time was bleak. She expressed her resentments in a pointed poem written late in 1938, "The Role of Red Tape":

> Though we move with all precision
> In this valuable Division
> And sometimes make real progress with a dash,
> Yet we'd like to state quite plainly
> That we'd progress less inanely
> If we had a little tape we all could slash.
>
> The red tape can get tangled
> Til official nerves are jangled
> And even local bookkeepers lament.
> With intricate gyrations
> They go into palpitations
> To make sure every nickle is well spent.
>
> When we're feeling rather glum
> About our curriculum
> And the adults lack of anything to read,
> You may ask for new releases
> And prepare some stuff that pleases
> But try to get it through with any speed.
>
> Illiterates are waiting
> Til some more "coordinating"
> Results in travel funds more freely used.
> For we meet with some impasses
> In our local rural classes
> Til even state officials are confused.
>
> In Negro education
> We feel real exhilaration
> When Negro classes start and seem to spread.
> Yet even model teachers
> Become most helpless creatures
> When bound around with tape of crimson red.
>
> But now we all can bear up
> For here's some tape to tear up;
> Some paper tape that's easy to unloose.
> So if this education
> Fails to edify the nation
> We now shall have no really good excuse.[31]

III

By 1939, Smith's program was endangered. Continued attacks on the alleged radical content of the workers' education classes, congressional cuts in the WPA budgets, and shifts in WPA organization and personnel weakened the already tenuous support for the workers' education program. In addition, the start of World War II completely changed the direction of the New Deal workers' education activities along with the nature of other WPA-sponsored emergency education projects.

In the reshuffling of New Deal programs, Director of WPA Women's and Professional Projects Woodward was appointed to the Social Security Board. A Smith ally and close colleague since 1933, Woodward had been a key figure in the New Deal sisterhood of social feminists and reformers that pressed for innovative programs for women, workers, and minorities. She was replaced by Florence Kerr, a former Red Cross worker and an English teacher at Grinnell College in Iowa, who had served as midwest director of WPA women's relief activities from 1935 to 1939.[32]

Kerr assumed her new office at a time when creative programs in her division faced cutbacks or abolition because of congressional and public attacks. Woodward's informal, supportive, and self-assured style of administration was replaced by Kerr's more formal approach to administrative procedures and staff relations. Responding to shifts in public attitudes and congressional pressures, Kerr tightened up the organization and program of her division and established more rigid supervision over staff, including Smith.[33]

Early in her new job, Kerr questioned the extent of support that organized labor was giving to the New Deal workers' education program. With no prior notice and while Smith was away from Washington, Kerr and other WPA officials laid off Friedmann and two secretaries who, at that time, staffed the national office of the WPA workers' education program. On her return to the capitol, Smith offered to resign, stating that "the WPA administration should be able to decide whether or not it wants to include any program of this kind in its future plans." She wrote to the Federal Works Administration (FWA) Director John Carmody that she did not want to push workers' education if he did not want it.[34]

Carmody, a New Deal administrator since 1933, interceded for Smith's program with Aubrey Williams, who in turn wrote to Kerr: "I hope that you will find it possible to have Miss Smith continue the work she has been doing. I think this work is one of the finest things we have ever done and it ought to be continued, if possible. I realize the difficulties you are under in cutting down the WPA and that everything must take its share, but I do hope you find it possible not to take more from the Workers' Education Program than its proportionate reduction."[35]

Smith responded to the crisis by continued lobbying with Carmody, Aubrey Williams, Mrs. Roosevelt, and other government influentials, tapping the support of her labor contacts, and accelerating discussions of a more permanent federal workers' education program. In mid-1939, she organized a meeting at the Washington home of John Edelman, a pioneer workers' educator who had been research director of the American Federation of Hosiery Workers. The meeting brought together Carmody, Kerr, and eighteen labor-union staff who came as individuals rather than as representatives of their union organizations.[36]

Citing unmet needs of their union groups and members, the labor staff members asked for a range of services from WPA programs: health instruction, radio publicity, information on labor laws, and cultural activities. Although no record exists of who initiated this new direction, the meeting proposed a broader set of activities for the WPA workers' education project. The report of the meeting summarized these recommendations:

> The decision was made to establish a Workers' Service Program on broader lines than the former program of classroom teaching. The new program is planned to develop statewide projects wherever there is sufficient interest among workers' groups and approval by state WPA officials. . . . The new program, which is an expansion of the Workers' Education Project now in its sixth year, has been initiated to meet the increasing number of requests from workers' groups for a service that offers greater variety of opportunities in education and leisure-time activities.[37]

In November 1939, the New Deal workers' education project became the Workers' Service Program. Administratively, as well as conceptually, it was designated a community service and was no longer a part of the WPA Emergency Education Program. Because of the shortage of persons on relief rolls who were capable of teaching workers' classes, and the lack of WPA support for a workers' education instructor-training program, the Workers' Service Program would use staff borrowed from other WPA projects. Florence Kerr announced this change in a General Letter:

> During the six years under the Adult Education Program, it became increasingly clear that groups of farmers and workers were isolated and not receiving benefits they needed from various community service projects. Requests were received by the workers' education unit for services in addition to classroom teaching which they could not give: recreation, art, library, visual aids, etc. Workers and farmers are ready to continue and sponsor these services. Workers' Service Program has been made one of

the Community Service Projects. It offers classes related to workers' interests along industrial and agricultural lines, channels services of other projects to reach workers. . . . For example, a recreation project becomes posture improvement when workers develop poor posture at their jobs.[38]

The conversion to the Workers' Service Program, announced as an expansion of the six-year New Deal workers' education activities, changed the goals and methods of the program. It marked a retreat from its earlier emphasis on workers' education. The shift diminished efforts to educate workers to think more critically about economic and social processes. It also diluted the union-oriented focus.

Workers' education moved from the classroom to the community but not in the way Smith had advocated in 1933. The community service concept propelled the program to more neutral, less politically threatening activities. These de-emphasized the adversarial relationship between labor and management. The new focus viewed workers as individuals with needs rather than as union members with economic and political agendas. It set aside any New Deal responsibility for educating them to be informed and effective trade union and community activists. The new concept was a far cry from the New Deal workers' education program that Smith had advocated and Hopkins had supported in 1933.

The change in program orientation and administration signaled a shift in status for Smith during the next three years. She lost her flexibility and autonomy. Although she attempted to adhere to Kerr's instructions to suggest new ways that community services for workers could be useful in developing a national defense program, she met with continued resistance in Washington and around the country. Clearly, "Mrs. Kerr or other WPA administrators intended to establish a firm measure of bureaucratic control over her."[39]

Workers' service projects, rather than workers' education, operated in ten states in 1940 and in thirteen states in 1941 and 1942. Sponsored by state departments of welfare, projects borrowed staff from other WPA units and included settlement houses, churches, housing projects, cooperatives, and unions as community co-sponsors. Fifteen state supervisors of workers' services projects were employed and paid from state WPA funds. The Washington office included Smith, a rehired Friedmann, and two stenographers. The office was moved four times within the next several years.[40]

Around the country, the workers' service activities varied widely. In Philadelphia, where sympathetic state officials continued many of the kinds of programs that had been developed in the preceding six years, successful classes, conferences, and recreation projects remained with the full cooperation with

CIO and AFL unions. In Detroit, the Workers' Service Program set up more than forty centers of activity for workers' groups, eighteen of them in UAW union halls.

Elsewhere, with the rapid growth of defense industries and the dramatic population explosion in many industrial cities, workers' service staff attempted to meet new needs. They maintained room registeries for workers and their families moving to new communities, helped organize tenant-landlord committees and other activities in new wartime housing projects, set up libraries and recreation rooms in union halls, and developed information and referral centers in settlement houses, churches, and unions.[41]

State reports from the three-year period indicate the diverse and amorphous range of projects. Workers' service staff in Georgia helped a group of black farmers remake old furniture and repaint their houses. In some Colorado cities, they helped conduct rudimentary wartime housing surveys. They helped union members in Indiana set up a small co-op credit union and a co-op coal buying club. They helped residents of a poor Chicago neighborhood clean up their area and organize more efficient garbage collection.

They developed some extension programs for Kansas farmers on consumer problems, erosion control, and crop rotation. They put together a handbook on bookkeeping for Utah cooperatives. They taught, or arranged for, classes on first aid and safety for workers in wartime industries. They showed workers, returning veterans, and retirees how to fill out forms for social security, veterans' benefits, and unemployment compensation. They distributed pamphlets from federal and state labor departments, housing authorities, health offices, immigration bureaus, and wages' and hours' boards. In a few places, they continued to teach classes on current events, parliamentary law, stewards' training, and union administration, and promoted educational films for workers' groups in union halls.

Casting about for new community projects, Smith also attempted unsuccessfully to develop workers' education programs on Indian reservations and in prisons, and to arrange for art appreciation programs for workers. She also turned to her social work colleagues to establish some links between that profession and workers' needs that could lead to "better standards of living, education for civic responsibility, and a more secure and creative life style." A section meeting on workers' education that she arranged for the June 1941 meetings of the National Conference of Social Work resulted in the growth of a union-counseling plan, developed on a small scale in Michigan and Illinois, that used social workers to train union members as peer counselors in referring workers to appropriate social agencies.[42]

Smith attempted to function as she had during the first six years of the New Deal administration, lobbying with other New Deal administrators and government agency staff, suggesting program directions, and publicizing her program through materials issued from her Washington office. She ran into trouble with all three activities.[43]

Although she organized a new interproject committee of Washington-based, government staff members that met once in November 1939 and again in January 1940, WPA administrators questioned the need for such meetings and discouraged her from calling them again. They also prevented her from distributing a pamphlet that she had written, "Workers' Service Projects Aid National Defense," that had previously been approved by various levels of WPA administrators and printed with private funds.[44]

Kerr sent her on field trips—sometimes two or three a month—and asked her to report on conditions for war workers around the country. Accordingly, Smith visited union meetings, defense plants, housing projects, migrant camps, and settlement houses, speaking to thousands of people about the need for workers' education.

In her reports to Kerr, Smith viewed the diverse Workers' Service projects around the country as helping "to build up the morale of industrial workers in production and also in their relations to employers, government departments, and the community as a whole." She recommended specific programs to develop this focus: discussions of labor problems, labor relations, and labor laws affecting wartime industries; consumer education for food conservation; health and nutrition education; first aid and safety instruction for industrial workers; recreation centers near war industries; and housing programs to aid in the functioning of newly developed housing projects. Her reports emphasized the need for civic education as part of the national defense program so that "industrial workers could learn to work with others for the maintenance of community standards important to the nation as measures of national defense."[45]

Smith, however, ran into trouble with some of her field reports. In her January 1941 report from California, she recorded her impressions of public and private housing projects, migrant camps, and Mexican communities in addition to documenting conversations with union and government officials and staff. In this and in other field reports, she noted squalid housing and community conditions and recommended expanded education and community services. California WPA officials asked her to rewrite part of her report after one WPA official chastised her in a letter to WPA Washington administrators: "It would be well to note clearly whether Miss Smith made the suggestions or whether they were derived from the group. Relationships with other agencies present a particular problem in California and WPA relationships are best left in the hands of local representatives."[46]

As a woman administrator in the New Deal, "her observations and activities were not welcomed by all, for she was the 'do-gooder' from Washington, trodding [sic] on local toes. Local interests resented her because they thought she was stirring up trouble—putting ideas in the heads and words in the mouths of downtrodden people. But even among WPA administrators who should have been the most sensitive to the deplorable conditions she reported, she was censured rather than commended." [47]

Smith continued to meet opposition from some state officials to even modest programs of workers' education or services. On a field trip to North Carolina, she confronted the resistance of one WPA official who advised her to take no action in that state until she had conferred and had obtained approval from WPA directors in Washington. Smith agreed not to force the issue of developing workers' education programs in that state, writing in her field report that "it is contrary to my own philosophy of education, as unwilling people would never give a genuine opportunity to a 'must' program." [48]

Despite this opposition, however, she persisted in attempting to develop a program in North Carolina, either misreading or choosing to ignore the lack of WPA administrative support for her work. In 1941, Dr. Frank Graham, president of the University of North Carolina, helped Smith initiate a workers' education instructor training program through that university's extension division. Smith spent two weeks teaching in that program before WPA state officials in North Carolina closed it down, claiming that only eight trainees had been recruited to participate. One of the trainees was also being investigated by the FBI at that time. [49]

Acting on information that several other Workers' Service Program staff members around the country were also being investigated by the FBI, or by persons purporting to be FBI agents, Smith conferred with Solicitor General Francis Biddle in June 1941. At his request, she submitted a full statement of her own background; the history, goals, and scope of the Workers' Service Program; lists of WPA state supervisors and staff; and names of persons connected with the Workers' Service Program who were being questioned by the FBI. Kerr forwarded these documents to Biddle along with her own statement supporting Smith and her program. There is no record available about the persons whom Smith had defended during this period. [50]

Ignoring political realities of the time, Smith persisted in developing ways of expanding the Workers' Service Program, searching for a permanent home for it in a national government agency, and developing support for its activities from union and government officials. In February 1941, Kerr permitted her to request personnel from national labor unions and other government agencies to help with the programs. A few months later, however, further quota reductions throughout the WPA precipitated a new program crisis. [51]

Fighting to maintain at least a minimal program, Smith wrote to Walter Kiplinger, a WPA administrator, listing the priorities of program activities that needed WPA support: education and information services for workers and farmers; labor information services especially in defense industry areas; and work with immigrants and aliens. She again turned to Eleanor Roosevelt, who demonstrated her continuing personal and political support by inviting Smith and Aubrey Williams to a White House luncheon on September 2, 1941. Smith wrote to FWA Director Carmody about the luncheon:

> Mrs. Roosevelt suggested this meeting because she is aware that we have been going through a crisis in the program. Four states terminated these projects (Kansas, Utah, North Carolina, and Washington) to reduce administrative costs or on other technicalities. (On the other hand, four new states are starting projects). . . . I can imagine that one or two people here would be glad to have me resign and have the whole program abandoned. . . . So the main objective of this luncheon is to bring out the fact that Workers' Service is needed in many urgent situations, and to consider the questions of its immediate resources for this year.[52]

Smith wrote to Carmody at a time when WPA administrators claimed that the size of the Workers' Service Program did not justify the costs of a Washington staff. They reassigned Smith's two stenographers to other government offices and threatened to lay off Friedmann within two months. Mrs. Roosevelt's support was not enough to reverse the effects of another WPA reorganization early in 1942 in which Friedmann was released and the Workers' Service Program was downgraded. Smith wrote to Starr: "This relegates workers' service to a very low status and that instead of being one of a group of projects or even on an equal level, we are now consolidated into a section where the project has no real status or identity of its own. . . . Ernestine is out. . . . So far as I can discover, she is the only one of the [WPA] Assistants for whom another place in the WPA has not been found."[53]

Smith's letter to Starr indicated that Kerr urged her to stay on with the WPA, although she had reprimanded Smith for sending out confidential letters to Workers' Service Program state supervisors, alerting them to new developments that had decimated the Program's Washington staff. "I have the feeling," Smith told Starr, "that I am being quietly disciplined by my various bosses here. Not that it worried me particularly, and Mrs. Kerr and I parted amicably." Smith urged Starr to help create support for the Workers' Service Program among national unions and in states where, she anticipated, lobbying efforts by unions and other interested groups could help save the national program.[54]

This was not so. For all intents and purposes, the Worker's Service Program was finished. Smith was never able to muster enough support within the WPA administration or within unions for its continued survival in a national relief administration. The program had been associated for too long with the growth of a strong labor movement and the New Deal thrust toward centralized government programming in emergency education and human services. As conservatives galvanized public reaction against the labor movement, and particularly as the New Deal gave way to the War Deal, support for workers' education even within the Democratic Party evaporated.

Smith wrote to her new supervisor, Lawrence Morris, complaining about the insecurity of her position and the ambiguity of her program's structure: "We have been given no idea as to the place of this project or its relation to other [WPA] projects. I have been told that we were to be considered a subunit of a section called 'etc.' under Education. . . . Until the position of Workers' Service is clarified, I am unable to rewrite again the many statements which I have submitted the past six months." [55]

Incensed by the lack of support from the WPA administration and by numerous bureaucratic problems, Smith allowed herself an expression of bitterness: "As in many other cases affecting this program, important decisions were made by people entirely ignorant of the purposes and methods of Workers' Service—often, indeed, by some who seemed to disapprove of everything for which the program stood." [56]

The Workers' Service Program ended officially on a national level on May 2, 1942, when Kerr wrote to WPA regional directors that it had been consolidated with the education phase of the WPA War Services Division. She indicated that Smith was to stay on the payroll for a limited period to work with other federal agencies and state labor departments to encourage unions to develop their own education programs. She stated clearly, however, that although Smith would report to the WPA War Services Division, she was no longer a representative of the WPA. [57]

Smith chose the title "Consultant in Workers' Education" and used her limited time left with the WPA to take some field trips and arrange some workers' education conferences. She continued to seek support for a permanent workers' education program based in a federal government unit. On September 27, 1942, Smith, Kerr, and twenty-five labor representatives met with Mrs. Roosevelt at the White House to confer with her about suggested legislation that would provide for a national, federally funded Labor Extension Service to be patterned after the Agricultural Extension Service. This meeting led to an intense national campaign over the next eight years that, although unsuccessful, was to further publicize the importance of workers' education and catalyze union and some community support for this legislation. [58]

By this time, however, Smith's tenure with the WPA was over. She now worked as chief of education and recreation for the Federal Public Housing Administration. Friedmann moved to Georgia to work with the Consumer Division of the U.S. Office of Price Administration. Carmody became U.S. maritime commissioner. The WPA had ended. [59]

Although Smith continued for the next eight years to head a vigorous campaign for a national labor extension service, the failure of that activity reflected the controversial nature of workers' education and its identification by the public as a partisan activity. Quixotic support from government and public officials and Smith's ambiguous relations with organized labor further undermined the campaign.

Smith had passionate supporters in her network of progressive educators, reformers, social workers, and trade unionists who shared her commitment and zeal about the need for workers' education. For many, as Highlander Folk School founder Miles Horton recently recalled, she was the aristocrat who had thrown in her lot with the poor and dispossessed. For some, she was the Brahmin friend of Eleanor Roosevelt who, as a result of this connection, garnered the backing of Hopkins and Aubrey Williams. Despite these contacts and her single-minded persistence, support for her work in the WPA had been tenuous from the start.[60]

Talking about Smith to Solicitor General Biddle following the demise of the WPA workers' education program, FWA Director Carmody described her as "one of God's noblewomen doing a fine job for difficult and stumbling people." Unfortunately, Carmody is not alive to tell us about the role he and his colleagues played in relation to the Workers' Service Program, and who the "difficult and stumbling people" were who frustrated Smith's dreams.[61]

7

Conclusions

The WPA demonstrated something about which I had been very doubtful; that it was possible for a government supported labor education program to service the needs of workers as they were organized in their unions. The whole program was based on the uncovering of a widespread appetite for education among workers, particularly when they are in trouble. With intelligent planning it was possible to discuss many problems which we are now again seeking to get before the workers.

—Larry Rogin, American Labor Education Service
Washington's Birthday Workers' Education Conference,
February 24, 1957[1]

With the end of the WPA, the National Labor Advisory Committee was officially disbanded, but several of its members continued to meet informally to lay plans for a national, federally funded labor extension service, draft a model resolution for union support, and establish an interim committee to promote the proposal. Their resolution, sent to labor organizations around the country, called for a labor extension service under an appropriate federal agency that would operate a broad labor education program with the assistance of organized labor in planning, policy making, and operation. The resolution was unanimously passed by the AFL and CIO Conventions in Toronto and in Boston in the fall of 1942.[2]

The interim committee, chaired by CIO Education Director Kermit Eby and with strong leadership from Smith, evolved over the next four years into the National Committee for the Extension of Labor Education (NCELE), an organization of individuals supporting congressional legislation mandating a labor extension service within the U.S. Department of Labor. Aided by an initial grant of $20,000 from the Special Service Committee, a support group of Smith's Bryn Mawr College alumni contacts in Ann Arbor, Michigan, the NCELE drafted a bill that was approved by both the AFL and CIO. Committee members facilitated its introduction, with bipartisan support, into the 80th Congress as the Labor Extension Bill of 1947.[3]

Led by Frank Fernbach, a Steelworkers' Union economist and lobbyist who was loaned by his union to head the campaign, the NCELE maintained the united support of the AFL and CIO for Senate Bill 1390 throughout the Senate subcommittee hearings in February 1948. The NCELE marshaled an impressive group of labor, government, and university witnesses to testify on the bill. NCELE members also agreed to the Senate subcommittee's recommendations to include unorganized workers and farm labor in the service, and to reduce organized labor's control over the proposed program. They further agreed that federal funds should be channeled through states to local public educational institutions, such as land grant universities and colleges, which would be guided in policy making and programming by state boards that would be free of political and/or professional domination.[4]

Strong opposition to the bill, however, surfaced during hearings in the House of Representatives of the 80th Congress in 1948. Adam Stricker, Jr., a General Motors Corporation economist, alleged in his testimony that a labor economics course taught by an instructor for the Workers' Education Service of the University of Michigan promoted a Marxist concept of class economics and used union materials that attacked corporation executives and Republican politicians. Stricker's testimony, which came as a surprise to the NCELE and Smith, bolstered the bill's congressional opponents. Claiming that labor education was potentially subversive and communist inspired, conservative congressmen killed the bill. Undaunted by this defeat and aided at that time by labor and bipartisan political support, the NCELE reintroduced the labor extension bill, as revised by the Senate of the 80th Congress, into both houses of the 81st Congress in January 1949.[5]

However, fearing the possibility that universities rather than organized labor would control the proposed service, the AFL changed its official position on the legislation three times during the 81st Congress. It withdrew its support for a federal labor extension service to be run on a state level by public colleges and universities and proposed instead a small labor information bureau within the U.S. Department of Labor. By taking this position, the AFL split labor support in the NCELE, destroyed the committee's lobbying credibility and fundraising efforts, and weakened congressional support for the bill. In July 1949 and January 1950, in addition to this major development, a number of witnesses and congressmen at congressional hearings on the bill again charged that labor education opened the door to left-wing influence and communist infiltration. The bill died in the 81st Congress's House Committee on Education and Labor. The Senate also failed to bring the bill to a vote.[6]

The bill's defeat was attributed to the change in support from AFL leaders, negative publicity generated by the Stricker testimony, the powerful opposition lobby of the National Association of Manufacturers, and the insistence of the National University Extension Association and the Association of Land Grant Colleges and Universities that federal funds for a labor extension service be controlled by public institutions of higher education. The NCELE, weakened internally by the unresolved competition between organized labor and organized education for control of a potential labor extension service, disbanded in 1950 at the end of the 81st Congress. The campaign to secure passage of a national, federally funded labor extension service died at that time.[7]

I

Evaluating the New Deal's emergency education programs, the Roosevelt Administration's Advisory Committee on Education presented a survey of the significant achievements and major problems of the FERA and WPA education activities, based on data and records available by 1937. Under the supervision of Dr. Doak S. Campbell, Dean of the Graduate School of the George Peabody College for Teachers, committee members summarized their report by pointing to the adverse affects of subordinating an emergency education program to the exigencies of a relief administration.[8]

Among these problems were uncertainty of planning and programming because of the temporary nature of the projects and insecurity of tenures that led to constant turnover of teachers and other personnel. Substandard teaching qualifications and the lack of professional experience of many persons on relief, as well as inadequate congressional appropriations and budgeting to hire supervisors, also plagued the FERA and WPA workers' education programs from 1933 to 1942.[9]

The litany of lesser grievances caused by the merger of relief and education was long. In this regard, Smith's reports and the reports of state and local workers' education supervisors supported the Advisory Committee's conclusions. Their reports pinpointed: the disuptive effects of changing FERA and WPA guidelines and regulations; vaguely defined spheres of administrative authority; administrative complexities at federal, state, and local levels; lack of channels of communication between the national office and programs within the states; inadequate support and funds for inservice teacher training; lack of travel funds; delay in delivery of educational materials and supplies; differences in pay scales of instructors and supervisors in different geographic regions; and lack of support for workers' education from WPA officials and from many state and local school system personnel.[10]

From the start, however, three problem areas proved especially troublesome for the New Deal's workers' education and workers' service projects: the relationship of a federally initiated and funded education effort to state and local education policies, programs, and personnel; the relationship of a federally funded workers' education program to the national leadership of the AFL; and the relationship of a national, government-supported workers' education program to political realities of the times.

The paramount problem from the inception of the EEP, and an issue that continued to affect the fate of labor extension service legislation until 1950, was the question of how a federally initiated and financed emergency education program related to the long standing tradition of state initiatives and state control of public education in this country. Hopkins and Alderman anticipated problems of coordinating a federal emergency relief education program with state policies, procedures, and patterns of education sponsorship and supervision. As it was conceived, the EEP aimed to supplement and not supplant existing public education services and facilities. In practice, however, this concept was frequently ignored, creating fears among state and local school officials and personnel that New Deal education programs such as the CCC, the NYA, the education camps for unemployed women, and the adult education and nursery school projects would develop into a dual, federally sponsored education system.[11]

As the Advisory Committee Report pointed out, many WPA officials in their haste to initiate emergency programs for the unemployed, failed to involve state and local school board sponsors in education planning and implementation. New Deal leaders, including President Roosevelt and Hopkins, were often irked by inertia in the state and local education hierarchy and these reactions created tensions and distrust. As Arthur McMahon observed, "The educational leaders in the Washington WPA headquarters were naturally enthusiasts. They had the sense of being crusaders; they sought to galvanize an awareness of human need and an educational opportunity. The situation was novel. Demonstration leaders who were subject matter specialists were dispatched throughout the country. . . . The singlemindedness of the purpose of these demonstration leaders . . . was often a cause for trouble in state and district WPA offices. These leaders were not always mindful of organizational niceties; they were interested in results within the field of interest." [12]

Reacting to what they viewed as increasing federalization of education, many education leaders sought to limit the federal government's involvement and perceived intervention into local control of education. The local system, they held, was better suited to traditions of freedom and liberty in a geographically vast and socially heterogeneous country. They were also protective of their professional jurisdictions and pressed for educational agencies to have more control over the hiring of part-time, temporary relief instructors.[13]

The president of the National Education Association wrote to President Roosevelt early in 1936 urging that all federal education efforts be channeled through the U.S. Office of Education to state and local communities, since "we are fearful that departure from this basic principle endangers the integrity of our education system and weakens one of the cornerstones of our democratic government." Roosevelt answered: "It has been the relief feature which has justified the Federal Government's supplying funds for programs so largely educational. Had these programs been wholly educational and had they represented essentially a Federal plan to aid in the support of education, it would have been my policy to use only the regularly constituted agencies of education to administer them." [14]

Roosevelt's response to the association glossed over some of the inherent contradictions in New Deal education efforts, contradictions in which the New Deal workers' education program was caught. Underlying Roosevelt's personal and political attitudes toward the public school establishment, attitudes that were shared to some extent by many New Deal architects and administrators, was the strong feeling that "if education were to be called on to do the job, the New Deal program would be largely, if unintentionally, sabotaged." [15]

This certainly would have been the fate of the New Deal workers' education program. Without the impetus from a national, federally financed program, albeit a temporary, emergency measure, support from professional educators for these controversial activities would have been even slimmer than it was in the mid and late 1930s. Without the political, financial, and, indeed, moral support of a federal government program, local school boards and officials would have been even more vulnerable to local antilabor forces that deemed workers' education partisan, radical, and anti-American.

The New Deal imprimatur, although lacking in sanctions on a state level, did lend a certain clout in areas where hesitant school officials needed such backing to experiment with these programs. Even with this official federal blessing, however, many state education officials were hostile and reluctant to support workers' education and chary of having their facilities used by relief instructors who were not under their immediate control.

Similar tensions between federal agencies and local governments were evident in a wide range of New Deal programs, but the institutional and political configuration of local power was least favorable to federal intervention in education. There was, to be sure, opposition to federal relief programs, unemployment insurance, labor law, and business regulation, but such opposition was not always unanimous and it frequently lacked organizational coherence. Private charity was in disarray, and municipal officials, aware that unemployed workers were also disgruntled voters, generally favored federal relief. At the same time, many business groups welcomed federal regulatory programs like the National Industrial Recovery Act, the Federal Communications Commission, and the Federal Housing Authority that stabilized markets and restored liquidity. Most businessmen did oppose federal labor law, but in this case, their opposition was countered by the labor movement's enthusiastic support.

In contrast, the New Deal's educational initiatives, as they met head on with local school systems, confronted a tax-supported establishment that was organizationally coherent, traditionally parochial, and increasingly opposed to federal "interference" in programming. Once the crisis of 1933–1934 passed and public schools reopened, institutional resistance (or indifference) to workers' education could only have been overcome by the support of a unified labor movement.

This support, however, was not forthcoming from the conservative leaders of the AFL. Smith later reminisced about this second major problem for the New Deal's education programs: "It was a struggle during the first two years to secure the support of organized labor for any workers' education sponsored by government. Labor leaders . . . were deeply suspicious, believing that any government-sponsored classes in economics and labor problems could never be anything but superficial or remote from workers' needs." [16]

In reality, the problems with the leadership of the AFL were much deeper than Smith's analysis. Federation leaders feared outside radical influences that would advocate a changed economic structure in the country or a changed union structure. They resisted any influences that might weaken the loyalty of craft-union members to their unions and to a capitalist economy. AFL officials viewed labor education as a process of training union members for more efficient union leadership and enhancing their unity and discipline, not for providing them with educational and cultural opportunities or preparing them for a new social order.

Suspicious of "outside intellectuals" and institutions of higher education, frequently repressive of independent workers' education endeavors not under its control, the AFL adhered to a philosophy of business unionism that emphasized building labor's own economic strength through orderly, collective bargaining processes. Many AFL leaders questioned the apparent eagerness of government-sponsored relief instructors to give information to their members. They challenged their interpretation of social problems and feared their advocacy of industrial unionism, alternative economic systems, and newly trained, ambitious young leaders who might seek to gain control of union affairs. [17]

Some leaders of the CIO's fledgling industrial organizations, on the other hand, viewed both their movement and workers' education programs as the means of altering the power relations in society and, through that process, bringing about social change. They welcomed government supported and financed workers' education and community services as a way of meeting their members' economic, political, educational, and community needs. Sensitive to the dependence of the CIO and its affiliates on government and legislative processes, leaders of new unions in the mass production industries were also aware of the need for union members to understand, as well as to take part in, the political defense of labor's interests. They welcomed programs that would train new leaders to interact with government and community agencies, understand new legislation and social policies affecting workers, and negotiate contracts in industries whose dynamics were shaped by sweeping economic and political developments of the times.

The CIO unions were on the move with organizing drives. They viewed the federally funded workers' education program as an aid in getting new members and building new local unions.

The New Deal workers' education projects were caught in the crossfire between AFL and CIO proponents. Although AFL opposition was not as pronounced as criticism from conservative and antilabor forces outside the labor movement, attacks from AFL national leaders undermined support for the program throughout the decade. Their criticism focused on a wide (and not always irrelevant) range of problems, but their ultimate complaint, as summarized in a 1939 resolution, was lack of AFL control over programming and appointments:

> Results [of the WPA workers' education program] have been less than notable. . . . Setting up a vast education program under relief authority has been the cardinal blunder. Relief rather than education standards have seriously impaired the methods employed and the ends pursued. Division of responsibility in local communities between relief and education authorities has proved unsound. The result has been inefficiency and inaction. Changes and modifications of relief aims and shifts in administrative control have impaired any long time gains from the program. Uncertainty and insecurity have characterized the whole effort. Expenses have been unduly high. . . . At times there has been a gesture at cooperation with the AFL but not permanently. The supervisors have been appointed without consultation with state AFLs.[18]

The third major problem that confronted New Deal workers' education activities in the mid and late 1930s was increasing antiunion sentiment throughout the nation. Many people in the United States were unprepared for the vastly increased federal bureaucracy, the huge increases in federal spending, and what they viewed as the unprecedented intervention of the federal government in local affairs and daily lives. Just as union members, minority groups, urban ethnics, farmers, and underprivileged groups became increasingly demanding of more federal aid, old Democratic Party leaders were rallying, especially in the years after 1936, to curtail New Deal spending.[19]

Frightened at the seizure of private property during the sitdown strikes of 1937, congressional conservatives and political opinionmakers predicted revolution unless Roosevelt intervened to protect corporate interests. Despite the fact that FDR was no patron of labor and had remained neutral during the sitdown strikes, many Americans believed the New Deal had conjured forth the CIO—a misconception that CIO leader Lewis perpetuated for his own ends by telling industrial workers: "The President wants you to join a union." Further, Labor's Nonpartisan League had been a highly visible source of financial support and votes for New Deal candidates in the 1936 elections, thereby underscoring the perceived relationship between militant labor and the New Deal administration. Fearful that Roosevelt would pander to this new source of support and power, many political leaders in both parties used this relationship to take potshots both at the Roosevelt Administration and at the newly organized CIO.[20]

The sitdown strikes, the campaign for higher labor standards, and continued press attacks about left-wing "subversion" catalyzed a conservative coalition in both houses of Congress that sought to end the WPA and to stop any direct or indirect government support of the labor movement. Lewis's intent to organize several million New Deal relief staff into CIO federal unions and his anticipation, unrealized, that Hopkins and Aubrey Williams would aid him in this endeavor further alarmed conservatives in both parties. Depressed by the 1937 death of his second wife and fighting his first bout with stomach cancer, Hopkins concentrated on wrapping up his WPA connections. Roosevelt appointed him U.S. Secretary of Commerce in 1938, and Hopkins thereafter contemplated his chances of winning the presidency in the 1940 campaign.[21]

All the while, Smith's small base of support within the New Deal rapidly eroded. Although she maintained her job through the intervention of Eleanor Roosevelt and WPA administrator Carmody, her programs shifted in the late 1930s to dealing with some of the community needs of individual workers rather than developing critical thinking or organizational competence.

The New Deal had changed since the days when Smith could use emergency funds to aid a fledgling labor movement and extend the learning horizons of individual workers. Liberal opinion of all shades had been prepared to assist the worker-as-victim, but it was a different matter when workers successfully established their own organizations and used collective action— rather than sweet reason—to win their aims. Some progressives welcomed this militancy as a necessary counter to the strong-arm tactics of employers, but the more squeamish did not. As these liberals and many other Americans saw it, when workers could collectively take care of themselves, when, in fact, they could force society to recognize their needs, then the government's proper role was to regulate rather than promote the workers' movement. Social control had always been a part of the progressive prescription for workers' education; for some, it was now the reasons such programs should be scuttled.

These conservative themes played all the more effectively as the nation mobilized for war in the early 1940s. In this context, government-sponsored workers' education—what remained of it—focused on improving civilian morale and stimulating workers to support the war effort. Labor peace became a desired goal and labor education a means of facilitating this outcome. The 1942 AFL resolution in support of a labor extension service touched on all these themes: "Therefore, be it RESOLVED . . . That a Commission on Labor Education and Morale be set up by the President under some appropriate agency of the Federal Government to initiate and operate a broad educational program assisting labor to understand and to take part in the war effort and in the post-war period, thus strengthening labor's cooperation with the community and with Government departments and further strengthening the war effort." [22]

The concept of workers' education thus changed in concert with the transformation of the labor movement and the rightward drift of the nation's politics. Workers' education was no longer defined, as Smith had proposed in 1933, as a process of aiding individual workers to think critically about the social and economic contexts of their lives so that they could participate more intelligently in a democracy. Nor was it geared to the need to train leaders for new and strong labor organizations. Instead, as a program seeking public support and federal government funding during the war years, labor education was defined in the broadest terms possible: a bulwark of national defense and a keeper of industrial peace.

II

Despite their multiple problems, shortcomings, and contradictions, the New Deal workers' education and workers' service programs made a considerable impact on the future of workers' education. They served as a bridge linking past developments in workers' education in the first three decades of the century to a nationwide, federally funded program during a dynamic period in the growth of the labor movement and of institutions of higher education.

Under the leadership of Smith and Friedmann, the New Deal's programs demonstrated a need for workers' education, introduced new concepts of program organization and teaching, and stimulated the sponsorship of workers' education by new union and university programs. Their innovative projects offered educational opportunities that aided many of the participants and instructors in their roles as union activists and elected officers, or as future staff of universities and related organizations. Finally, they enriched the lives and increased the social, economic, and political awareness of the hundreds of thousands of workers and community members who took part in these programs.

In areas of the country where workers' education was a new concept, as well as in regions where some workers' education had previously taken place, the WPA projects introduced new classes and services for heterogeneous groups of craft, industrial, service, and white-collar workers. The programs made education accessible through course offerings in neighborhood schools, community centers, and union halls. They gave many unions as well as university and community education programs the first inkling of the need for special programming for workers, the range of possible projects, and their potential institutional roles in developing labor education programs.

Basic to these innovations was the principle that workers and trade union representatives had the right to participate in all plans made for the projects. Smith transferred the concept of workers participation in advisory committees from the successful experiences at the Bryn Mawr Summer School for Women Workers to the New Deal workers' education projects. In many locales, the workers' education advisory committees—or their outgrowths, community workers' education councils—helped protect the New Deal programs from political interference. They also served to interpret the needs of unions and their members to WPA and educational administrators and the nature and scope of the New Deal program to unions and their members.

Although the advisory committees varied greatly in their effectiveness, in a few areas they were the only means of bringing AFL and CIO representatives together to discuss common educational needs. In some areas, the advisory committees developed a bridge to local school board, university, and community officials and established a framework and a foundation for future cooperation between government, education, and union institutions.

The FERA and WPA workers' education programs also introduced pedagogical techniques that had been developed for adult worker students in the 1920s to a wider arena of adult and workers' education activities in the 1930s. Smith's field manuals, materials, memoranda, and numerous articles during the decade advocated the use of small discussion groups, role playing, field trips, participant observation, self-governing committees, graphics workshops, and panel discussions—techniques that had been pioneered at the residential schools for women workers in the 1920s to meet the learning needs of adult students with limited formal schooling.

In the nationwide context of the New Deal emergency education programs, discussion of these teaching and learning methods disseminated information about the philosophy and techniques of student-centered adult education to a wider audience. The network of workers' education teacher-training centers initiated by Smith in 1934 and 1935, and the follow-up teacher-training programs sponsored by state WPA emergency education projects in the years following 1935, served to further spread these concepts, demonstrate their effectiveness, and give some instructor trainees and staff the opportunity to participate in new kinds of learning experiences.

The President's Advisory Committee recognized these achievements in summarizing the impact of the New Deal workers' education projects:

[The WPA workers' education projects] provided leadership in the field of teacher training as well as effective methods in the instruction of adults which are being successfully adapted to the adult education program as a whole. Among the chief contributions may be listed the following: limitation of class size to a small group; the provision of instruction through informal group discussion; the discussion of topics of local and immediate interest to group participants; the employment of simple but pertinent and well illustrated experimental material; and the adaption of subject matter to make it immediately applicable in the relationship of the individual to the social groups with which he is associated.[23]

The FERA and WPA workers' projects responded to the needs of the times by developing new classes in union administration, parliamentary law, legislation, and social policies affecting workers. Through this process, they served to spread information about New Deal accomplishments in new legislation and social policies. In many rural areas of the country, the workers' projects attempted to develop classes and community services for farm workers and, in a few regions, planned programs that brought industrial workers and farmers together to discuss common concerns. During the Depression years and as the country mobilized for war, state and local workers' education projects offered classes to help working people meet their consumer, health, safety, and housing needs.

In many ways, the New Deal workers' education and workers' service projects changed the structure and sponsorship of workers' education in this country. They established a principle that the federal government and publicly supported educational institutions had a responsibility for serving employed as well as jobless workers. Along with the other emergency education programs, they provided an extraordinary variety of innovative, publicly funded programs that filled the gaps in educational services to working-class adults. As part of the New Deal's thrust to meet the needs of the unemployed, the FERA and WPA workers' education projects offered an unsurpassed range of programs that aimed in 1933 to rehabilitate individuals, both instructors and participants, to provide remedial education services for those who had been forced to leave school at an early age, to develop an interest among workers in understanding and helping solve social problems, and to create a better understanding of working-class life and workplace organizations.

With the burgeoning of new unions and the unprecedented growth of the labor movement in the mid and late 1930s, the WPA program helped train new union leaders and alerted unions to the need for education as an ongoing union function. Largely due to the interest aroused by the WPA programs, many hundreds of union locals and state and community labor councils formed education committees to promote classes for their members. Both directly and indirectly, the WPA program contributed to the founding of national union education divisions, especially in the new CIO unions as well as in its national office. For example, as Thomas Linton writes about the formation of the education department in the UAW:

> Several teachers who had worked in the federal program found employment in various unions as staff members. Men like Merlin Bishop and Roy Reuther received much of their early training from this government program. They were both active as students and later as teachers in the federal program. When they became UAW staff educators they continued to employ many of the same approaches used in the government work. Their early recognition of the value of education caused them to promote the acceptance of a full time program within the UAW.[24]

Bishop became the first education director of the newly formed UAW. Reuther taught WPA workers' classes in Flint, Michigan from 1935 to 1937. Frank Marquart, also a WPA workers' instructor, became education director of UAW Local 3 in Detroit.

The WPA programs introduced several universities to their possible role in establishing labor extension services. As the labor movement expanded during the late 1930s and early 1940s and began to be perceived as a significant interest group and political force, publicly funded state universities began to recognize the importance of organized labor as allies in obtaining needed state budget appropriations as well as necessary political support. A number of universities responded to labor's requests for educational services and set up labor education programs through their extension divisions. During the war years, they offered classes in collective bargaining, arbitration of grievances, and War Labor Board procedures, while also setting up programs aimed largely at preventing strikes in war industries. In the postwar campaign for a national labor extension service, a number of universities established labor extension programs in the expectation that land grant institutions would be recipients of financial support if this legislation passed.[25]

III

Smith brought her idealism and visions of progressive education from the successful experiments for women workers on the Bryn Mawr College campus to her work with the New Deal administration. She shared the liberal's faith in social reconstruction through education, reason and the use of intelligence, and the keen belief that an informed people is the basis of a democracy. She attempted to graft an amalgam of these principles and practices, honed in the earlier part of the century, onto the nationwide relief efforts and to publicize these concepts in her numerous field manuals, program reports and articles.

In the economic and social chaos of the first part of the Depression decade,

New Deal administrators were open to the lobbying of educators and others who suggested that they could bring new populations into support for Roosevelt's programs. In 1933, Smith appeared with an agenda for workers' education that seemed to fit in with New Deal goals. As the decade progressed, however, her educator's mission conflicted with the short-term relief and recovery aspects of many of the New Deal's emergency education measures.

In the severe school of the 1930s, the Roosevelt mode of political education frequently substituted progressive social engineering for a process of popular education in attaining social policies and programs. With their pragmatic emphasis in dealing swiftly and effectively to preserve the domestic economy and the domestic political system, New Deal administrators were more interested in popular consent for, and participation in, their fait accompli than in widespread leisurely deliberations about social planning. New Deal critics of all political shades charged that the Roosevelt Administration had abandoned political principles that had infused progressive liberals—thoughtful political leadership, political honesty, and a process of cultivating and responding to popular judgment. The educative philosophy of the government appeared confined to disseminating facts about economic realities and New Deal accomplishments rather than fostering Jeffersonian concepts of schools for citizenship and self government. "Popular government survived at a heavy cost to the democratic theory of educated politics. . . . The New Deal won not by principle but by practice." [26]

Smith aimed high and ignored the realities of many failed WPA workers' education projects. Single-mindedly, she held to the education-oriented liberal's beliefs that the individual citizen is a unique contributor to a democratic form. "Perhaps in time," she wrote as late as 1940 to WPA administrator Aubrey Williams, "these little experiments in democratic thought and action may have a decided effect on the whole pattern of our national life in government and in politics, directing national planning along democratic lines for the benefit of all." [27]

Smith's idealism garnered little backing from New Deal administrators. Throughout the nine years of the workers' education program she lacked sustained support that could have provided more national staff and program resources that might have helped improve many of the hastily planned and haphazardly presented WPA workers' education projects. She lacked political clout to deal effectively with the constant political and administrative confrontations and crises and the frequent subversions of her projects on state and local levels. Always the pedagogue and moralist, Smith also failed to understand the profound changes in the society and the resulting power politics within the New Deal. Time and again, only Mrs. Roosevelt's interventions and Smith's personal status as a selfless and highminded patrician rescued the federal workers' education projects from total demise.

Both Smith and Eleanor Roosevelt, however, failed to confront the fact that workers' education would not produce a more reasoned and cooperative world through individual enlightenment, a position they adhered to in their attempts to salvage the WPA workers' education program. At precisely the time that workers' education received federal backing and expanded nationwide, labor-management conflicts and industrial violence also increased dramatically across the nation. Eleanor Roosevelt's claim that education could produce a generalized capacity to avoid "narrow" conflicts of self-interest and develop national solutions to major economic and political crises became less effective as a defense of workers' education because it was an unconvincing position in the context of the 1930s.[28]

Smith was caught in a crisis of liberalism in the latter part of the New Deal period. Faced with the power struggles of the period, many liberals questioned their pious hopes that established group experiences and group interests could be reconciled through an educative process that would develop a rationally ordered society. Workers' education had changed during the decade from the early experiments initiated and supported by progressive liberals to compensate working-class adults for their lack of educational and cultural opportunities and to provide classroom experiences designed to encourage democratic dialogue and citizenship training.

With the swift growth of industrial unionism during the 1930s, workers' education in general, and the WPA program in particular, became instrumental in developing labor's organizational competence and cohesion, and training informed and skilled union activists and leaders who could challenge more effectively managements' traditional prerogatives. In their own ways, anti-union forces understood the need to act on these developments more clearly than did the liberals. Liberal support for the program was far outweighed by conservative attacks that viewed federal sponsorship and financing of workers' education as a partisan activity that aided the labor movement's challenge to the industrial status quo, and abetted its potential to divide a wounded nation along class lines.

Smith became increasingly isolated in the late 1930s by political pressures and bureaucratic uncertainties. As the nation moved further into the European war, her program was viewed as an aid for stimulating workers' support of the war effort and maintaining industrial peace. In the process, WPA workers' education projects shifted focus to provide a diffuse range of community services that would enhance the civilian morale of union members and help them make the transition to war work and a wartime economy.

Yet, for all of its many limitations and failings, the WPA workers' education program kept a workers' education movement alive during the 1930s when many union and community projects were cut back or cut out for lack of funds. It also laid the groundwork for a lobbying effort to continue this unique initiative of the federal government in underwriting a nationwide program of workers' education. The WPA activities helped workers' education gain some legitimacy in public and union policies, and demonstrated the efficacy of workers' education for the labor movement and for institutions of higher education. In fact, "the vitality of present day labor education derives from people who were associated with the WPA projects." [29]

The New Deal spawned many new and innovative measures to deal with the exigencies of the Depression. Some survived and established a principle of federal involvement in ameliorating inequities in the nation's life. Others did not outlast the 1930s. Some of the projects took root in different forms.

The WPA workers' education program did not survive to establish the principle of federal support for workers' education. But Smith's program played a crucial role in the transition from the multiple and frequently amorphous goals of earlier attempts to educate adult workers to a concept of labor education that serves the learning needs of workers in the contexts of their union institutions. In doing so, this program succeeded in transmitting the legacy of the democratic education ideals and practices of the progressive adult educators of the 1920s to the education of union activists today.

Notes

Chapter One

1. Nettie Silverbrook, "What Do I Want from Workers' Education," *American Federationist* 35 (January, 1928): 100.

2. As quoted in Emily M. Danton, "Uncle Sam, School Teacher," *Journal of Adult Education* 8 (1936): 149.

3. Doak S. Campbell, Frederick H. Bair, and Oswald L. Harvey, *Educational Activities of the Works Progress Administration*, U.S. Advisory Committee on Education, Staff Study Number 14 (Washington, D.C.: GPO, 1939), pp. 6–11, 30, 31, 37–40. This work includes data as of 1937.

4. Ibid., pp. 141–157.

5. C. Hartley Grattan, *In Quest of Knowledge* (New York: Association Press, 1955), p. 229; Malcolm Knowles, *The Adult Education Movement in the United States* (New York: Holt, 1962), p. 137.

6. *The Spokane Spokesman—Review*, August 10, 1938, p. 4, as quoted by Harry Zeitlin. "Federal Relations in American Education, 1933–1943: A Study of New Deal Efforts and Innovations" (Ph.D. diss., Columbia University, 1958), p. 317.

7. Official figures are not available for the actual number of workers served by the FERA and WPA workers' education and workers' service programs from 1933 to 1942. Many states combined data on participation in workers' education and workers' service activities with data on participation in general adult education and other Emergency Education Program (EEP) activities. Hilda Smith estimated that more than one million workers were reached by these programs from 1933 to 1942. Hilda W. Smith, "People Come First: A Report of Workers' Education in the Federal Emergency Relief Administration, the Civil Works Administration and the Works Progress Administration, 1933–1942," H. W. Smith, Papers, Franklin D. Roosevelt Library, Hyde Park, N.Y., p. 141; also Mark Starr, "The Current Panorama," in *Workers' Education in the United States: Fifth Yearbook of the John Dewey Society*, ed. Theodore Brameld (New York: Harper, 1941), p. 90; and Jack Barbash, *Universities and Unions in Workers' Education* (New York: Harper, 1955), p. 38.

8. Ernest E. Schwartztrauber, "Administering Workers' Education," in *Workers' Education in the United States: Fifth Yearbook of the John Dewey Society* (New York: Harper, 1941), p. 208.

9. Starr, "Current Panorama," p. 95; Joseph Mire, *Labor Education* (Madison: Interuniversity Labor Education Committee, 1956), pp. 90–93; Alice Hanson Cook and

Agnes M. Douty, *Labor Education Outside the Unions* (New York: New York State School of Labor and Industrial Relations, Cornell University, 1958), pp. 85–86.

10.   Clarke A. Chambers, *Seedtime of Reform: American Social Service and Social Action, 1918–1933* (Ann Arbor: University of Michigan Press, 1967), p. 267.

11.   Robert Bruce, *1877: Year of Violence* (New York: Bobbs-Merrill, 1959), p. 19; John Schneider, *Detroit and the Problem of Order, 1830-1880: A Geography of Crime, Riot, and Policing* (Lincoln: University of Nebraska Press, 1980), p. 106; Paul Ringenbach, *Tramps and Reformers, 1873–1916: The Discovery of Unemployment in New York* (Westport, Conn.: Greenwood, 1973), pp. 10–11.

12.   Philip Foner, *The Great Labor Uprising of 1877* (New York: Monad, 1977), pp. 215–217.

13.   Leon Fink, *Workingmen's Democracy: The Knights of Labor and American Politics* (Urbana: University of Illinois Press, 1983), p. 10.

14.   Maldwyn Allen Jones, *American Immigration.* (Chicago: University of Chicago Press, 1960), p. 179.

15.   Jacob Riis, *The Battle with the Slum* (New York: Macmillan, 1902), p. 6.

16.   Ringenbach, *Tramps and Reformers*, pp. 85–91.

17.   Ibid., p. 89.

18.   William Tolman, *Social Engineering* (New York: McGraw, 1909), p. 271.

19.   Stephen Meyer, *The Five Dollar Day: Labor Management and Social Control in the Ford Motor Company, 1908–1921* (Albany, State University of New York Press, 1981); Tom Klug, "The Employers' Association of Detroit, the Open Shop, and the Making of Managerial Authority, 1900–1916," Typescript, Wayne State University, 1981, pp. 25–29; Tom Klug, "The Contradictions of Free Wage Labor and the Managing of the Labor Market and Worker Mobility in Detroit, 1850–1930," Typescript, Wayne State University, 1984, pp. 24–26.

20.   Tom Klug, "The Ideology and Practices of Labor Market Control and the Origins of Personnel Management in Detroit, 1900–1920," Typescript, Wayne State University, 1981, p. 58.

21.   Elizabeth and Kenneth Fones-Wolf. "Trade Union Evangelism: Religion and the AFL in the Labor Forward Movement, 1912–1916," in *Working-Class America: Essays on Labor, Community, and American Society*, ed. Michael Frisch and Daniel Walkowitz (Urbana: University of Illinois Press, 1983), pp. 153–184; Stephen Fraser, "Dress Rehearsal for the New Deal: Shop-Floor Insurgents, Political Elites, and Industrial Democracy in the Amalgamated Clothing Workers," ibid., p. 232.

22.   "Recent Developments in Adult Workers' Education in the United States," *Monthly Labor Review* 23 (July 1926): 91–100.

23.   Ibid.

24.   Ibid.

25.   Harry Overstreet, *Workers' Education: A Quarterly Journal* 13 (October 1936):37; "Recent Developments in Workers' Education in Various States," *Monthly Labor Review* 40 (April 1935): 948–953; *Labor Review* 37 (April 1937): 95.

26.   Lawrence Rogin and Marjorie Rachlin, *Labor Education in the United States* (Washington, D.C.: National Institute of Labor Education, American University, 1968), p. 12; Irvine Kerrison, *Workers' Education at the University Level* (New Brunswick, N.J.: Rutgers University Press, 1951), p. 12.

27.   Susan Estabrook Kennedy, *If All We Did Was to Weep at Home: A History of*

White Working Class Women in America (Bloomington: Indiana University Press, 1979), pp. 141–143; John Garraty, *The American Nation: A History of the United States Since 1865* (New York: Harper & Row, 1977), p. 484; Kenneth E. Reid, *From Character Building to Social Treatment: The History of the Use of Groups in Social Work* (Westport, Conn.: Greenwood, 1981), pp. 111–115.

28. Kennedy, *If All We Did Was to Weep at Home:*, p. 165. Also see articles by Robin Jacoby, Rita Heller, Susan Stone Wong, Marian Roydhouse, and Mary Frederickson in *Sisterhood and Solidarity: Workers' Education for Women, 1914–1984*, ed. Joyce L. Kornbluh and Mary Frederickson (Philadelphia: Temple University Press, 1984).

29. Robert L. Church, *Education in the United States* (New York: Free Press, 1976), pp. 343–369.

30. Workers' Education Bureau, *Report of Proceedings, Second National Conference on Workers' Education in the United States* (New York: Workers' Education Bureau, 1922), p. 94.

31. Ibid.

32. For a review of these developments in the U.S. and abroad, see: Marius Hansome, *World Workers' Educational Movements: Their Social Significance* (New York: Columbia University Press, 1931); Margaret T. Hodgen, *Workers' Education in England and the United States* (New York: Dutton, 1925); Bert MacLeech, "Workers' Education in the United States" (Ph.D. diss., Harvard University, 1951).

33. For a discussion of the influences of the *The 1919 Report*, see Michael Joseph Day, "Adult Education as a New Educational Frontier: Review of the *Journal of Adult Education* 1929–1941" (Ph.D. diss., University of Michigan, 1981), chap. 3.

34. Ibid.

35. Ibid.

36. Information for this section was obtained from a review of correspondence, minutes and other archives of the Workers' Education Bureau (WEB), from a partial collection on the WEB in the Archives of the New York State School of Industrial and Labor Relations, Cornell University, Ithaca, N.Y.

37. Interview with Hilda W. Smith, August 14, 1969, by Doris A. Brody, as cited in "American Labor Education Service, 1927–1962: An Organization in Workers' Education" (Ph.D. diss., Cornell University, 1973), p. 80.

38. Biographical information from Hilda W. Smith's privately printed autobiography, *Opening Vistas in Workers' Education* (Washington, D.C.: n.p., 1978).

39. Ibid., pp. 113–156.

40. MacLeech, "Workers' Education," p. 235.

41. Ibid. Amy Hewes, "Early Experiments in Workers' Education," *Adult Education* 6 (Summer 1956): 217.

42. Speech by Mrs. Roosevelt, October 24, 1933 at Barnard College, quoted in Smith's unpublished autobiographical mss., Smith Papers, Schlesinger Library, Box 16. In her biography of Eleanor Roosevelt, historian Tamara Hareven writes: "Miss Smith's carte blanche to bring her troubles to the White House, her close friendship with the First Lady, and the latter's interest in the project secured for it the respect of other administrators and the interest and attention of FDR." *Eleanor Roosevelt: An American Conscience* (Chicago: Quadrangle, 1968), p. 78.

43. Marian Roydhouse, "Partners in Progress: The Affiliated Schools for Women

Workers, 1928–1939," chap. 6 in *Sisterhood and Solidarity*; Caroline Ware, *Labor Education in Universities* (New York: American Labor Education Service, 1946), pp. 3–4.

44. Jean Carter and Eleanor Coit, "The Affiliated Schools Establish Experimental Projects," *Journal of Adult Education* 6 (October 1934): 506.

45. Ronald J. Peters, "Factors Affecting Labor Extension Legislation, 1945–1950" (Ph.D. diss., Michigan State University, 1976), p. 39.

46. Mark Starr, "Workers' Education on Wheels," "Concerning Workers' Education" 1 (May-June 1934): 9; Hansome, *World Workers' Educational Movements*, p. 60.

47. James O. Morris, *Conflict within the AFL: A Study of Craft Versus Industrial Unionism 1901–1938* (Ithaca, N.Y.: Cornell University Press, 1958), pp. 86–135. Cook and Douty, *Labor Education*, p. 81; Hewes, "Early Experiments," p. 212.

48. Hewes, "Early Experiments."

49. Ibid.

50. Resolution of the Workers' Party Council, quoted in Hansome, *World Workers' Educational Movements*, pp. 294–295.

51. Alice Cheyney, "Workers Education in the United States," *International Labour Review* 32 (July 1935): 39–59.

52. AFL, *Proceedings of the Fifty-First Annual Convention* (Washington, D.C.: AFL, 1928), pp. 86–87.

53. Peters, "Factors Affecting Labor Extension Legislation," p. 45.

54. AFL, *Proceedings of the Fifty-First Annual Convention*, pp. 86-87.

55. Peters, "Factors Affecting Labor Extension Legislation," p. 45.

56. J.B.S. Hardman, "Workers' Education," *Forum* 75 (March 1926): 450.

57. Spencer Miller, Jr., *The Promise of Workers' Education* (New York: WEB, 1924), pp. 11, 15.

58. Smith to Williams, February 18, 1938, Hilda W. Smith Papers, Franklin D. Roosevelt Library, Hyde Park, N.Y. Container 9, File "Organization and Management, 1938."

59. Peters, "Factors Affecting Labor Extension Legislation," pp. 218–265; Robert A. Bowman, "The National Committee for the Extension of Labor Education 1942–1950" (Ph.D. diss., Rutgers University, 1979), pp. 169–342.

60. Ibid.

61. Leonard Woodcock, "Call for a Coalition to Establish a National Labor Extension Service," *Labor Studies Journal* 1 (Winter 1977): 281–285.

62. Howard Zinn, ed., *New Deal Thought* (New York: Bobbs-Merrill, 1966), pp. xvii–xviii.

Chapter Two

1. Excerpt from a speech by Harry Hopkins to a conference on unemployment and education at Teachers' College, Columbia University, May 15, 1937, as quoted in Mavis M. Profitt, "Adult Education," *Biennial Survey of Education 1934–1936*, vol. 1, bulletin 2 (Washington, D.C.: GPO, 1938), p. 22.

2. Alex Baskin, ed., *The Unemployed: 1930–1932* (New York: Archives of Social History, 1975), p. 2.

3. Irving Bernstein, *The Lean Years: A History of the American Worker, 1920–1933* (Boston: Houghton Mifflin, 1960); Roger Keeran, *The Communist Party and the Auto Workers Unions* (Bloomington: Indiana University Press, 1980); Maurice Sugar, *The Ford Hunger March* (Berkeley: Meikeljohn Institute, 1980).

4. Bernstein, *The Lean Years*, chap. 7.

5. Rita Heller, "Blue Collars and Bluestockings: The Bryn Mawr Summer School for Women Workers," in *Sisterhood and Solidarity: Workers Education for Women, 1914–1984*, ed. Joyce L. Kornbluh and Mary Frederickson (Philadelphia: Temple University Press, 1984), pp. 121-122; Hilda W. Smith, "People Come First: A Report of Workers' Education in the Federal Emergency Relief Administration, The Civil Works Administration and the Works Progress Administration, 1933–1943," pp. 8-9. For a detailed review of the political and financial issues of Brookwood Labor College in the 1930s, see James O. Morris, *Conflict within the AFL: A Study of Craft Versus Industrial Unionism 1901–1938* (Ithaca, N.Y.: Cornell University Press, 1958), chap. 5.

6. Lewis R. Alderman, "Adult Education in the Public Schools, 1930–1932," *School Life* 18 (March 1933): 128–129; Profitt, "Adult Education", p. 1; George F. Zook, "Federal Emergency Aid to College Students," National Association of State Universities, *Transactions and Proceedings* (1934), pp. 213–219. Harry Zeitlin, "Federal Relations in American Education, 1935–1943: A Study of New Deal Efforts and Innovations" (Ph.D. diss., Columbia University, 1958), pp. 128–129.

7. Frances Perkins, *The Roosevelt I Knew* (New York: Viking Press, 1946), pp. 190–191; Zeitlin, "Federal Relations," pp. 327–347; James T. Patterson, *The New Deal and the States: Federalism in Transition* (Princeton, N.J.: Princeton University Press, 1969), pp. 50, 71; Harry L. Hopkins, *Spending to Save: The Complete Story of Relief* (New York: Norton, 1936), pp. 165–166; Theodore E. Whiting, *Final Statistical Report of the FERA* (Washington, D.C.: GPO, 1942), p. 103.

8. Barton J. Bernstein. "The New Deal: The Conservative Achievements of Liberal Reform," in *Towards a New Past: Dissenting Essays in American History*, ed. Barton J. Bernstein (New York: Pantheon, 1968), p. 264.

9. *Congressional Record*, 73d Congress, 1st Session (1933), pp. 77: 1022.

10. Beulah Amidon, "Emergency Education," *Survey Graphic* 23 (September 1934): 415.

11. Robert E. Sherwood, *Roosevelt and Hopkins* (New York: Harper, 1948), pp. 1–168; Perkins, *Roosevelt*, pp. 190–191; William E. Leuchtenburg, *Franklin D. Roosevelt and the New Deal, 1933–1940* (New York: Harper & Row, 1963), pp. 120–123; Arthur M. Schlesinger, Jr., *The Coming of the New Deal* (Boston: Houghton Mifflin, 1958); Hopkins excerpt is quoted by Profitt, "Adult Education," p. 22.

12. *New York Times*, May 23, 1933, p. 21; also as quoted by Profitt, "Adult Education," p. 22; Zeitlin, "Federal Relations," pp. 123–126.

13. Zeitlin, "Federal Relations," pp. 123–126.

14. Doak S. Campbell, Frederich H. Bair, and Oswald L. Harvey, *Educational Activities of the Works Progress Administration*, U.S. Advisory Committee on Education, Staff Study Number 14 (Washington, D.C.: GPO, 1939), pp. 6–8; Zeitlin, "Federal Relations," pp. 122–124.

15. Campbell, Bair and Harvey, *Educational Activities*, pp. 6–8.

16. G. W. Maxwell, "In Appreciation of a Great Leader," *Adult Education* 7 (December 1942): 39–40; Zeitlin, "Federal Relations," p. 130.

17. Zeitlin, "Federal Relations," p. 128–131; Campbell, Bair, and Harvey, *Educational Activities*, p. 2.

18. Ibid.

19. U.S. Works Progress Administration, Document 13499 (Washington, D.C.: GPO, 1938), p. 8.

20. Robert L. Church, *Education in the United States* (New York: Free Press, 1976), pp. 343–397.

21. Harry L. Hopkins, as quoted in *Inventory: An Appraisal of the Results of the Works Progress Administration* (Washington, D.C.: GPO, 1938), pp. 39–40.

22. Ibid.

23. Arthur W. MacMahon, John D. Millet, and Gladys Ogden, *The Administration of Federal Work Relief* (Chicago: Public Administration Service, 1941), p. 250; Frank Goldin, "Emergency Adult Education in Lynn, Massachusetts," *School and Society* 44 (1936): 277–285.

24. As quoted in Arthur Armstrong, "Who Are Our Students?" *Journal of Adult Education* 9 (1937): 302–303.

25. Ibid.

26. Eunice F. Barnard, "Back to School Desks Millions Go," *New York Times Magazine*, May 17, 1936, p. 5.

27. *New York Times*, May 9, 1936, p. 33.

28. Campbell, Bair, and Harvey, *Educational Activities*, pp. 63–141.

29. Ibid., pp. 74–86.

30. Sidney B. Brooks, "Michigan's Great Adventure in Mass Education," *Michigan Education Journal* 12 (May 1935): 404; *New York Times*, September 20, 1936, p. 14; John D. Millet, *The Works Progress Administration in New York City* (Chicago: Public Administration Service, 1938), pp. 113–118; *New York Times*, March 27, 1937, p. 4.

31. Campbell, Bair, and Harvey, *Educational Activities*, p. 74.

32. Ibid., p. 155.

33. Ibid., pp. 65–66; Lyman Bryson, *Adult Education* (New York: American Book, 1936), pp. 32–33.

34. Campbell, Bair, and Harvey, *Educational Activities*, pp. 65–68; Zeitlin, "Federal Relations," pp. 138–139.

35. Emily M. Danton, "Uncle Sam, School Teacher," *Journal of Adult Education* 8 (1936): 151; Zeitlin, "Federal Relations," p. 139.

36. Campbell, Bair, and Harvey, *Educational Activities*, p. 70; *New York Times*, May 31, 1939, p. 8; Maurice Judd, "WPA Trains Immigrants for Citizenship Examinations," *School and Society* 46 (September 4, 1937): 317–318.

37. Campbell, Bair, and Harvey, *Educational Activities*, p. 68.

38. Ibid., pp. 103–119; Zeitlin, "Federal Relations," pp. 140–141.

39. Ibid.

40. Campbell, Bair, and Harvey, *Educational Activities*, pp. 87–91; Zeitlin, "Federal Relations," p. 141.

41. Campbell, Bair, and Harvey, *Educational Activities*, pp. 87–91.

42. *American Machinist* 79 (October 9, 1935): 749–751; (November 6, 1935): 823–824.

43. Ibid.

44. Ibid.

45. U.S. Federal Emergency Relief Administration, "Memorandum of Policies to Guide the Organization and Instruction of Workers' Education" (Washington, D.C.: FERA, 1933), pp. 1–2; Hilda W. Smith, pp. 56–57.

46. Ernest E. Schwartztrauber, *Workers Education: A Wisconsin Experiment* (Madison: University of Wisconsin Press, 1942), p. 217.

47. U.S. Federal Emergency Relief Administration, *The Emergency Education Program and the College Student Aid Program of the Federal Emergency Relief Administration* (Washington, D.C.: GPO, 1935), pp. 13-14; U.S. Works Progress Administration, *WPA Program Operation and Accomplishments, 1935–1943, Education*, vol. 3 (Washington, D.C.: GPO, 1943), pp. 14, 20, 25–26.

48. Ibid.

49. Hubert H. Humphrey, *The Education of a Public Man* (Garden City, N.Y.: Doubleday, 1976), p. 70.

50. U.S. Works Progress Administration, *WPA Education Program*, pp. 14, 20, 25–26.

51. General Education Board, *Annual Report* (1935–1936), p. 62, as quoted by Zeitlin, "Federal Relations," p. 159. Criticism of the program can be found, among other places, in Morse A. Cartwright, "Annual Report of the Director of the American Association for Adult Education," *Journal of Adult Education* 10 (October 1938): 336–337; and in the "Report from the Adult Education Association Director," *Journal of Adult Education* 7 (October 1935): 350.

52. U.S. Works Progress Administration, *WPA Education Program*, p. 82.

53. Zeitlin, "Federal Relations," pp. 288–326.

54. Ibid., pp. 145–146, 157–162.

55. U.S. Works Progress Administration, *Workers on Relief in the U.S.* (Washington, D.C.: GPO, 1935), p. 17; California Department of Education, *The Emergency Education Program in California* (Sacramento: California Department of Education, 1936), p. 3.

56. Sidney B. Hall to President Roosevelt, January 30, 1939 as cited by Zeitlin, "Federal Relations," p. 162. President Roosevelt to Sidney B. Hall (n.d.), as cited in ibid.

57. U.S. Works Progress Administration, *WPA Education Program*, pp. 117–118.

58. Campbell, Bair, and Harvey, *Educational Activities*, p. 95, 133–135. See also chapter four of this study.

59. Ibid., pp. 154–157.

60. Ibid.

61. "Emergency Education: How Will it Affect the Adult Education Movement?" *Journal of Adult Education* 8 (January 1936): 73–78.

62. As quoted in Lewis R. Alderman, "Carry Over from the Emergency Education Program," *Journal of Adult Education* 7 (October 1935): 476-479.

63. Campbell, Bair, and Harvey, *Educational Activities*, p. 157.

Chapter Three

1. U.S. Federal Emergency Relief Administration, Division of Emergency Educational Programs, "Concerning Workers' Education," vol. 1, no. 1. (Washington, D.C.: FERA, December 1934–January 1935, mimeographed), p. 4.

2. Broadus Mitchell, *Depression Decade* (New York: Rinehart, 1947), pp. 323–326. Arthur M. Schlesinger, Jr., *The Coming of the New Deal* (Boston: Houghton Mifflin, 1958), p. 298; Susan Ware, *Beyond Suffrage: Women in the New Deal* (Cambridge: Harvard University Press, 1981).

3. Hilda W. Smith, "People Come First: A Report of Workers' Education in the Federal Emergency Relief Administration, the Civil Works Administration and the Works Progress Administration, 1933–1942," Hilda W. Smith, Papers, Franklin D. Roosevelt Library, Hyde Park, N.Y., pp. 8–19; transcript, Hilda W. Smith oral history interview, November 17, 1963, Franklin D. Roosevelt Library, Hyde Park, N.Y., pp. 21–23. Tamara Hareven, *Eleanor Roosevelt: An American Conscience* (Chicago: Quadrangle, 1968), p. 77.

4. Ibid.

5. Smith, "People Come First," appendix 1, pp. 1–2.

6. Ibid.

7. Ibid., text, p. 19.

8. Ibid.; Smith to Spencer Miller, Jr., September 14, 1933, Franklin D. Roosevelt Library, Hyde Park, N.Y., Container 10, File "Public Relations—Labor, 1933–1938."

9. Smith, "People Come First," pp. 21–22; Harry L. Hopkins to Governors and State Emergency Relief Administrators, August 19, 1933, Record Group 69, FERA Records, Box 10, National Archives; "Memorandum on Policies to Govern Work Relief to Needy Unemployed Teachers," September 20, 1933, Record Group 69, FERA Records, Box 10, National Archives, pp. 1–4.

10. U.S. Federal Emergency Relief Administration, "Memorandum of Policies to Guide the Organization and Instruction of Workers' Education" (Washington, D.C.: FERA, 1933), p. 3.

11. Alice Hansen Cook and Agnes M. Douty, *Labor Education Outside the Unions* (Ithaca, N.Y.: New York State School of Industrial and Labor Relations, Cornell University, 1958), p. 86.

12. Smith, "People Come First," p. 33.

13. Ibid., p. 22.

14. Ibid., p. 23.

15. Ibid., p. 22.

16. Doak S. Campbell, Frederick H. Bair, and Oswald L. Harvey, *Educational Activities of the Works Progress Administration*, U.S. Advisory Committee on Education, Staff Study Number 14 (Washington, D.C.: GPO, 1939), pp. 11–22.

17. Hilda W. Smith, "Memorandum of Policies to Guide the Organization and Instruction of Workers' Education Classes Under Point 3 of the Federal Emergency Relief for Unemployed Teachers" (Washington, D.C.: FERA, n.d.), p. 3.

18. Ibid.

19. Smith, "People Come First," p. 29.

20. Hilda W. Smith, "Federal Cooperation in the Education of Workers," *Journal of Adult Education* 6 (October 1934): 500.

21. As quoted by Ronald J. Peters, "Factors Affecting Labor Extension Education, 1945–1950" (Ph.D. diss., Michigan State University), p. 57; Smith, "People Come First," pp. 56–57.

22. Smith, *Opening Vistas in Workers' Education*, p. 240.

23. "Concerning Workers' Education," vol. 1, no. 5 (September-October 1934), p. 2.

24. Smith, "People Come First," p. 31.

25. Ibid., 32–37; ibid., appendix 2, "Why a Special Program for Workers?" pp. 1–2.

26. Ibid.

27. "Minutes of the Conference on Workers' Education, February 2, 1934," Hilda W. Smith, Papers, Franklin D. Roosevelt Library, Hyde Park, N.Y., Container 10, File "Conferences 1932–1936."

28. Ibid., pp. 15–23.

29. Ibid., p. 9.

30. Smith, "People Come First," p. 39.

31. "Report of the Program of Work Conducted by the Affiliated Schools for Workers in Cooperation with the Federal Emergency Relief Administration, January 1, 1934-October 1, 1935," American Labor Education Service Collection, Martin P. Catherwood Library, New York State School of Industrial and Labor Relations, Cornell University, File "Reports on Workers' Education," Box 13.

32. Ibid.

33. Ibid.

34. Pearl Hertz, "Report of a Study Analyzing the Recruiting Methods of the Schools for Workers in Industry at the University of Wisconsin and the Relation of Community Activities of the 1934 Students to Attendance at that School"; and Eleanor Coit, "Government Support of Workers' Education," American Labor Education Service Collection, Martin P. Catherwood Library, New York State School of Industrial and Labor Relations, Cornell University, Box 88.

35. Smith, "People Come First," p. 63; Appendix 8, "Washington Staff—Workers' Education, 1933–1943."

36. Affiliated Schools' Minutes, December 2, 1939, American Labor Educaton Service Collection, Martin P. Catherwood Library, New York State School of Industrial and Labor Relations, Cornell University, Box 124.

37. As quoted in Eleanor Coit, "Progressive Education at Work," *Workers' Education in the United States* (New York: Harper, 1941), p. 171.

38. William Green, "The Clearing House-Adult Education for Special Groups," *Journal of Adult Education* 6 (October 1934): 314.

39. *Workers' Education News*, November 1934, p. 1.

40. "Workers' Education: A Symposium," *Journal of Adult Education* 6 (October 1934): 491–528.

41. Harry Russell, "New England Labor Prepares for the New Deal," *Journal of Adult Education* 6 (October 1934): 527.

42. William Green to George Zook, Reply from Zook to Green, May 9, 1934, Hilda W. Smith, Papers, Franklin D. Roosevelt Library, Hyde Park, N.Y., Container 10, File "Public Relations-Labor, 1933–1938."

43. *Proceedings of the Fifty-Ninth AFL Convention* (Washington, D.C.: AFL, 1934), pp. 137–138.

44. Minutes of Meeting with AFL Representatives, June 14, 1935, Franklin D. Roosevelt Library, Hyde Park, N.Y., Container 10, File "Public Relations-Labor, 1933–1938."

45. AFL, *Proceedings of the Fifty-Ninth AFL Convention*, p. 464.

46. See chap. 5 of this study and Hareven, *Eleanor Roosevelt*.

47. U.S. Federal Emergency Relief Administration, "Workers' Education under the FERA, 1934–1935" (Washington, D.C.: FERA, n.d.), Hilda W. Smith, Papers, Franklin D. Roosevelt Library, Hyde Park, N.Y., Container 12, File "Technical Committee on Workers' Education, 1935-1941."

48. Ibid.

49. Smith, "People Come First," p. 53.

50. Hilda W. Smith, "Mill Hand," "Concerning Workers' Education," vol. 1, no. 6 (December-January, 1934–1935), p. 37.

Chapter Four

1. U.S. Federal Emergency Relief Administration, Division of Emergency Educational Programs, "Concerning Workers' Education," vol. 1, no. 1 (Washington, D.C.: FERA, December 1934-January 1935): 37.

2. U.S. Federal Emergency Relief Administration, *Teacher Training Centers in Workers' Education, 1934 and 1935* (Washington, D.C.: FERA, 1935); Hilda W. Smith, "People Come First: A Report of Workers' Education in the Federal Emergency Relief Administration, the Civil Works Administration, and the Works Progress Administration, 1933–1943," Hilda W. Smith, Papers, Franklin D. Roosevelt Library, Hyde Park, N.Y. pp. 59–72.

3. Doak S. Campbell, Frederick H. Bair, and Oswald L. Harvey, *Educational Activities of the Works Progress Administration*, U.S. Advisory Committee on Education, Staff Study Number 14 (Washington, D.C.: GPO, 1939), pp. 95–96, 133–39, 154.

4. In 1933, Eduard Lindeman proposed to Spencer Miller, Jr., a program of traveling teacher training institutes to be conducted by the Workers' Education Bureau and to include courses on teaching methods, industrial and economic problems, and the humanities. Lindeman to Miller, October 29, 1923, in Workers' Education Bureau Papers, Martin P. Catherwood Library, New York State School of Industrial and Labor Relations, Cornell University, File "Correspondence-Spencer Miller, Jr." In February and June 1924, Brookwood Labor College held two conferences on methods of teaching workers' classes. Articles about these meetings appear in *Workers' Education News* 1 (February 1924): 1 and (June 1924): 1. In April 1924, the WEB sponsored a regional, one-day institute at the New School for Social Research for teachers of workers. It focused on teaching methods and included an opening address by Charles Beard as well as simulation demonstrations led by Harry Overstreet and Alexander Fichandler. *Workers' Education News* 1 (June 1924): 1. These conferences aimed to "discover a new and vital method of teaching workers' classes," and advocated experimenting with new teaching methods appropriate to adult worker-students.

5. Smith, "People Come First," pp. 5–9.

6. Hilda W. Smith and Spencer Miller, Jr., "Memorandum sent to the Commissioner of Education, the Secretary of Labor, and the Federal Emergency Relief Administrator," Smith, "People Come First," appendix 1; ibid., pp. 9–11.

7. Hilda W. Smith to George Zook, November 15, 1933, Hilda W. Smith, Papers,

Franklin D. Roosevelt Library, Hyde Park, N.Y., Container 8, File "Organization and Management, 1933."

8. Campbell, Bair, and Harvey, *Educational Activities*, p. 4; Smith, "People Come First," pp. 24–25.

9. Campbell, Bair, and Harvey, *Educational Activities*, pp. 151–154.

10. Ibid.

11. U.S. Federal Emergency Relief Administration, *Teacher Training Centers in Workers' Education, 1934 and 1935*, p. 3.

12. Ibid., p. 18.

13. Ibid.

14. Ibid.; Smith, "People Come First," pp. 33–35.

15. Hilda W. Smith, "Workers' Education as Determining Social Control," *The Annals of the American Academy of Political and Social Science* 182 (November 1935): 82; U.S. Federal Emergency Relief Administration, *Teacher Training Centers in Workers' Education, 1934 and 1935*, p. 20.

16. Smith, "People Come First," p. 47.

17. U.S. Federal Emergency Relief Administration, *1934 Workers' Education Teacher Training Centers* (Washington, D.C.: FERA, 1934), p. 1.

18. Smith, "People Come First," p. 42.

19. Ibid., p. 62; Campbell, Bair, and Harvey, *Educational Activities*, p. 95.

20. Interview with Ernestine Friedmann by Alice M. Hoffman, February 14, 1972, the Pennsylvania Labor Archives, Pattee Library, Pennsylvania State University, State College, Pa.

21. Ibid.; Smith, "People Come First," p. 63 and appendix 8.

22. Smith, "People Come First," p. 64 and appendix 4. Smith hired the following workers' education federal field representatives in 1934, who worked on her project until WPA budget cuts in 1936; Nelson Cruickshank, New York and New England; John Jacobsen, New Jersey, Pennsylvania, Kentucky, West Virginia and Ohio; Marguerite Gilmore, midwest; Henry Rutz, midwest; Howard Bridgeman, southeast; Freda Sigworth, southwest; Ethel Clark, far west; J. C. Kennedy, west coast.

23. Ibid., pp. 64–66.

24. U.S. Federal Emergency Relief Administration, *1934 Workers' Education Teacher Training Centers*, pp. 2, 13.

25. Ibid., p. 25.

26. Ibid., p. 4.

27. Smith, "People Come First," pp. 65–66.

28. Hilda W. Smith, "Memorandum on Policies for Organizing a Teacher Training Center" (Washington, D.C.: Office of the Specialist in Workers' Education, 1934), p. 13; U.S. Federal Emergency Relief Administration, *1934 Workers' Education Teacher Training Centers*, p. 12; idem, *Teacher Training Centers in Workers' Education, 1934 and 1935*, p. 18.

29. Campbell, Bair, and Harvey, *Educational Activities*, p. 95.

30. U.S. Federal Emergency Relief Administration, *Teacher Training Centers in Workers' Education, 1934 and 1935*, p. 6.

31. Ibid.

32. Eleanor Coit, "Report of a Trip to FERA Teacher Training Center, West

Chester, Pa., October 15, 16 and 17, 1935," American Labor Education Service Collection, Archives of the New York State School of Industrial and Labor Relations, Record Group 5225, Box 15, File "Emergency Education Program, 1935"; Florence Nelson, "Report of Workers' Education Teacher Training Center, A. M. and N. College, Pine Bluffs, Arkansas, 1935," p. 2, National Archives, Record Group 69, File "Workers' Service Program—Arkansas."

33. Constance Williams, "Report of the Workers' Education Teacher Training Center, Yale University, New Haven, Connecticut, 1935," p. 1, National Archives, Record Group 69, File "Workers' Service Program—Connecticut."

34. U.S. Federal Emergency Relief Administration, *1934 Workers' Education Teacher Training Centers*, p. 6.

35. Smith, "Policies for Organizing a Teacher Training Center," pp. 2–5.

36. Ibid.

37. U.S. Federal Emergency Relief Administration, *1934 Workers' Education Training Centers*, pp. 13–14; idem, *Teacher Training Centers in Workers' Education, 1934 and 1935*, p. 16.

38. U.S. Federal Emergency Relief Administration, *1934 Workers' Education Teacher Training Centers*, pp. 13–14; idem, *Teacher Training Centers in Workers' Education, 1934 and 1935*, p. 6.

39. Nelson, "Workers Education Teacher Training Center, Pine Bluffs, Arkansas, 1935," p. 2.

40. Smith, "Policies for Organizing a Teacher Training Center," p. 6.

41. This information is derived from the 1934 and 1935 reports of the directors of workers' education teacher training centers in Arkansas, California, Colorado, Connecticut, Georgia, Illinois, Michigan, Minnesota, Mississippi, New York, Pennsylvania, and Wisconsin in National Archives, Record Group 69, in state file of the Works Progress Administration Workers' Service Program. Hereafter, Center Directors' Reports, 1934, 1935.

42. Ibid.

43. Ibid.

44. Ibid.

45. Ibid.

46. Ibid.; Smith, "Policies for Organizing a Teachers' Training Center," p. 7.

47. Smith, "Policies for Organizing a Teachers' Training Center"; U.S. Federal Emergency Relief Administration, *Teacher Training Centers in Workers Education, 1934–1935*.

48. U.S. Federal Emergency Relief Administration, *Teacher Training Centers in Workers Education, 1934–1935*, p. 8.

49. Williams, "Workers' Education Teacher Training Center, Connecticut, 1935," p. 15.

50. Ibid., p. 17.

51. Dorsie Dowdle to Hazel Howard (n.d.) in American Labor Education Service Collection, New York State School of Industrial and Labor Relations, Record Group 5225, Box 15, File "FERA Report of Projects Under Grant, February 1934-May 1935."

52. U.S. Federal Emergency Relief Administration, *Teacher Training Centers in*

Workers' Education, 1934 and 1935. Some of the teacher trainees in the workers' education teacher training centers had had experience in the labor movement before attending the 1934 and 1935 teacher-training center programs. A number joined union staffs following the programs of the WPA.

53. Information for this section is derived from reading reports of some of the Emergency Education Division Programs in teacher training, which are filed by state in the National Archives, Emergency Education Division Collection, Record Group 69; Campbell, Bair, and Harvey, *Educational Activities*, p. 154.

54. Campbell, Bair, and Harvey, *Educational Activities*, p. 154.

55. U.S. Works Progress Administration, *Report of the Teacher Training Center at the University of Michigan, Ann Arbor, Michigan, July-August 1940* (Ann Arbor: University of Michigan, 1940).

56. Campbell, Bair, and Harvey, *Educational Activities*, pp. 136–137.

57. Smith to Alderman, November 18, 1937, Hilda W. Smith, Papers, Franklin D. Roosevelt Library, Hyde Park, N.Y., Container 9, File "Organization and Management, 1937."

58. Campbell, Bair, and Harvey, *Educational Activities*, p. 137.

59. Smith, "People Come First," p. 150.

Chapter Five

1. U.S. Federal Emergency Relief Administration, Division of Emergency Educational Programs, "Concerning Workers' Education," vol. 1, no. 1 (Washington, D.C.: December 1934–January 1935, mimeographed): 44. 1935), 1: 44.

2. Oral history of Hilda W. Smith conducted by Ashley Doherty, May 30, 1969, Hilda W. Smith Papers, Franklin D. Roosevelt Library, Hyde Park, N.Y., Container 1, File "Interviews."

3. U.S. Federal Emergency Relief Administration, *Report on Educational Camps for Unemployed Women, 1934 and 1935* (Washington, D.C.: FERA, 1936), appendix 2. Susan Ware, *Beyond Suffrage: Women in the New Deal* (Cambridge: Harvard University Press, 1981), p. 113.

4. Excellent summaries of conditions for women during the Depression and New Deal years are found in Lois Scharf, *To Work and To Wed* (Westport, Conn.: Greenwood Press, 1980), chap. 6; and Alice Kessler–Harris, *Out to Work: A History of Wage-Earning Women in the U.S.* (New York: Oxford University Press, 1982), chap. 9; "Employment Conditions and Unemployment Relief: Unemployment among Women in the Early Years of the Depression," *Monthly Labor Review* 39 (April 1934): 792, n. 7; Meridel Le Sueur, *Ripening* (New York: Feminist Press, 1982), p. 141; Helena H. Weed, "The New Deal that Women Want," *Current History* 41 (November 1934): 181–182.

5. Weed, "New Deal," p. 183.

6. Chicago Council of Social Agencies, *Work Camps* (Chicago: Chicago Council of Social Agencies, 1941), pp. 1–2.

7. William E. Leuchtenburg, *Franklin D. Roosevelt and the New Deal, 1932–1940* (New York: Harper & Row, 1963), p. 52.

8. Women's Trade Union League, "Memorandum of Suggestions to Labor Confer-

ence, March 1933," Hilda W. Smith, Papers, Franklin D. Roosevelt Library, Hyde Park, N.Y., Container 10, File "Public Relations-Labor, 1933–1938"; Hilda W. Smith, "Plan for Resident Schools for Unemployed Women in Need of Relief," Hilda W. Smith, Papers, Schlesinger Library, Radcliffe College, Cambridge, Mass., Record Group A–76, file 290.

9. Joseph P. Lash, *Eleanor and Franklin* (New York: Norton, 1971), pp. 510–511, 699.

10. Ibid.

11. *New York Times*, June 2, 1933, 2:2; "Memorandum, May 31, 1933," Federal Emergency Relief Administration, Women's Camps Section, Old Subject File, National Archives.

12. Letters and telegrams from individuals and organizations offering facilities for the women's camp program can be found in U.S. Federal Emergency Relief Administration Collection, National Archives, Record Group 69, File 984.

13. Ether to Congressman Lemke, July 12, 1933, U.S. Federal Emergency Relief Administration Collection, National Archives, Record Group 69, File 284.

14. Hilda W. Smith, "Plan for Resident Schools for Unemployed Women in Need of Relief," Hilda W. Smith, Papers, Schlesinger Library, Radcliffe College, Record Group A–76, File 290.

15. Ware, *Beyond Suffrage*, pp. 106–107; Weed, "New Deal," p. 183.

16. Hilda W. Smith, "People Come First: A Report of Workers' Education in the Federal Emergency Relief Administration, 1933–1942," p. 78; U.S. Federal Emergency Relief Administration, *Educational Camps for Unemployed Women, 1934 and 1935*, p. 8.

17. Ibid., p. 10; *New York Times*, April 29, 1934, 20:7.

18. "Summary of White House Conference on Problems of Jobless Women, April 30, 1934," U.S. Federal Emergency Relief Administration Collection, National Archives, Record Group 69, File 360.

19. Members of the National Advisory Committee included: Dr. Lewis R. Alderman, Director, WPA Emergency Education; Josephine Brown, Intake and Certification, WPA; Richard Brown, National Youth Administration; Mary Bethune, U.S. Department of Labor, Women's Bureau; Helen Gifford, National Board, YWCA; Eleanor Coit, Affiliated Schools for Workers; Dorothea de Schweinitz, National Youth Administration; Ellen Woodward, director of Women's Work, WPA; and Elizabeth Wickenden, WPA.

20. Smith, "People Come First," pp. 75–76 and appendix G.

21. Ibid., p. 78.

22. *New York Times*, June 16, 1934, 17:8.

23. Hilda W. Smith, *Suggestions for Organization, Curriculum, and Teaching in Residential Schools and Educational Camps* (Washington, D.C.: FERA, 1934); American Labor Education Service Papers, Martin P. Catherwood Library, New York State School of Industrial and Labor Relations, Cornell University, Record Group 5525, Box 15, File "Schools and Camps for Unemployed Women."

24. U.S. Federal Emergency Relief Administration, *Educational Camps for Unemployed Women, 1934 and 1935*.

25. Ibid., pp. 21–22.

26. As quoted by Lash, *Eleanor and Franklin*, p. 205; U.S. Federal Emergency Relief Administration, *Educational Camps for Unemployed Women, 1934 and 1935*, p. 4; *Monthly Labor Review* 39 (November 1934): 1110.

27. U.S. Federal Emergency Relief Administration, *Educational Camps for Unemployed Women, 1934 and 1935*, p. 5.

28. Ibid.

29. Ibid.

30. Ibid., p. 17.

31. Ibid.; in addition, I examined reports from about fifteen of the educational camps, which I found in the National Archives, the Hilda W. Smith, Papers, Schlesinger Library, Radcliffe College, Cambridge, Mass., and in the American Labor Education Service Collection, Martin P. Catherwood Library, New York State School of Industrial and Labor Relations, Cornell University.

32. U.S. Federal Emergency Relief Administration, *Educational Camps for Unemployed Women, 1934 and 1935*, pp. 34–36.

33. Harry Gersh, "The She-She-She Camps: An Episode in New Deal History," unpublished term paper, Hilda W. Smith, Papers, Schlesinger Library, Radcliffe College, Cambridge, Mass., Record Group A-76, File 292.

34. *New York Times*, July 3, 1936, 3:4; see also articles, Hilda W. Smith, Papers, Schlesinger Library, Radcliffe College, Cambridge, Mass. Record Group A-76, File 297.

35. U.S. Federal Emergency Relief Administration, *Educational Camps for Unemployed Women, 1934 and 1935*, p. 6.

36. Ibid.

37. Funds for the women's educational camp program under the National Youth Administration were provided through a separate allocation from its budget. Presidential Letter No. 5064, July 13, 1936, established a limit of $1,111,000 of which only $700,000 was actually allocated for the women's camp project. The camp program operated as an official work project and closed October 1, 1937. Palmer O. Johnson and Oswald L. Harvey, *The National Youth Administration*, U.S. Advisory Committee on Education, Staff Study Number 13 (Washington, D.C.: GPO, 1938), p. 17.

38. Ella Ketchin, *Report on the National Youth Administration Camps for Unemployed Women* (Washington, D.C.: NYA, 1937), p. 48.

39. Ibid. p. 62.

40. "Minutes of the Advisory Committee, Monday September 21, 1936," American Labor Education Service Collection, Martin P. Catherwood Library, New York State School of Industrial and Labor Relations, Cornell University, Record Group 5225, Box 156, File "Schools and Camps."

41. Smith to Eleanor Roosevelt, November 18, 1936, Hilda W. Smith, Papers, Franklin D. Roosevelt Library, Hyde Park, N.Y., Container 21, File "Correspondence"; see also, Adeline Taylor, *NYA Camps for Jobless Women* (Washington, D.C.: NYA, 1936), p. 18.

42. Statement of Charles Taussig to the National Youth Administration Advisory Committee, February 8, 1938, National Youth Administration Collection, National Archives, Box 608, File "NYA Papers."

43. Ketchin, *National Youth Administration Camps*, p. 42.

44. "Memorandum to Mrs. Roosevelt, June 1, 1937," and "Minutes of the National Advisory Committee meeting, August 3, 1937," Hilda W. Smith, Papers, Schlesinger Library, Radcliffe College, Cambridge, Mass., Record Group A–76, File 290.

45. *New York Times*, August 17, 1937, 24:4.

46. U.S. Federal Security Agency, *Final Report of the National Youth Administration, 1936–1943* (Washington, D.C.: GPO, 1944), pp. 84–85.

47. Smith to Eleanor Roosevelt, May 15, 1940, Hilda W. Smith, Papers, Schlesinger Library, Radcliffe College, Cambridge, Mass., Record Group A–76, File 290.

Chapter Six

1. Eleanor Roosevelt, "My Day," January 29, 1936, Hilda W. Smith, Papers, Franklin D. Roosevelt Library, Hyde Park, N.Y., Container 12, File "Publicity, 1936–1938."

2. William E. Leuchtenburg, *Franklin D. Roosevelt and the New Deal, 1933–1940* (New York: Harper & Row, 1963), chap. 5.

3. Ibid., pp. 107, 252.

4. Ibid., chap. 11; Susan Ware, *Beyond Suffrage: Women in the New Deal* (Cambridge: Harvard University Press, 1981), p. 117. See also, James T. Patterson, *Congressional Conservatism and the New Deal* (Lexington: University of Kentucky Press, 1967).

5. Max Kampelman, *The Communist Party vs. the C.I.O.* (New York: Praeger, 1957), documents the role of Communist Party members in the organization of mass production industries in the late thirties.

6. Broadus Mitchell, *Depression Decade* (New York: Rinehart, 1947), pp. 323–326; U.S. Works Progress Administration, *Final Report on the W.P.A. Program, 1935–1943* (Washington: GPO, 1946); Donald Howard, *The W.P.A. and Federal Relief Policy* (New York: Russell Sage Foundation, 1943), pp. 105–108.

7. Ibid. Adult-training projects (literacy and citizenship, parent education, vocational training, general adult education and workers' education) were administered by the WPA White Collar and Professional Division, later renamed the Division of Service Projects. WPA recreation, library, museum, art, music, and theater projects were administered by the same division. U.S. Works Progress Administration, *Final Report on the W.P.A. Program*, pp. 59–61; and Hilda W. Smith, "People Come First: A Report of Workers' Education in the Federal Emergency Relief Administration, the Civil Works Admistration and the Works Progress Administration, 1933–1942," Hilda W. Smith, Papers, Franklin D. Roosevelt Library, Hyde Park, N.Y., pp. 48–49.

8. Smith, "People Come First," pp. 49–56.

9. Barbara Donald to Hilda W. Smith, "Memorandum," Smith Papers, Franklin D. Roosevelt Library, Hyde Park, N.Y. Container 9, File "Organization and Management, 1936."

10. Hilda W. Smith, "Report from the 1935 AFL Convention," Hilda W. Smith, Papers, Franklin D. Roosevelt Library, Hyde Park, N.Y., Container 10, File "Public Relations-Labor, 1933–1938."

11. Paul Vogt to Spencer Miller, Jr., June 20, 1935, Hilda W. Smith, Papers, Franklin D. Roosevelt Library, Hyde Park, N.Y., Container 10, File "Public Relations-Labor, 1933–1938."

12. Hilda W. Smith, "1936 Report," Hilda W. Smith, Papers, Franklin D. Roosevelt Library, Hyde Park, N.Y., Container 9, File "Organization and Management, 1936."

13. Ibid.

14. "Suggestions for a Technical Committee on Workers' Education," Smith Collection, Franklin D. Roosevelt Library, Container 11, File "Public Relations—Federal Agencies, 1936." Members of the Technical Committee on Workers' Education included: Dr. Isador Lubin, chair; Josephine Roche, J. C. Luekhardt, Mary Switzer and Kathleen Lowrie from the U.S. Interdepartmental Committee on Health and Welfare; Anna Burdick, C. F. Klinfelter, and Chester Williams from the U.S. Office of Education; Clara Beyer, Mollie Ray Carroll, Mary Anderson, and Thomas Holland from the U.S. Department of Labor; C.W. Warburton, D.E. Montgomery, Carl F. Taeusch, and A. Drummond Jones from the U.S. Department of Agriculture; Beatrice Stern and Malcolm Ross from the National Labor Relations Board; Lewis Resnick, Louise Griffith, and Ethel Smith from the U.S. Social Security Board; Estelle Warner and David Bishop from the U.S. Department of Public Health.

15. Clipping from *Press Digest*, January 4, 1937, reporting on a *New York Times* article the preceding Sunday, Hilda W. Smith, Papers, Franklin D. Roosevelt Library, Hyde Park, N.Y., Container 6, File "Newspaper Publicity, 1937."

16. See Hilda W. Smith, Papers, Schlesinger Library, Radcliffe College, Cambridge, Mass., Record Group A-76, File "Attacks" and Hilda W. Smith, Papers, Franklin D. Roosevelt Library, Hyde Park, N.Y., Container 6, File "Newspaper Publicity, 1936," Hyde Park, N.Y. Hubert Humphrey, workers' education supervisor for the twin cities in Minnesota, later described the tensions among instructors in his program: "There were essentially three groups of teachers at that time on WPA: the Stalinist Communists, the Trotskyist bloc, and a third group of everyone else. The Stalinists and Trotskyists hated each other, and when we had teachers' sessions, they'd sit on opposite sides of the room and harass each other." Hubert H. Humphrey, *The Education of a Public Man* (Garden City, N.Y.: Doubleday, 1976), pp. 68–69.

17. Ibid.

18. Ibid., *New York American*, May 11, 1935 and *New York Times*, May 19, 1935, carried articles about the reaction of the Federal Grand Jury Association for the Southern District of New York to the WPA workers' education classes at the School for the Unemployed in New York City.

19. *Washington Times*, August 22, 1935, clipping, Hilda W. Smith, Papers, Schlesinger Library, Radcliffe College, Cambridge, Mass., Record Group A–76, File "Attacks"; Smith, "People Come First," p. 62.

20. Interview with Jack Barbash, November 1980; clipping from *New York Daily News*, August 9, 1934, Hilda W. Smith, Papers, Schlesinger Library, Radcliffe College, Cambridge, Mass., Record Group A-76, File "Attacks."

21. Clipping from the *Baltimore Sun*, May 12, 1935, Hilda W. Smith, Papers, Schlesinger Library, Radcliffe College, Cambridge, Mass., Record Group A–76, File "Attacks"; Smith, "People Come First," p. 62.

22. Tamara Hareven, *Eleanor Roosevelt: An American Conscience* (Chicago: Quadrangle, 1968), pp. 74–77. Hareven states: "Miss Smith's carte blanche to bring her troubles to the White House, her close friendship with the First Lady and the latter's interest in the project secured for it the respect of other administrators and the

interest and attention of FDR. Hilda Smith did not hesitate to invoke the First Lady's name when her project was threatened by budget cuts or encountered other opposition," p. 78. Hareven also writes: "Mrs. Roosevelt's shrewd tactic was to visit the state, look at the operation of various New Deal agencies, and then innocently ask to see the workers' education project. Sometimes this question alone was sufficient to stimulate the launching of such a program, as happened in Michigan," p. 79.

23. Eleanor Roosevelt, "My Day" (n.d.), Hilda W. Smith, Papers, Franklin D. Roosevelt Library, Hyde Park, N.Y., Container 12, File "Publicity, 1937."

24. Eleanor Roosevelt, "My Day," April 27, 1938 as quoted by Hareven, *Eleanor Roosevelt*, p. 77; n. 34, p. 77; see also, "Report of a Conference of WPA Workers' Education Supervisors held at West Park, N.Y., July 18–22, 1938," Hilda W. Smith, Papers, Franklin D. Roosevelt Library, Hyde Park, N.Y. Container 2, File "Workers' Service Program, WPA; Conferences, 1937–1938." Eleanor Roosevelt, "My Day," January 29, 1936, Eleanor Roosevelt, Papers, Franklin D. Roosevelt Library, Hyde Park, N.Y., Container 2, File "My Day."

25. Lewis R. Alderman to Aubrey Williams, "Memorandum on Conditions for More Effective Operation of WPA Education Programs" and Hilda W. Smith to Aubrey Williams, "Memorandum, August 13, 1937," both in Hilda W. Smith, Papers, Franklin D. Roosevelt Library, Container 9, File "Organization and Management, 1937."

26. Ibid.

27. Smith, "People Come First," appendix 5.

28. Hilda W. Smith to Lewis R. Alderman, "Memorandum," in Hilda W. Smith, Papers, Franklin D. Roosevelt Library, Hyde Park, N.Y., Container 10, File "Organization and Management, 1938–1939."

29. Ernestine Friedmann, "Report from Georgia, April 1938," Hilda W. Smith, Papers, Franklin D. Roosevelt Library, Hyde Park, N.Y., Container 20, Spindle file.

30. Smith, "People Come First," pp. 93–94. Members of Smith's national Labor Advisory Committee were: George L. Googe, James A. Graham, Marion Hedges, Lillian Herstein, Carl Mullen, Nancy Lee Smith, H.M. Thackery, and Robert Watt from the AFL; Thomas Burns, Clinton Golden, J.B.S. Hardman, Ralph Hetzel, Jr., Katherine Lewis, Larry Rogin, Elizabeth Nord and Nicholas Zenarich from the CIO; Gladys Edwards, Donald Henderson, Kenneth Hones, Mary Mower, Merlin G. Miller from the unions of agricultural workers, tenant farmers and groups of cooperatives; Elizabeth Christman from the National Women's Trade Union League; Russell Watson and A. Philip Randolph from unions of WPA workers and Negro workers.

31. Hilda W. Smith, Papers, Franklin D. Roosevelt Library, Container 20, Spindle file, November-December 1938.

32. Ware, *Beyond Suffrage*, pp. 105–106; 101, 111, 120.

33. Ibid., p. 188, n. 4.

34. Elsie George, "The Women Appointees of the Roosevelt and Truman Administrations (Ph.D. diss., American University, 1972), p. 204; See also Hilda W. Smith to John M. Carmody, August 17, 1939, Hilda W. Smith, Papers, Franklin D. Roosevelt Library, Hyde Park, N.Y. Container 1, File "Carmody Correspondence." Members of Smith's Washington staff included Ernestine Friedmann, Assistant in charge of field work and training, 1934–1942; Helen Hermann, Assistant in research, materials and office administration, 1934–1940; Oliver Peterson, assistant in labor contacts and state program coordination, 1936–1938; Barbara Donald, assistant in research and materi-

als preparation, 1936–1939; Charlotte Brooks, office secretary, 1934–1939.

35. Aubrey Williams to Florence Kerr, August 29, 1939, Hilda W. Smith, Papers, Franklin D. Roosevelt Library, Hyde Park, N.Y., Container 1, File "Williams Correspondence."

36. Smith, "People Come First," pp. 93–94.

37. "Report of the Meeting at Edelmans," Hilda W. Smith, Papers, Franklin D. Roosevelt Library, Hyde Park, N.Y., Container 9, File "Organization and Management, 1938–1939."

38. General Letter No. 292 (211.43), National Archives, Record Group 69, "Workers' Service Program—Kerr, 1939–1940."

39. George, "Women Appointees," p. 206.

40. Hilda W. Smith to John M. Carmody, February 1941, National Archives, Record Group 69, File "Historical Background Data, Workers' Service Program, WPA."

41. Mark Starr, *Workers' Education Today* (New York: League for Industrial Democracy, 1941), p. 12.

42. This summary comes from a reading of the Workers' Service Program state supervisors' reports 1940–1942, National Archives, Record Group 69, from files on the Workers' Service Program in California, Illinois, Indiana, Michigan, New York, and Pennsylvania.

43. Hilda W. Smith to Walter Kiplinger, National Archives, Record Group 69, File "Workers' Service Program, WPA-Kerr."

44. George, "Women Appointees," p. 207; also, Hilda W. Smith, Papers, Franklin D. Roosevelt Library, Hyde Park, N.Y., Container 9, File "Organization and Management, 1939–1942."

45. Ibid.

46. Hilda W. Smith to Walter Kiplinger, "Field Trip Report, March 13, 1941," and Walter Kiplinger to Hilda W. Smith, March 20, 1941, National Archives, Record Group 69, File "Workers' Service Program, WPA, 1941–1942."

47. George, "Women Appointees," p. 209.

48. Hilda W. Smith to Florence Kerr, May 10, 1939, and Hilda W. Smith, "Field Trip Report, May 1939," National Archives, Record Group 69, File "Smith Travel Correspondence."

49. Ibid.

50. Hilda W. Smith to Florence Kerr, June 10, 1941, "Investigation of Workers' Service Program," National Archives, Record Group 69, File "Historical Background Data, Workers' Service Program, WPA."

51. Hilda W. Smith to Florence Kerr, February 26; March 13, 24, 27; April 10, 1941. National Archives, Record Group 69, File "Historical Background Data, Workers' Service Program, WPA."

52. Hilda W. Smith to John M. Carmody, August 28, 1941, Hilda W. Smith, Papers, Franklin D. Roosevelt Library, Hyde Park, N.Y., Container 1, File "Carmody Correspondence."

53. Hilda W. Smith to Mark Starr, February 13, 1942, Hilda W. Smith, Papers, Franklin D. Roosevelt Library, Hyde Park, N.Y., Container 1, File "Starr Correspondence."

54. Ibid.

55. Hilda W. Smith to Lawrence Morris, March 18, 1942, National Archives, Record Group 69, File "Workers' Service Program, WPA-Smith General Correspondence, 1941–1943."

56. As quoted by George, "Women Appointees," p. 216.

57. Florence Kerr to WPA Regional Directors and Supervisors, May 2, 1942, in National Archives, Record Group 69, File "Workers' Service Program, WPA-Kerr Correspondence, 1941–1943."

58. Smith, "People Come First," pp. 155–156.

59. George, "Women Appointees," pp. 216–217.

60. Interview with Miles Horton, April 6, 1983; and interview with Harry Gersh, June 18, 1983.

61. Margaret Smokin Moore to John M. Carmody, May 28, 1942, refers to a conversation about Smith between Carmody and Francis Biddle, John M. Carmody, Papers, Franklin D. Roosevelt Library, Hyde Park, N.Y. Container 69, File "Hilda Smith."

Chapter Seven

1. Larry Rogin, "Survey of Workers' Education," *History of an Ideal* (New York: American Labor Education Service, 1957), pp. 5–6.

2. Ronald J. Peters, "Factors Affecting Labor Extension Legislation, 1945–1950" (Ph.D. diss., Michigan State University, 1976), pp. 159–190; Norman Eiger, *Toward a National Commitment to Workers' Education: The Rise and Fall of the Campaign to Establish a Labor Extension Service, 1942–1950* (New Brunswick, N.J.: Institute of Management and Labor Relations, Rutgers University, 1975).

3. Ibid.

4. Peters, "Factors Affecting Labor Extension Legislation," pp. 218–264.

5. Ibid.

6. Ibid.

7. Ibid.

8. Doak S. Campbell, Frederick H. Bair, and Oswald L. Harvey, *Educational Activities of the Works Progress Administration*, U.S. Advisory Committee on Education, Staff Study Number 14 (Washington, D.C.: GPO, 1939), pp. 151–153.

9. Ibid.

10. Information for this section is taken from Hilda W. Smith's annual program reports and the reports of FERA and WPA state supervisors of workers' education that are found in the National Archives and in the Smith Papers at the Franklin D. Roosevelt Library.

11. Harry Zeitlin, "Federal Relations in American Education, 1933-1943: A Study of New Deal Efforts and Innovations" (Ph.D. diss., Columbia University, 1958), pp. 288–325.

12. Arthur W. MacMahon, John D. Millet, and Gladys Ogden. *The Administration of Federal Work Relief* (Chicago: Public Administration Service, 1941), p. 250.

13. Ibid.

14. Agnes Samuelson to President Roosevelt, January 13, 1936, and Roosevelt to Samuelson, February 4, 1936, as quoted by Zeitlin, "Federal Relations," p. 299.

15. Roscoe Pulliam, "The Influence of the Federal Government in Education," *School and Society* (January 15, 1938): 71.

16. Hilda W. Smith to Aubrey Williams, February 23, 1940, Hilda W. Smith, Papers, Franklin D. Roosevelt Library, Hyde Park, N.Y., Container 9, File "Organization and Management, 1938."

17. Thomas R. Adams, *The Workers' Road to Learning* (New York: American Association for Adult Education, 1940), p. 77.

18. *A Brief Outline of the Resolutions and Pronouncements of the AFL in Support of the General Principles and Practices of Education from 1881–1938* (Washington, D.C.: AFL, 1939), p. 52.

19. William E. Leuchtenberg, *Franklin D. Roosevelt and the New Deal, 1933–1940* (New York: Harper & Row, 1963), pp. 95–116.

20. Ibid., pp. 252–274.

21. Searle F. Charles, *Minister of Relief: Harry Hopkins and the Depression* (Syracuse: Syracuse University Press, 1963), pp. 174–219.

22. Robert A. Bowman, "The National Committee for the Extension of Labor Education, 1942–1950" (Ph.D. diss., Rutgers University, 1979), pp. 376–377.

23. Campbell, Bair, and Harvey, *Educational Activities*, (mss), National Archives, Workers' Service Program, Record Group 69, File "Final Reports and Evaluations," p. 115.

24. Thomas E. Linton, *An Historical Examination of the Purposes and Practices of the Education Program of the United Automobile Workers of American, 1936–1959*, University of Michigan Comparative Education Dissertation Series, no. 8, (Ann Arbor: University of Michigan School of Education, 1965), p. 35.

25. Peters, "Factors Affecting Labor Extension Legislation," p. 267.

26. Rush Welter, *Popular Education and Democratic Thought in America* (N.Y.: Columbia University Press, 1962), p. 310–317.

27. Smith to Aubrey Williams, February 23, 1940, Hilda W. Smith, Papers, Franklin D. Roosevelt Library, Hyde Park, N.Y., Container 9, File "Organization and Management."

28. I am indebted to labor historian Steve Babson for discussions that shaped this analysis.

29. Brendan Sexton, "Staff and Officers' Training to Build Successful Unions," *Industrial Relations* 5 (February 1966): 85.

Bibliography

Books

Adams, Thomas R. *The Workers' Road to Learning*. New York: American Association for Adult Education, 1940.

Baskin, Alex, ed. *The Unemployed: 1930–1932*. New York: Archives of Social History, 1975.

Barbash, Jack. *Universities and Unions in Workers' Education*. New York: Harper, 1955.

Bernstein, Irving. *The Lean Years: A History of the American Worker, 1920–1933*. Boston: Houghton-Mifflin, 1960.

Bowers, C. A. *The Progressive Educator and the Depression: The Radical Years*. New York: Random House, 1969.

Brameld, Theodore, ed. *Workers' Education in the United States*. New York: Harper, 1941.

Bruce, Robert. *1877: Year of Violence*, New York: Bobbs-Merrill, 1959.

Bryson, Lyman. *Adult Education*. New York: American Book, 1936.

California Department of Education. *The Emergency Education Program in California*. Sacramento: California Department of Education, 1936.

Campbell, Doak S., Bair, Frederick H., and Harvey, Oswald L. *Educational Activities of the Works Progress Administration*. U.S. Advisory Committee on Education, Staff Study Number 14. Washington: D.C.: GPO, 1939.

Chambers, Clark A. *Seedtime of Reform*. Ann Arbor: University of Michigan Press, 1967.

Charles, Searle F. *Minister of Relief: Harry Hopkins and the Depression*. Syracuse: Syracuse University Press, 1963.

Church, Robert L. *Education in the United States*. New York: Free Press, 1976.

Coit, Eleanor. *Government Support of Workers' Education*. New York: American Labor Education Service, 1940.

Cook, Alice H., and Douty, Agnes M. *Labor Education Outside the Unions*. Ithaca, N. Y.: N. Y. State School of Industrial and Labor Relations, Cornell University, 1958.

Counts, George S. *Dare The School Build a New Social Order?*. New York: John Day, 1932.

Cremin, Lawrence A. *The Transformation of the School*. New York: Random House, 1964.

Educational Policies Commission. *A Bibliography on Education in the Depression.* Washington, D. C.: National Education Association, 1937.

Eiger, Norman. *Toward a National Commitment to Workers' Education: The Rise and Fall of the Campaign to Establish a Labor Extension Service, 1942–1950.* New Brunswick, N.J.: Institute of Management and Labor Relations, Rutgers University, 1975.

Ely, Mary L., ed. *Adult Education in Action.* New York: American Association for Adult Education, 1936.

Feder, L. H. *Unemployment Relief in Periods of Depression.* New York: Russell Sage Foundation, 1936.

Fernbach, Alfred P. *University Extension and Workers' Education.* Bloomington: National University Extension Association, 1945.

Fink, Leon. *Workingmen's Democracy: The Knights of Labor and American Politics.* Urbana: University of Illinois Press, 1983.

Foner, Philip. *The Great Labor Uprising of 1877.* New York: Monad, 1977.

Garraty, John. *The American Nation: A History of the United States Since 1865*, New York: Harper & Row, 1977.

Grattan, C. Hartley. *In Quest of Knowledge.* New York: Association Press, 1955.

Hansome, Marius. *World Workers' Educational Movements.* New York: Columbia University Press, 1931.

Hareven, Tamara. *Eleanor Roosevelt: An American Conscience.* Chicago: Quadrangle, 1968.

Hill, Frank E. *The School in the Camps.* New York: American Association for Adult Education, 1935.

———. *Listen and Learn: Fifteen Years of Adult Education on the Air.* New York: American Association for Adult Education, 1937.

———. *Education for Health: A Study of Programs for Adults.* New York: American Association for Adult Education, 1939.

Hodgen, Margaret, T. *Workers' Education in England and the United States.* New York: Dutton, 1925.

Hopkins, Harry L. *Spending to Save: The Complete Story of Relief.* New York: Norton, 1936.

Howard, Donald. *The W.P.A. and Federal Relief Policy.* New York: Russell Sage Foundation, 1943.

Jones, Maldwyn A. *American Immigration.* Chicago: University of Chicago Press, 1960.

Kallen, Horace. *Education, the Machine, and the Worker.* New York: New Republic, 1925.

Keeran, Roger. *The Communist Party and the Auto Workers Unions*, Bloomington: University of Indiana Press, 1980.

Kennedy, Susan E. *If All We Did Was to Weep at Home: A History of White Working Class Women in America.* Bloomington: Indiana University Press, 1979.

Kerrison, Irvine. *Workers Education at the University Level.* New Brunswick, N.J.: Rutgers University Press, 1951.

Kerrison, Irvine and Levine, Herbert A. *Labor Leadership Education: A Union-University Approach.* New Brunswick, N.J.: Rutgers University Press, 1960.

Kessler-Harris, Alice. *Out to Work: A History of Wage-Earning Women in the United States*. New York: Oxford University Press, 1982.

Knowles, Malcolm. *The Adult Education Movement in the United States*. New York: Holt, 1962.

Kornbluh, Joyce L., and Frederickson, Mary, eds. *Sisterhood and Solidarity: Workers' Education for Women, 1914–1984*. Philadelphia: Temple University Press, 1984.

Kotinsky, Ruth. *Adult Education and the Social Scene*. New York: Appleton-Century, 1933.

Kurzman, Paul A. *Harry Hopkins and the New Deal*. Fairlawn, N.J.: Burdick, 1974.

Leuchtenburg, William E. *Franklin D. Roosevelt and the New Deal, 1932-1940*. New York: Harper & Row, 1963.

Lies, Eugene T. *The New Leisure Challenges the Schools*. Washington: National Education Association, 1933.

Meyer, Stephen. *The Five Dollar Day: Labor, Management and Social Control in the Ford Motor Company, 1908–1921*. Albany: State University of New York, 1981.

Millet, John. *The WPA in New York City*. Chicago: Public Administration Service, 1938.

Mire, Joseph. *Labor Education*. Madison, Wisc.: Inter-University Labor Education Committee, 1956.

Mitchell, Broadus. *Depression Decade*. New York: Rinehart, 1947.

Morris, James O. *Conflict within the AFL: A Study of Craft Versus Industrial Unionism 1901–1938*. Ithaca, N. Y.: Cornell University Press, 1958.

National Council of Parent Education. *Handbook for Leaders of Parent Education Groups in Emergency Education Programs*. Washington, D.C.: U.S. Office of Education, 1934.

National Education Association. *What American Leaders Say About Adult Education Especially During the Present Crisis*. Washington: National Education Association, 1933.

Ogburn, William F., ed. *Social Change and the New Deal*. Chicago: University of Chicago Press, 1933.

Patterson, James T. *Congressional Conservatism and the New Deal*. Lexington: University of Kentucky Press, 1967.

——. *The New Deal and the States: Federalism in Transition*. Princeton, N. J.: Princeton University Press, 1969.

Pells, Richard H. *Radical Visions and American Dreams: Culture and Social Thought in the Depression Years*. New York: Harper & Row, 1974.

Perkins, Frances. *People at Work*. New York: John Day, 1934.

——. *The Roosevelt I Knew*. New York: Viking, 1946.

Perlman, Selig. *A History of Trade Unionism in the United States*. New York: A. M. Kelley Publishers, 1950.

Riis, Jacob. *The Battle With the Slum*. New York: Macmillan, 1902.

Ringenbach, Paul. *Tramps and Reformers, 1873–1916: The Discovery of Unemployment in New York*. Westport, Conn.: Greenwood, 1973.

Roosevelt, Franklin D. *Looking Forward*. New York: John Day, 1933.

——. *On Our Way*. New York: John Day, 1934.

Rogin, Lawrence, and Rachlin, Marjorie. *Labor Education in the United States.* Washington, D.C.: National Institute of Labor Education, American University, 1968.

Salmond, John, *A Southern Rebel: The Life and Times of Aubrey Williams, 1890–1965* (Chapel Hill: University of North Carolina Press), 1983.

Scharf, Lois. *To Work and To Wed.* Westport, Conn.: Greenwood, 1980.

Schlesinger, Arthur M., Jr. *The Age of Roosevelt*, vols. 1, 2, 3. Boston: Houghton Mifflin, 1957, 1958, 1960.

Schneider, Florence H. *Patterns of Workers' Education: The Study of the Bryn Mawr Summer School.* Washington, D.C.: American Council on Public Affairs, 1941.

Schneider, John. *Detroit and the Problem of Order, 1830–1880: A Geography of Crime, Riot, and Policing.* Lincoln: University of Nebraska Press, 1980.

Schwartztrauber, Ernest E. *Workers' Education: A Wisconsin Experiment.* Madison: University of Wisconsin Press, 1942.

Sherwood, Robert. *Roosevelt and Hopkins: An Intimate History.* New York: Harper, 1948.

Smith, Hilda W. *Opening Vistas in Workers' Education.* Washington, D.C.: n.p., 1978.

———. *Women Workers at the Bryn Mawr Summer School.* New York: Affiliated Schools for Workers and American Association for Adult Education, 1929.

Starr, Mark. *Labor Looks at Education.* Cambridge, Mass.: League for Industrial Democracy, 1947.

Studebaker, John. W. *Plain Talk.* Washington, D.C.: National Home Library Association, 1936.

———. *Safeguarding Democracy Through Adult Civic Education.* Washington, D. C., 1936.

Sugar, Maurice. *The Ford Hunger March.* Berkeley: Meikeljohn Institute, 1980.

Tolman, William. *Social Engineering.* New York: McGraw, 1909.

Tyack, David. *Public Schools in Hard Times: The Great Depression and Recent Years* (Cambridge: Harvard University Press), 1984.

Ware, Caroline F. *Labor Education in Universities: A Study of University Programs.* New York: American Labor Education Service, 1946.

Ware, Susan. *Beyond Suffrage: Women in the New Deal.* Cambridge: Harvard University Press, 1981.

Welter, Rush. *Popular Education and Democratic Thought in America.* New York: Columbia University Press, 1962.

Zinn, Howard, ed. *New Deal Thought.* New York: Bobbs-Merrill, 1966.

Articles

"Adult Education and the Depression." *Adult Education Quarterly* 8 (November-December 1932): 1–28.

"Adults at Study." *Time* 24 (September 17, 1934): 60.

"Adults Study Their World." *Progressive Education* 11 (April-May 1934): 229–323.

Alderman, Lewis R. "Carry-over from the Emergency Education." *Journal of Adult Education* 7 (October 1935): 476–479.

———. "Emergency Education Program for Unemployment Relief." *National Municipal Review* 24 (July 1935): 379–381.

———. "Emergency Relief and Adult Education." *School and Society* 38 (December 2, 1933): 717–719.

———. "How the School Could Help Solve the Unemployment Problem." *School Life* 16 (December 1930): 62.

———. "Problems of the FERA." National Education Association *Proceedings* (1934): 290.

Alsburg, Harry G. "The Federal Writers' Project and Education." *Journal of the National Education Association* 25 (March 1936): 86.

Amidon, Beulah, "Emergency Education." *Survey Graphic* 23 (September 1934): 415–419.

Anderson, L.O. "The WPA and Adult Education." *School Executive* 5 (January 1933): 450–451.

Armstrong, Arthur. "Who Are Our Students?" *Journal of Adult Education* 9 (June, 1937): 302.

Arnold, Henry J. "A Free-time People's College." *Journal of Adult Education* 5 (January 1933): 67–68.

Bernstein, Barton J. "The New Deal: The Conservative Achievements of Liberal Reform," in *Towards A New Past: Dissenting Essays in American History*, ed. Barton J. Bernstein. New York: Pantheon, 1968.

Bestor, Arthur E. "The ABCs of Federal Emergency Education." *Journal of Adult Education* 6 (April 1934): 150–154.

Boutwell, William D. "Open Your Schools to the Unemployed." *School Life* 17 (May 1932): 1963–1964.

Bridgman, Donald S. "Education for Work and Citizenship." *Yale Review* 1 (Summer 1938): 93–110.

Brown, Muriel. W. "Emergency Parent Education at Work." *Journal of Home Economics* 27 (February 1935): 78–82.

Burdell, E. S. "Adventure in Education for the Unemployed." Association of Governing Boards of State Universities and Allied Institutions. *Proceedings* (1933).

Burns, Arthur E. "The Federal Emergency Relief Administration." *Municipal Year Book*. Chicago: n.p., 1937.

Campbell, Harold G. "The Importance of Adult Education." *Adult Education Quarterly* 8 (September-October 1932): 8–9.

Carroll, Mollie Ray. "The Emergency Education Program and Labor." *Journal of Adult Education* 6 (October 1934): 493–498.

Carroll, Mollie Ray and Miller, Spencer, Jr., eds. "Workers Education: A Symposium." *Journal of Adult Education* 6 (October 1934): 491–529.

Cartwright, Morse A. "Adult Education." *Library Journal* 62 (March 15, 1937): 232–234.

Chamberlain, Arthur H. "Emergency Education Program." *Overland Monthly* 92 (April 1934): 75.

Coffman, Lotus D. "Adult Education and Unemployment." *Adult Education* 6 (March-April 1931): 7–8, 26.

Coit, Eleanor. "Workers' Education and Government Support." *Journal of Adult Education* 8 (June 1936): 263–266.

Coit, Eleanor, and Hourwich, Andrea Taylor. "Workers' Education, Changing Times: The Story of the American Labor Education Service." *Yearbook of Workers' Education, 1926–1943.* New York: American Labor Education Service, 1943, 12–17.

Corbin, William. "A City Goes to School." *American Magazine* 120 (October 1935): 63, 139.

Covert, Timon. "School Crisis Facts." *School Life* 19 (September 1933): 7.

Cummings, James E. "Federal Educational Work Relief Program." *Catholic Educational Review* 41 (November 1933): 641–644.

Cummings, Milton C. "How Can the Schools Build a New Social Order." *School and Society* 36 (December 10, 1932): 756–758.

Daniel, Walter G. "Current Trends and Events of National Importance in Negro Education." *Journal of Negro Education* 4 (April 1935): 278–288.

Daniels, Roger. "Workers Education and the University of California 1921–1941." *Labor History* 4 (Winter, 1963): 32–50.

Danton, Emily M. "The Federal Emergency Adult Education Program," in *Handbook of Adult Education in the U.S,* ed. Dorothy Rowden. New York: American Association for Adult Education, 1936: 28–53.

"Department of Teacher Training of the Emergency Education Program." *School and Society* 41 (March 16, 1935): 359–360.

Dwyer, Richard. "Workers' Education, Labor Education, Labor Studies: An Historical Delineation." *Review of Educational Research* 47 (Winter, 1977), 179–207.

"Educational Work Relief for Jobless Teachers." *Monthly Labor Review* 37 (October 1933): 810–811.

Eiger, Norman. "Toward a National Commitment to Workers' Education: The Rise and Fall of the Campaign to Establish a Labor Extension Service 1942–1950." *Labor Studies Journal* 1 (Fall, 1976): 130–150.

"Emergency in Education." *School and Society* 39 (June 30, 1934): 835–836.

"Emergency Education: How Will It Affect the Adult Education Movement?" *Journal of Adult Education* 8 (January 1936): 73–78.

"Emergency Education Program: First Nationwide Adult Education Program in the U.S." *School Life* 19 (March 1934): 137.

"Emergency Federal Aid for Education." *NEA Journal* 23 (October 1934): 181.

"Employment of Teachers by the FERA." *School and Society* 40 (August 25, 1934): 243–244.

Evans, Anne. "Quicksand or Causeway?" *Journal of Adult Education* 6 (January 1934): 12–16.

Fansler, T. "The Problem of Adult Education." *Public Health Nursing* 28 (April 1936): 224–228.

Farman, C. H. "Dilemma of Emergency Adult Education." *Texas Outlook* 19 (December 1935): 25

"Federal Funds for Education." *School Life* 19 (November 1933): 42.

"Federal Funds in Education." *Congressional Digest* 13 (March 1934): 85–87.

Fones-Wolf, Elizabeth, and Fones-Wolf, Kenneth. "Trade Union Evangelism: Religion and the AFL in the Labor Forward Movement, 1912-1916," in *Working-Class America: Essays on Labor, Community, and American Society,* ed. Michael Frisch and Daniel Walkowitz, Urbana: University of Illinois Press, 1983.

"Fortune Survey of CWA, FERA, WPA, PWA." *Fortune* 14 (October 1946): 132.

Foster, R. G. "Family-life Education and Research." *Journal of Home Economics* 30 (January 1938): 6–10.

Fraser, Stephen. "Dress Rehearsal for the New Deal: Shop-Floor Insurgents, Political Elites, and Industrial Democracy in the Amalgamated Clothing Workers," in *Working-Class America: Essays on Labor, Community, and American Society*, ed. Michael Frisch and Daniel Walkowitz. Urbana: University of Illinois Press, 1983.

Frazier, B. W. "When a Teacher Goes Job Hunting." *Nation's Schools* 16 (December 1935): 25–26.

Freuder, Irene. "Adult Education." *Nation* 140 (April 1935): 389.

Hansome, Marius. "The Development of Workers' Education," in *Workers Education in the United States: Fifth Yearbook of the John Dewey Society*, ed. Theodore Brameld. New York: Harper, 1941: 48–66.

Hart, J. K. "Freeing Adults for the Uncharted Future." *Progressive Education* 11 (April-May 1934): 229–233.

Hedges, Marian H. "Workers Education before the U.S. Congress." *Public Affairs* 11 (July, 1948): 144–148.

Henry, David D. "Michigan's Work Relief in Education." *Michigan Education Journal* (February 1934): 243–245.

Henry, David D., and Condon, W. H. "Socializing the School Program Through Adult Education." *Nation's Schools* 15 (May 1935): 14–16.

Hertzeberg, Sidney. "The Wisconsin Experimental College." *Current History and Forum* 36 (July 1932): 438–443.

Hewes, Amy. "Early Experiments in Workers' Education." *Adult Education* 6 (Summer 1956): 211–220.

Holderman, Carl. "Organized Labor and the Continuation Schools." *American Federationist* 37 (August 1930): 951–953.

Keppel, Francis P. "New Knowledge and New Ignorance." *Journal of Adult Education* 7 (January 1935): 10–12.

Lash, Frederick M. "Emergency Adult Education in Seattle, Washington." *School and Society* 41 (June 22, 1935): 839–841.

Leith, Donald M. "Implementing Democracy: The Des Moines Forums." *Religious Education* 29 (April 1934), 113–119.

Lewis, William M. "Lafayette Unemployment College." *Journal of Adult Education* 5 (January 1933): 69–70.

Lindeman, Eduard C. "Adult Education." *Encyclopedia of the Social Sciences*, 1:463. New York: Macmillan, 1937.

Judd, Maurice. "WPA Trains Immigrants for Citizenship Examinations." *School and Society* 46 (September 4, 1937): 317–318.

"Labor Education." *Adult Education Journal* 2 (January 1943): 81.

Langdon, Grace. "News of Family–Life Education Under the WPA." *Journal of Home Economics* 31 (February 1939): 106.

Leach, Henry G. "In Praise of Boon-doggling Cultural Relief Activities." *Forum* 93 (June 1935): 321–322.

Lies, Eugene T. "Education for Leisure." *National Education Association Journal* 21 (November 1934): 253–254.

Lloyd, John H. "Adult Education Conference." *School Life* 19 (November 1933): 58.

May, Mark A. "Education for the Unemployed." *Yale Review* 23 (March 1934): 553–567.

Meiklejohn, Alexander. "Adult Education: A Fresh Start." *New Republic* 90 (August 15, 1934): 14–17.

Nash, Philip C. "The Combination of Community Adult Education with the FERA Emergency School Program." *School and Society* 41 (June 8, 1935): 773–776.

"Oldsters Go to School at Night." *Library Digest* 123 (May 28, 1937): 25.

Orr, Charles A. "University Sponsored Labor Education in the United States." *Labor Law Journal*, 21 (June, 1970): 365–373.

Overstreet, Harry A. "Capturing the Depression Mind." *Journal of Adult Education* 4 (January 1932): 12–15.

"People's University" (Lansing, Michigan). *Time* 23 (January 29, 1934): 24.

Perkins, Frances. "Unemployment and Relief." *American Journal of Sociology* 39 (May 1934): 768–775.

Peters, Ronald J. and McCarrick, Jeanne M. "Roots of Public Support for Labor Education 1900–1945." *Labor Studies Journal* 1 (Fall 1976): 109–129.

"Plans of the Joint Commission on the Emergency in Education." *School and Society* 39 (January 20, 1934): 78–79.

Profitt, Mavis M. "Adult Education." *Biennial Survey of Education, 1934–1936* Vol. 1. Bulletin 2. Washington: GPO, 1938: 22.

"Program in Action: How the FERA Projects Are Being Developed in Cooperation with the U.S. Office of Education." *School Life* (January 1934): 91–92.

"Program Proposed by the Federal Advisory Committee on Emergency Aid in Education." *School and Society* 39 (January 20, 1934): 90–91.

Punke, Harold H. "Literacy, Relief and Adult Education in Georgia." *School and Society* 42 (October 12, 1935): 514–517.

———. "Membership and Interests of Adult Education Classes." *School Review* 47 (February 1939): 110–120.

"Recent Developments in Workers' Education in Various States." *Monthly Labor Review* 40 (April 1935): 948–953.

Reeves, Floyd W. "Adult Education as Related to the Tennessee Valley Authority." *School and Society* 44 (August 29, 1936): 257–266.

———. "TVA Training." *Journal of Adult Education* 7 (January 1935): 48–52.

"Residential Schools for Unemployed Women." *Journal of Adult Education* 6 (June 1934): 340.

Reynolds, Major B. T. "Classes for the Unemployed." *Nineteenth Century* 114 (August 1933): 191–200.

Richmond, James H. "Meeting the Emergency in 1935." National Education Association. *Proceedings* (1934): 69–75.

Rutz, Henry. "Workers' Education in Wisconsin." *Brookwood, Labor's Own School.* Katonah, N. Y.: Brookwood Labor College, 1936, 35–36.

Sands, William F. "Education for Living." *Commonweal* 22 (June 28, 1935): 229–231.

"Schools for Unemployed Women." *Journal of Adult Education* 7 (June 1935): 337.

Schwartztrauber, Ernest E. "Administering Workers' Education." *Workers Education in the United States: Fifth Yearbook of the John Dewey Society*, ed. Theodore Brameld. New York: Harper, 1941.

Shapiro, Theodore. "The Challenge of Workers' Education." *Adult Education* 1 (February 1951): 91–99.

"Shoulder to Shoulder with Other Emergency Agencies." *School Life* 21 (October 1935): 24–26.

"Since March 4: The Chronological Record of the Development of the Federal Emergency Education Program." *School Life* 20 (January 1934): 89.

Smith, Hilda W. "Education Via Relief." *Journal of Adult Education* VI (January 1934): 118–20.

———. "The Emerging Program of Workers' Education." *Journal of Adult Education* 8 (June 1936): 347.

———. "Federal Cooperation in the Education of Workers." *Journal of Adult Education* 6 (October 1934): 499–505.

———. "New Aspects of Workers' Education." *Women's Press* 28 (July 1934): 369–370.

———. "New Directions for Workers' Education." *Journal of Adult Education* 12 (April 1940): 162–166.

———. "New Plans for Adult Education." *American Federationist* 41 (March 1934): 261–267.

———. "Resident Schools and Camps for Unemployed Women." *Journal of Adult Education* 4 (October 1934): 461–462.

———. "Teacher Training in Workers' Education." *Journal of Adult Education* 8 (June 1936): 384–385.

———. "Workers' Education and the Federal Government." *Progressive Education* 11 (April-May 1934): 239–245.

———. "Workers' Education and the Public Schools." *Journal of Adult Education* 7 (April 1935): 241–243.

———. "Workers' Education as Determining Social Control." *Annals of the American Academy of Political and Social Science* 182 (November 1935): 82–92.

———. "Workers' Education under FERA." *Labor Information Bulletin* 2 (June 1935): 1–3.

———. "Workers' Education with Federal Support." *Workers' Education* 13 (October 1936): 31–34.

———. "Workers' Education in the States." *American Federationist* 42 (May 1935): 490–493.

Smith, Hilda W., and Donald, Barbara. "Federal Training Schools for Household Employment." *Journal of Home Economics* 27 (April 1935): 215–217.

———. "Workers' Education in the States." *American Federationist* 42 (August 1935): 1073–1075.

———. "Workers' Education under the Federal Government." *Labor Information Journal* 3 (June 1936): 7–9.

———. "Workers' Education under WPA." *American Federationist* 43 (February 1936): 198–199.

Smith, Hilda W., and Friedmann, Ernestine L. "Methods in Workers' Education." *Adult Education Bulletin* (January 1937): 3–6.

Smith, Hilda W., and Hart, Nancy. "Workers' Education in the FERA." *Opportunity* 13 (January 1935): 1920.

Smith, Lorna M. "CWA School for the Home Folks." *Scribner's Magazine* 96 (August 1934): 105–108.

Starr, Mark. "Higher Education and Organized Labor." *Current History* 29 (September 1955): 168–172.

———. "The Current Panorama," in *Workers Education in the United States: Fifth Yearbook of the John Dewey Society*, ed. Theodore Brameld. New York: Harper, 1941: 89–113.

———. "Workers' Education." *Harvard Educational Review* 12 (Fall 1951): 243–267.

Thorndike, Edward L. "In Defense of Facts." *Journal of Adult Education* 7 (October 1935): 381–388.

Watson, Goodwin B. "Families, Education and the Use of Leisure in the Present Crisis." *Journal of Home Economics* 25 (December 1933): 831–839.

White, Edna N. "Parent Education in the Emergency." *School and Society* 40 (November 24, 1934): 379–381.

Williams, Chester S. "Uncle Sam Promotes Education." *Journal of Educational Sociology* 10 (May 1937): Ms. 527–534.

Wilson, Lewis "Enlarged Adult Education Opportunities." *Recreation* 27 (February 1934): 507, 537.

Woods, Roy C. "Education: A Cure for Unemployment." *Literary Digest* 119 (January 26, 1935): 32.

Woodcock, Leonard. "Call for a Coalition to Establish a National Labor Extension Service." *Labor Studies Journal* 1 (Winter 1977): 281–285.

Woodward, Ellen S. "WPA's Program of Training for Housework." *Journal of Home Economics* 31 (February 1939): 86–88.

"Work of the New York State Emergency Colleges." *School and Society* 39 (February 17, 1934): 215–216.

"Workers' Education." *Monthly Labor Review* 45 (July 1937): 140–142.

"Workers Education, A Plea for Government Support." *Yearbook of Workers' Education, 1926–1943*. (New York: American Labor Education Service, 1943), 27–28.

"Workers' Education in Puerto Rico." *American Federationist* 43 (April 1936): 409–412.

"Workers' Education under the WPA." *Journal of Adult Education* 9 (October 1937): 466.

Wright, John C. "Contributions of Vocational Education to the Relief of Unemployment." *Education* 55 (April 1935): 472–475.

Zook, George F. "Adult Schools." *School Management* 3 (June 1934): 11.

———. "National Welfare Depends Upon the Classroom." *Nation's Schools* 13 (March 1934): 31–34.

Government Reports (A Selected List)

U.S. Federal Emergency Relief Administration. *The Emergency Education Program and the College Student Aid Program of the Federal Emergency Relief Administration.* Washington: GPO, 1935.

————. *The Emergency Work Relief Program of the Federal Emergency Relief Administration, April 1, 1934-July 1, 1935.* Washington, D.C.: GPO, 1936.

————. *Purposes and Activities of the Federal Emergency Relief Administration.* Washington, D.C.: GPO, 1935.

U.S. Office of Education. *A Step Forward for Adult Civic Education.* Bulletin Number 1, 16. Washington, D.C.: GPO, 1936.

U.S. Works Progress Administration. "Aids to Teachers of Literacy, Naturalization and Elementary Subjects for Adults." Education Circular Number 5 (January 13, 1938). Mimeo.

————. "Bibliography for Teachers of Adult Education." Education Circular Number 7 (August 5, 1938). Mimeo.

————. "Bibliography on Family-life Education." Education Circular Number 8 (August 16, 1938). Mimeo.

————. "Conferences for the Education of Teachers." Education Circular Number 6 (n.d.). Mimeo.

————. "Inventory: An Appraisal of the Results of the Works Progress Administration" (June 30, 1938). Mimeo.

————. *Final Statistical Report of the Federal Emergency Relief Administration.* Washington, D.C.: GPO, 1942.

————. *WPA Program Operation and Accomplishments, 1935–1943. Education,* vol. 3. Washington, D.C.: GPO, 1943.

Unpublished Manuscripts

Bowman, Robert A. "The National Committee for the Extension of Labor Education, 1942–1950." Ph.D. diss., Rutgers University, 1979.

Brody, Doris A. "American Labor Education Service, 1927–1962: An Organization in Workers' Education." Ph.D. diss., Cornell University, 1973.

Day, Michael Joseph. "Adult Education as a New Educational Frontier: Review of the *Journal of Adult Education* 1929–1941." Ph.D. diss. University of Michigan, 1981.

Friedmann, Ernestine I. "The Story Behind Labor's Request for a State Sponsored Labor Extension Service." Draft of a paper submitted to the *Connecticut Education Survey,* February, 1951, Labor Education Collection, Schlow Memorial Library. Pennsylvania State University, State College, Pa.

George, Elsie L. "The Women Appointees of the Roosevelt and Truman Administration: A Study of Their Impact and Effectiveness." Ph.D. diss., American University, 1972.

"History of Workers Education." Transcript of a group recording of a meeting consisting of Hilda Smith, Ernestine Friedmann, Mark Starr, Dorothy Oko, Nelson Cruikshank, Lee Stanley, Oliver and Esther Peterson, and Alice Hoffman conducted by Local 189 of the American Federation of Teachers, November 21, 1969, Labor Education Collection, Schlow Memorial Library, Pennsylvania State University, State College, Pa.

Jacoby, Robin M. "The British and American Women's Trade Union Leagues, 1890– 1925: A Case Study of Feminism and Class." Ph.D. diss., Harvard University, 1977.

Jones, V. *An Analysis of the Federal Emergency Education Program in Oklahoma.* Master's thesis, Oklahoma Agricultural and Mechanical College, 1935.

Klug, Tom. "The Contradictions of Free Wage Labor and the Managing of the Labor Market and Worker Mobility in Detroit, 1850–1930." Typescript, Wayne State University, 1984.

———. "The Employers' Association of Detroit, the Open Shop, and the Making of Managerial Authority, 1900–1916." Typescript, Wayne State University, 1981.

———. "The Ideology and Practices of Labor Market Control and the Origins of Personnel Management in Detroit, 1900–1920." Typescript, Wayne State University, 1981.

MacLeech, Bert. "Workers' Education in the United States." Ph.D. diss., Harvard University, 1951.

Peters, Ronald J. "Factors Affecting Labor Extension Legislation, 1945-1950." Ph.D. diss., Michigan State University, 1976.

Smith, Hilda W. "History of the Labor Extension Bill." Unpublished manuscript, 1950.

———. "Labor Education: A Summary and a Forecast." Draft of an article mailed to the Cleveland Industrial Council upon request for an article for the *Cleveland IUC Yearbook*, January 3, 1947.

———. "People Come First: A Report on Workers' Education in the Federal Emergency Relief Administration, the Civil Works Administration and the Works Progress Administration, 1933–1942."

———. Transcript of an Oral History by Ashley Doherty, Bryn Mawr, Pa., May 30, 1969, Hilda W. Smith, Papers, Franklin D. Roosevelt Library, Hyde Park, N.Y., Container 1, File "Interviews."

Smith, Hilda W. and Fernbach, Frank. Transcript of an Interview by Alice Hoffman, Washington, D.C., April 30, 1971, Labor Education Collection, Schlow Memorial Library, Pennsylvania State University, State College, Pa.

Wong, Susan S. "Workers' Education Movement: 1921–1951." Columbia University, 1977.

Zeitlin, Harry. "Federal Relations in American Education, 1933–1943: A Study of New Deal Efforts and Innovations." Ph.D. diss., Columbia University, 1958.

Manuscript Collections

American Labor Education Service. Papers. Martin P. Catherwood Library. New York State School of Industrial and Labor Relations. Cornell University. Ithaca, N.Y.

———. Papers. Wisconsin State Historical Society. Madison, Wisc.

Borchardt, Selma. Papers. Archives of Labor History and Urban Affairs. Wayne State University. Detroit, Michigan.

Bryn Mawr Summer School for Women's Workers. Papers. Institute for Management and Labor Relations. Rutgers University. New Brunswick, N.J. Papers.

Cohn, Fannia. Papers. New York Public Library. New York, N.Y.

Coit, Eleanor. Papers. Sophia Smith Collection. Smith College. Northampton, Mass.

Copenhaver, Eleanor. Report. Industrial Department. Archives of the National Board of the YMCA. New York, N.Y.

Edelman, John. Papers. Archives of Labor History and Urban Affairs. Wayne State University. Detroit, Michigan.

Federal Emergency Relief Administration. Papers. National Archives. Washington, D.C.

National Women's Trade Union League. Papers. Library of Congress. Washington, D.C.

———. Papers. Schlesinger Library. Cambridge, Mass.

Robins, Margaret Dreier. Papers. University of Florida Library. Gainesville, Fla.

Saposs, David. Papers. Wisconsin State Historical Society. Madison, Wisc.

Schneiderman, Rose. Papers. Tamiment Library. New York University. New York, N.Y.

Smith, Hilda W. Papers. Franklin D. Roosevelt Library. Hyde Park, N.Y.

———. Papers. Schlesinger Library, Cambridge, Mass.

Starr, Ellen and Mark. Papers. Archives of Labor History and Urban Affairs. Wayne State University Library. Detroit, Michigan.

Southern Summer School. Papers. Martin P. Catherwood Library. New York State School of Industrial and Labor Relations. Cornell University. Ithaca, N.Y.

Textile Workers Union of America. Papers. Wisconsin State Historical Society. Madison, Wisc.

Thomas, M. Carey. Papers. Bryn Mawr College Library. Bryn Mawr, Pa.

Workers' Education Bureau. Papers. Martin P. Catherwood Library. New York State School of Industrial and Labor Relations. Cornell University. Ithaca, N.Y.

Index

A Note on the Author

Joyce L. Kornbluh is a research scientist of the Institute of Labor and Industrial Relations at the University of Michigan, Ann Arbor. She founded and directs the Program on Women and Work of the ILIR's Labor Studies Center. She received her bachelor's degree from the University of Pennsylvania, and her doctorate from the University of Michigan. Her previous publications include *Rebel Voices: An IWW Anthology*; *Negroes and Jobs*; and *Sisterhood and Solidarity: Workers' Education for Women, 1914–1984*.